THE SOCIOLOGY OF EMILE DURKHEIM

The Sociology of
Emile Durkheim

ROBERT NISBET

New York
OXFORD UNIVERSITY PRESS
1974

Copyright © 1974 by Oxford University Press, Inc.
Library of Congress Catalogue Card Number: 73-87611

Printed in the United States of America

Again, to CAROLINE

Preface

Emile Durkheim is, along with Max Weber, one of the two dominating influences on contemporary sociology. He has held this position in America for approximately a third of a century, having become at the turn of the century the preeminent influence in French sociology and somewhat later a major force in English social anthropology. There is every reason to assume that Durkheim's intellectual status will continue, will become, as I believe, even stronger during the remainder of the century. It is impossible to overlook the connection between the assimilation of Durkheim (and of course Weber) into American sociology in the 1930s and the subsequent burst of creative energy in all fields of the discipline.

Equally impressive, I cannot help believing, will be the relation between Durkheim's rigorous objectivism and the liberation of American sociology from its recent and short-lived plunge into subjectivism—call it what we will, ethnomethodology, consciousness-, reflexive-, or egocentric-sociology. Signs of this liberation are already vivid, as I write, and there seems to me little doubt that they will become even more evident. "Epochs which are regressive and in the process of dissolution," declared Goethe to Eckermann, "are always subjective, whereas the trend in all progressive epochs is objective."

Taking sociology as a whole, and looking back on its creative periods in the past, I find it exceedingly unlikely that its continuing development will be much longer hindered by fashions of the past decade or two. And in the work of reaffirming the vital tradition of sociology, a tradition that has no room in it for self-preoccupation, the ideas of Durkheim are bound to be crucial. No one, not even Weber, has so eloquently set forth for us the essentials of the scientific method as it bears upon social phenomena. No one else has seen so clearly the legitimate boundaries of sociology among the sciences. And no single sociologist I can think of has so skillfully and suggestively lighted up the necessary fusion of fact and theory as has Durkheim.

None of this is to diminish the contributions of Weber, Simmel, Tönnies, Mead, and Thomas, or anyone else in the early-twentieth century history of sociology, or of those in cultural and social anthropology such as Malinowski, Radcliffe-Brown, Boas, and Kroeber who were also concerned with setting the study of human behavior upon foundations as objective as possible. We could hardly do without these contributions, and with many others as well. Nevertheless, as one surveys the present scene, noting the thrust of antiscientific, antirational, and, indeed, anti-empirical arguments parading under the spurious labels of either "humanism" or "radicalism" or both, it is impossible not to feel that, of all the works written by the titans of the early part of our century, those written by Durkheim speak most powerfully and also most illuminatingly at the present time. The test of a classic in any field is that it continue to speak meaningfully and pertinently and that it continue to serve as an exemplar of what is important. That there are more than a few such classics for us in sociology, I do not deny. I only say that of all these the ones bearing Durkheim's name have been made in many ways the most timely by recent currents of thought.

There is no want of books dealing with Durkheim the philosopher, the moralist, the systematic theorist, the empirical sociologist, and the man. Elsewhere, in my *The Sociological Tradition,* and in a long introductory essay to my *Emile Durkheim: Selected Essays* (now out of print), I considered Durkheim's ideas in the thematic contexts afforded in the nineteenth century by the allied, if distinguishable, ideas of Alexis de Tocqueville, Karl Marx, Frédéric Le Play, Ferdinand Tönnies, Georg Simmel, and Max Weber. In those works, particularly in *The Sociological Tradition,* I used certain unit-ideas—*community, authority, status,* the *sacred,* and *alienation*—as hooks, so to speak, on which to hang the ideas of the writers just mentioned, including Durkheim, along with those of other European thinkers of the late nineteenth and early twentieth century.

The aim of this book is very different. I do not hesitate to call it a Durkheim primer—using that last word in its oldest and best sense of concern strictly with what is essential and constitutive. I have stayed clear of interpretative works on Durkheim, of the constantly building corpus of Durkheim scholarship, not from any lack of appreciation of these works and the often impressive scholarship involved, but from desire to write a book on Durkheim for the student or general reader whose knowledge of subject may be presumed incomplete or fragmentary and who desires a concise introduction to Durkheim's fundamental ideas and also to consideration of the impact of these ideas on fields of contemporary sociological thought.

That is why I have arranged the contents of the book as I have: to show as clearly as possible the direct relation between Durkheim's fundamental ideas and fields or areas of contemporary sociology which are by common assent vital ones. *Method, social structure, social psychology, political sociology, religion, morality, deviance,* and *social change* are all, plainly enough, important areas of theory and research in contemporary sociology. What I have tried to do is indicate as precisely as possible Durkheim's substantive contributions to these areas. I have ended the book with a brief chapter on Durkheim's relation to modern culture. Although he cannot be said to have anything like the widely perceived impact on this culture that is associated with the names of Freud and Marx, there is nevertheless reason, as I have suggested, for regarding Durkheim as in many ways the most fruitful of those who at the turn of the century began to shape themes which subsequent history has shown to be powerful in Western consciousness. Durkheim, after all, is the sociologist *par excellence* of anomie and of modern man's loss of the sustaining ties of community, authority, and dogma. Rigorous a scientist as he was, he was nevertheless deeply affected by a sense of crisis that he from the beginning pronounced a moral crisis in the West.

Contents

THE SOCIOLOGY OF EMILE DURKHEIM

Introduction

BIOGRAPHICAL

Emile Durkheim was born April 15, 1858 in the city of Epinal, France, not far from Strasbourg, of Jewish parents. His father was a rabbi, and we are told that Emile Durkheim was himself destined at one point to become a rabbi. What changed his, or his parents' mind, we cannot be sure. There seems to have been a short period in his schooling when he was deeply impressed by a Catholic woman teacher and was apparently inclined briefly toward a somewhat mystical form of Roman Catholicism. In neither instance, Jewish nor Catholic, did anything overt come of the religious influence to which he was subjected as a boy. By the time he entered college he was well on the way toward the rigorous agnosticism that would stay with him to the end of his life. Even so, as so much of his work makes clear, Durkheim was fascinated throughout his life by religion and by the special values and constraints in human society which are born of religion. And no one, believer or nonbeliever, has ever written a more powerful demonstration, and explanation, of the eternality of religion in human society than Durkheim.

In the *collège*, or secondary school, of his native city Durkheim was known as an outstanding student, brilliant in his studies and rich in promise of scholarly career ahead. At age eighteen he left home for Paris, on the strong recommendation of his teachers, to prepare for the *École Normale Supérieure*. Despite rigorous study, he failed, however, to gain admission to this famous and notably difficult school when he first competed for entrance in 1878. Only after a third try did he succeed, in 1879, and

among his classmates were a substantial number who would attain an intellectual eminence comparable to Durkheim's.

Durkheim was not, it must be said, an enthusiastic student at
the École Normale. He did not like the curriculum or the kind of
teaching he received. As Henri Peyre tells us: "Even in a con-
genial group of some fifty young and promising scholars selected
annually from the whole of France, Durkheim was dissatisfied
with his instruction." He considered it highly conventional in
substance, ritualized in form, and with too few opportunities for
individual initiative to break through the surface. He was nevertheless regarded by his classmates as, even by their high standards,
brilliant and learned. It must have come as a surprise to many
when, at the end of the third year and the all-important, required
examinations were taken, Durkheim wound up near the bottom
of the list. He was, Professor Peyre tells us, "in no way daunted by
this disregard of his originality. He was already planning his thesis and bubbling over with ideas. He realized he would never be
a conformist or an official greedy for academic honors. He was
never elected to the Institut de France, and he had to wait a long
time before a special professorship was created for him at the
Sorbonne."[1]

Two points should be interjected here. The first is, Durkheim was not the first, nor will he be the last, student of brilliance
and restless originality to do badly, or relatively badly, in the required work of his college and then to fail of election or award
during subsequent career when prestige-laden memberships and
honors were being distributed. Given his talent and buoyancy of
mind, it is hard to resist concluding that only a small amount of
ingratiation would have enabled him to receive all the ordinary
distinctions of the intellectual and academic world during his
time. One infers, however, that even this small amount was, for
Durkheim, too much. He would not yield. The result was that
honors and awards went to others who, even in that day, were
known to have not the slightest hope of the kind of lasting quality of work that Durkheim's admirers knew to lie in his remarkable contributions. The second point to make here is a very dif-

ferent one. Despite his own restlessness with curriculum and what he felt to be the conventionalized, ritualized instruction of the École Normale, Durkheim never lost his basic respect for the necessity of such curriculum and instruction. We are told that he looked back on his years there with gratitude. And we know that he insisted that his son André enter the same school. Rebel against the system, yes, and be willing to suffer the consequences, but destroy or abandon the system, no! This was an attitude toward structure and toward deviance that was to become a hallmark of Durkheim's sociological thinking.

We must not overlook the fact that at the *École Normale* there were a few, at any rate, whose teaching impressed Durkheim profoundly. There were, among others, the philosopher Emile Boutroux and two remarkable historians, Fustel de Coulanges and Gabriel Monod. Fustel de Coulanges's *The Ancient City,* along with his studies of medieval institutions in France, clearly had immense impact on Durkheim's direction of thought and research. And there is little doubt but that Boutroux's philosophical system had seminal effect on Durkheim's own philosophy and his distinctive sociological method. I am inclined to believe, however, that highest among all influences on Durkheim's developing mind were those that came from like-minded, almost equally original, buoyant, and energetic fellow-students.[2] Durkheim himself must have realized this, for we are told that to the end of his life he remained in touch with many of them—those in very final years, at least, who had not been killed during the first years of World War I.

Following completion of his required courses and the examinations, Durkheim held a succession of teaching positions in small *lycées,* all near Paris. This meant the easy possibility of his drawing on the bibliographical and other scholarly resources of that city in the prosecution of his own research toward the all-important doctor's dissertation. It meant also, however, early exposure to teaching pupils of brilliance of mind and already-acquired dedication to academic discipline. We are told that Durkheim was, almost from the beginning, a deeply respected teacher of these *lycée* pupils. And although Durkheim endeavored, as indeed he did throughout his teaching career, to appear austere, even aloof, the better to make discipline, idea, and fact supreme in the classroom, not teaching personality, those pupils who were occasionally invited to his home to engage in philosophical discussions soon discovered that Durkheim was a man of sensitivity and compassion, deeply interested in human beings.

In 1885–86 Durkheim managed a year's leave from his teaching in the *lycée,* which he spent in Germany. There he became greatly attracted by the works of the renowned experimental psychologist Wilhelm Wundt. Wundt's interest in ethics and in the motivations to moral behavior was profound, as was his conviction that morality was subject to scientific investigation. It is probable that much of Durkheim's own devotion to problems in morality and the relation of morality to individual and to social structure sprang in the first instance from his exposure to Wundt's work. It is possible, if not probable, too, that his temporary fascination with typology of social solidarity—fascination that would result in his distinction between "mechanical" and "organic" solidarity in his first published book, the *Division of Labor*—is also rooted in his German year. Ferdinand Tönnies's profound *Community and Society* would not be published in Germany until the year after Durkheim's visit, and Durkheim's own notable review of Tönnies's book would not appear until 1889. Even so, one is justified in assuming that the distinction Tönnies put into the memorable terminology of *Gemeinschaft* and *Gesellschaft* was in some degree in the air in Germany during the year of Durkheim's visit. The fundamental perspective behind the terminology lay in other works, in Germany and elsewhere.

In 1887 Durkheim's career as university teacher began at the University of Bordeaux. The years immediately following were inevitably busy ones both in classroom and in Durkheim's study, where he kept continuously at work writing as well as preparing for his popular and much respected lectures. In 1893 his *Division of Labor* was published, his first major work. It had been written as one of the two doctoral dissertations required in Paris—the other being a shorter one, written in Latin, on Montesquieu—and its publication gave substantial impetus to his scholarly career. Two years later came *The Rules of Sociological Method*. This little book, based in part on articles written earlier, probably did more than its predecessor to make Durkheim's a celebrated, if not always praised, name in French social science circles. For it was here that Durkheim elaborated his thesis of the externality of all social facts, their separation from psychological states in the individual, and, above all, his insistence that collective, that is, social states or structures are the beginning of all genuinely sociological analysis. The book yielded its full share of critics, chief among them Gabriel Tarde who, along with his students and other followers, would wage relentless intellectual war, from an individualistic point of view, against Durkheim's ideas thenceforth.

In 1896 Durkheim got his full professorship at Bordeaux, and two years later founded the journal, *L'Année Sociologique*, some twelve imposing annual issues of which would appear before the outbreak of World War I in 1914. Among initial contributors to this journal were such minds, all destined to become famous as scholars, as Celestin Bouglé, Henri Hubert, Marcel Mauss, and also the German Georg Simmel. During succeeding years the *Année* would become in essence the primary organ of the Durkheim school of social science in France, a vehicle for his own ideas on occasion but also for those of his many students and admirers. It is interesting to note that awareness of this journal played a considerable role in the much later founding of the historical journal, *Annales*, by Marc Bloch, Lucien Febvre, and Fernand Braudel, all of whom as young men had admired Durkheim's journal and many of its central concepts.

Continuing, in 1897, *Suicide* was published, the book that to this day is regarded by many sociologists as the single most successful fusion of theory and empirical research—and also, it should be noted, of sociology and psychology, and of basic science and social policy—to be found in the literature of sociology. During the next few years a steady stream of articles poured forth, a

few of them in *L'Année,* to which he gave almost as much attention as he did to his classes at the university, seeing it, properly,
as being as much a medium of teaching as the classroom was.

Durkheim's reputation in French social philosophy and science was by now made, and today, in viewing the quality and
amount of his scholarship during the thirteen years following
publication of his *Division of Labor,* not to mention the spreading fame of his teaching at Bordeaux, there is nothing surprising
in the fact that by 1902, despite heavy competition, as was common in such matters, he was called to teach at the University of
Paris—the apex of the educational system in France and the
dream of every academic person. In 1906 Durkheim was appointed to the chair of full professor, though in the field of education, there being no work offered in sociology as such at that
time. It is this in part, but only in part, that explains his continuing interest, and writing, in the field of education. Durkheim
correctly saw in the study of education, in the learning process,
which is the root, a splendid means of gaining insight into the
whole socialization process.

At Paris, as at Bordeaux, Durkheim quickly acquired the
reputation of being one of the exhilarating teachers in that historic institution. Students came, if only for a few lectures, from
such far-flung areas as history, law, philosophy, and literature,
as well as from the social sciences, to hear this man who had so
much to say that bore upon one's own work, however distant
from Durkheim's it might be in name. Taking his career as a
whole, it is hard to resist the conclusion that great as was Durkheim the philosopher-scholar, he was perhaps even greater as a
teacher—whether in direct classroom role, as founding editor of
L'Année, or in any of the numerous intellectual relationships he
had with younger scholars of his day, whose work could become
of as obsessing interest to him as his own.

Nor, despite overriding devotion to teaching, scholarship,
and family, was Durkheim totally aloof to the political and social
issues which burned in the France of the turn-of-the-century. He
was a Dreyfusard, meaning a member of the group of generally

liberal, anticlerical, humanitarian thinkers of the Left that had become a formidable influence in French national politics as the result of its early, courageous defense of Alfred Dreyfus, a Jew, captain in the French army, who had been accused by the army of treasonable conduct, given a transparently prejudiced trial, and sent to Devils Island. Apart only, though, from Durkheim's passionate support of France in World War I, it is difficult to find any other evidence of ideological commitment, of political partisanship in his career. Scholarship and teaching were his primary devotions and he would not allow anything to threaten a personal objectivity that he prized deeply.

What Durkheim wrote on French socialism, particularly on Saint-Simon, reveals a mind sympathetic to the underlying ideal of socialism but skeptical of its doctrines and conclusions. The centralizing, collectivizing, and nationalizing cast of modern European socialism, especially strong after the triumph of German socialism over French in the period following France's humiliating defeat by Prussia in 1870, was alien to Durkheim's pluralist-decentralist cast of mind. The nearest Durkheim came to any then-reigning theory of socialism was French guild socialism, with its emphasis on occupational groups intermediate to individual and state, an emphasis that, as we shall see, is very strong in Durkheim's political sociology.

Liberal-humanitarian and anticlerical though Durkheim may have been in his role as Dreyfusard, it is impossible to miss in his writings a strong vein of thought that can only be called conservative, whether by the standards of that day or our own. His view of modernism—of individualism, secularism, equalitarianism, and of direct political action—was, to say the least, a jaundiced one. In no sociologist has respect for the roots of stability and authority in the social order been higher. He saw the crisis of the modern age basically in terms of a disintegration of these roots with nothing yet in view adequate to their replacement. Theories, he wrote, "that celebrate the beneficence of unrestricted liberties are apologies for a diseased state." Discipline is the first element of any morality. He did not exempt "the anarchist, the esthete, the mystic, the socialist revolutionary" from his cataloguing of elements of modern life, in the final pages of *Suicide,* which "have in common with the pessimist a single sentiment of hatred and disgust for the existing order, a single craving to destroy or to escape reality." His love for the French nation, to be seen at its height in his deep patriotic writings after World War I began, has an almost mystical element in it.

More to the point, however, and more consistent with his life's work in sociology is the essential conservatism of value and symbol that we find from the beginning. Whether in his first major work, the *Division of Labor,* with its concluding reflections on the breakdown of order in European society, in *The Rules of Sociological Method,* where the facts of constraint and coercion in society's relationship to the individual come almost to seem coterminous with the data of sociology, in *Suicide,* with its diagnosis of moral and social disintegration in French, and Western European, society and its prescription of renewal of authority and of discipline equivalent to the old authorities that time had eroded away, or, finally, in *The Elementary Forms of Religious Life,* with its demonstration of the functional indispensability of the sacred, of ritual, and of dogma to the social order, we are, very plainly, dealing with a mind in which the symbols of order and authority have primary place.

Add to this Durkheim's lifelong opposition, in his scholarly writing, to utilitarianism and also to rationalism considered as intellectual systems concerned with the roots and motivations of human behavior. It would be hard to find anywhere in the nineteenth century more stringent criticisms of the rationalist approach to religion than those we find in Durkheim—and these, be it emphasized, by a mind committed to no religion. In his own day, Durkheim's sociology, with its profound stress on tradition, authority, constraint, and on the personality's unceasing need for these, was occasionally called "Talmudic sociology." Whether, however, Durkheim's preoccupation with the symbols of conservatism sprang from his own Jewish roots, touched, as we have noted, with rabbinical influences, or from the impact made upon his youthful mind by his cherished Roman Catholic teacher, or from his exposure to the then immensely popular currents in French life of a nationalist traditionalism that was in part a response to France's defeat by Prussia in 1870 and to a general reexamination by French intellectuals of the Revolutionary-Napoleonic currents that so many felt had led up to this defeat, it is difficult to say. It suffices to say that, whatever their origin, the marks of conservatism are very clear indeed in Durkheim's life and work.[3]

None of the immediately foregoing discussion must be allowed to distract, however, from what is vital and central in Durkheim: his absolute commitment to teaching and scholarship. Durkheim shared with Weber—and with many other leading scholars and scientists of his day—a conviction that only the most abstemious relation to politics and the marketplace could save the scholar from being swamped by ideological passions, his role as intellectual-scientific arbiter thus weakened. It is hard to imagine from Durkheim much if any disagreement with the view set forth by Weber so memorably in his "Science as Vocation." That view is, as I write, not a very popular view at the present time in American sociology, but one can take comfort in the recognition of redressing currents of thought and belief already becoming important—once again.

Dispassionate study, objective research, these were, above all others, Durkheim's ideals. From the time he commenced his *Division of Labor,* we find him alive to the methodological issues which, in his view, were vital to whether the study of human behavior was, or was not, to be scientific. I shall deal with this in some detail in the first chapter of this book. My only interest here is to underscore the point that Durkheim, whatever may have been his due concern as citizen with the ideological issues of French politics, never for a moment confused his role as scholar or scientist with the partisanships which are inescapable in the political sphere. Nor did he, even at the height of his Dreyfusard activity, ever deem anything so important to the long run welfare of society as he did the scholarship and science in whose vineyards he labored.

Durkheim's rich yield as scholar is sufficiently evident. What is perhaps less well known is his yield as teacher. Had he published little or nothing but managed nevertheless to attract the students and followers he did, his reputation would be a secure one in history. In law there were Georges Davy and J. Declareuil; in economics and political science, Hubert Bourgin, François Simiand, Leon Homo, among many others; in historical geography, Roger Dion and Lucien Febvre; in ethnology, Marcel Mauss, Paul Fauconnet, Claude Lévi-Strauss, and Roger Caillois; in archaeology, Henri Hubert; in history, Marcel Granet, Gustave Glotz, Henri Berr, and, as noted above, the young historians, including Marc Bloch and Fernand Braudel whose admiration for Durkheim's journal *Année Sociologique* played so important a role in the later founding of the immensely influential *Annales* school of historians in France, along with their journal of that name. Finally, and perhaps most important in Durkheim's teaching legacy was the tradition of sociology he established in France, with the names of Marcel Mauss, Paul Fauconnet, Georges Davy, Celestin Bouglé, and Maurice Halbwachs among the most notable exemplars of that tradition.

The range of Durkheim's teaching was as wide as his intellectual interests generally. Harry Alpert has given us a listing of the courses Durkheim taught, beginning with the years at Bordeaux and continuing through his last days at the University of Paris. The listing includes social solidarity, sociology of the family, suicide, law and ethics, history of socialism, punishment, moral education, crime and deviance, the history of sociological thought, history of education, and primitive society.[4] The formal listing does not, of course, include the many specialized subjects on which Durkheim gave students the benefit of his learning in circumstances of a more informal kind. It would be hard, from all accounts, to find any single mind in the modern history of science and scholarship that achieved a more fruitful union of research and teaching. If the years reaching from 1887, when Durkheim began his university career as teacher, to 1914, when World War I broke out, are splendid years of research and writing, they are not less splendid as years of teaching.

Durkheim's final years were dominated by the issues, the passions, and the appalling slaughter of World War I. We are justified in saying that when this war broke out, Durkheim the teacher-scholar was succeeded by Durkheim the ardent French patriot. In this respect he was exactly like Weber and Simmel in Germany, both of whom—among many other scholars and scientists—threw themselves passionately into the war. It is difficult for us today, nationalist though we still are in high degree, to appreciate the almost religious intensity of both French and German nationalism in 1914. Scholars of the gentlest and most humane nature could be found on both sides of World War I, and from all countries, the United States included once it entered that war in 1916, engaged in the fiercest of nationalist passions.

Durkheim was no exception. To the normal intensity of devotion to the French cause against Germany there was added the bitterness and grief that attended the news of the death on the eastern front of his only son shortly after hostilities broke out. We are told that Durkheim never fully recovered from his grief. His health broke down in 1916, and, sensing that his own end was not far away, he commenced arranging his papers and notes for the benefit of students and others who would continue his work in sociology after the war. Fortunate it is that he did this, for the stream of posthumously published works, devotedly put in final form by students, is a long and distinguished one. He died, just short of age sixty, at Fontainebleau where he was staying temporarily, on November 15, 1917.

SOCIAL MILIEU

Social milieu is one of Durkheim's central concepts, and we can do no better at this point, having looked briefly at his biography, than to apply it to the understanding of his major ideas and perspectives. "The elements which make up this milieu," writes Durkheim, "are of two kinds: things and persons. Besides material objects incorporated into the society, there must also be included the products of previous social activity: law, established customs, literary and artistic works, etc..''[5] We cannot hope to understand the specific themes of Durkheim's work except in terms of the milieu in which Durkheim thought and worked—in which, indeed, he was born, lived, and died.

Fundamentally, this milieu was the consequence of the two great revolutions of modern times—the industrial revolution and the political revolution—the former which had soared into greatest visibility in the late 18th century in England, the latter which had made itself so dramatically and lastingly felt about the same time in France with the outbreak of the Revolution. It would be difficult, impossible, I think, to find revolutions anywhere in human history of like magnitude so far as discernible effect upon social organization, human allegiances, social customs, and ideas are concerned. The changes associated with the rise of the machine-based factory system and its vast output of goods and with the explosion of mass democracy, highlighted by new techniques of power over human beings, spread throughout Europe and America in the 19th century and to the rest of the world in the 20th. The consequences of the two revolutions were to destroy, or reduce to obsolescent inutility, a great many of the structures of belief, authority, and community within which human beings had lived for centuries, even millennia.

We know that Durkheim was profoundly affected by currents generated by both revolutions. We see these currents throughout the pages of his first great work, the *Division of Labor,* especially in the final chapters, where he confronts directly the types of anomie which he declared to be the results of the revolutions, particularly the industrial. The currents are manifest again in his *Suicide.* The two major types of suicide for modern man, he writes, are *egoistic* and *anomic,* each the direct result of erosion, through historical forces of industrialization and democratization, of those social contexts in which human beings tend to derive suicide-insulating sense of community and of protective authority. Even in so austere and specialized a work as *The Elementary Forms of the Religious Life,* devoted entirely to the rites and beliefs of primitive religion, the attentive reader will find more than a few observations which spring from Durkheim's deep conviction of the erosive effects of hyper-individualism upon any form of social association or community.

Individualism was, in a strict sense, the very essence of the two revolutions. Whether through spread of the factory system, with its novel forms of function and authority springing so largely from technology, or through the spread of mass democracy, with its steadily increasing number of political activities and powers, the individual was being dislocated everywhere, as it seemed to those living in the 19th and early 20th centuries, from traditional and established contexts of association and meaning.

Paralleling the individualism of circumstance generated by the two revolutions was the immense outburst of individualism of thought to be found in 19th-century social and moral philosophy. By a great many minds individualism was thought to be the crowning achievement of the laws of human development, the manifestation of a form of freedom never before known to man but also of a form of social organization never before known. In the writings of the English utilitarians Jeremy Bentham, James Mill, Benjamin Kidd, Walter Bagehot, and, above all, Herbert Spencer, we find individualism made into the constitutive principle of a science of society.

Herbert Spencer, who did so much through his voluminous writings to carry the prestige of the new science of sociology all over the world, declared the individual to be the unit of all social analysis as well as the sovereign element of the social order. What did not spring directly from the individual himself, Spencer declared, arose out of contract: the kind of contract that free, separated, individuals make with one another. In France there were to be found analytical individualists also, the greatest of them in sociology being Gabriel Tarde. Between Tarde and his followers and Durkheim and his followers there was uncompromising opposition with respect to principle, method, and conclusion. There had to be, for where Tarde, like Herbert Spencer, saw fundamental reality only in individuals, with society a derivation, Durkheim saw society as the fundamental reality, with individuals sociologically discoverable largely as personifications of society's roles, statuses, and norms.

We shall come back shortly to this basic perspective of Durkheim's work. For the moment it is enough to emphasize the radical character of Durkheim's sociological thought. It was radical in its unrelenting opposition to the whole view of individual and society that was in Durkheim's time so largely current. Durkheim rejected individualism on every possible ground. He found it insupportable as a principle of social solidarity, as an ethic or moral value, as a cornerstone of the social order, and, not least, as the vantage point of social analysis. Hence the sharp criticisms we encounter in all of Durkheim's principal writings of individualism in the several manifestations of this almost universal philosophy in the 19th century. Hence the specific criticisms of the individualistically oriented titans of his day, such as Herbert Spencer and Gabriel Tarde.

Still another powerful element of Durkheim's milieu must be cited here: biologism. There were two major forms that were taken by biologism: racial and individual. Durkheim opposed both with equal intensity. Not all racialist doctrines of the time were of the kind of absurdity that lifted one race, commonly the white, into social, cultural, and mental preeminence, the kind reflected in ideas of Aryan supremacy. There were theories that endeavored, without special favor to any single race, simply to establish the principle that there is close and ineradicable relation between a given race and its form of culture—whether high or low. These theories, in short, sought merely to advance race as a major factor in accounting for social change in history, for development or progress. So common were these theories that the words "race" and "culture" and "nation" were often used interchangeably. It was assumed that the French, say, by virtue of being a nation and a culture formed a distinct race, one significantly different from the "races" of Germans, Italians, and others.

The other equally influential form of biologism was that which made the individual its center or focus. Here it was the presumed existence of instincts, drives, or needs in the individual, biologically transmitted through the germ plasm from one generation to another, that was made the central element of social explanation. If we find the arts of industry, they must spring from an "instinct for workmanship"; if it is war we are concerned with accounting for, the cause lies in an instinct for "belligerence" or "aggressiveness." So too with other aspects of the social order or of social behavior. Family, law, government, language, sociability, protectiveness, delinquency, insanity, and all the other phenomena of society are to be explained through biological causes such as variable instinct, variable biological capacity. If some individuals succeed visibly and lastingly, it is because their innate, biologically transmitted, mental powers are superior to those of others. So the argument went.

Durkheim, from the beginning of his scholarly career, opposed both of these forms of biologism. Neither in the collective germ plasm of race nor in the germ plasm of the individual did Durkheim find more than a point of departure for sociology. Biological explanations may be adequate—that is, a part of the larger picture—Durkheim argued, but they can never be *sufficient*. For sufficient, for crucial, explanations of social behavior—within which he placed culture, language, and human thought itself—we must always go to social elements, to the groups, statuses, roles, functions, and norms which comprise the social order.

Sigmund Freud and Vilfredo Pareto, towering intellects of Durkheim's age, are sufficient evidence of the power that was exerted by doctrines which were, at bottom, not merely individualistic but also biologistic. Freud was, plainly, a radical mind. To him above all others we are indebted for modern realization of the role of the nonrational, the prerational motivations of the unconscious mind of the individual. In his revolt against ordinary analytical rationalism Freud must be regarded as a creative mind of highest luster. But at no point did Freud ever depart from either the individualism or the residual biologism of his age. Neither did Pareto, who also found reality in states of mind or feeling contained within the individual in the forms of what he called "residues." For both Pareto and Freud society was a

derivation from the prior reality of the individual, his drives, instincts, needs, and other biologically inherited mechanisms.

It was during this age, commencing in the 1870s, that psychology became a notable academic and research discipline. Psychology seemed to many to be the master-science when it came to
the understanding of both individual and society. Individual
psychology was the study of the consciousness, inner states of
feeling, and internal motivations of the individual. Social psychology, which came into being as a discipline about the same
time, was the study of the mental or affective *relations* of individuals to one another. But, back in that day, even social psychology was erected on foundations of individualist-biologism.
To look through any of the major works of social psychology of
that time, ranging from Wundt in Germany, through Tarde in
France, and Spencer in England, all the way to William McDou-
gall (whose textbook on the subject went through a large number
of editions) in the United States, is to be confronted by ideas,
then powerful, even regarded as self-evident, which made the individual the be-all and end-all of the understanding of social
phenomena.

It is a mark of the originality and radical character of Durkheim's mind that he opposed psychological doctrines—that is, as
explanations of social and cultural phenomena—as vigorously as
he opposed biological explanations of society. I stress these
points here, for unless the reader is aware of how powerful were
the currents of thought I have described as individualism and
biologism, he cannot understand the intensity of Durkheim's re-
buttals of these currents.

Nor can these currents of thought be relegated to the past.
It is surely evident that they hold a great deal of influence even
at the present time. Racialism as such—that is, explanations of
culture and society in terms of asserted biological structure of
given races—may not today be taken very seriously in the social
sciences and related disciplines. But there is still a great deal of
interest in biological and psychological explanations of social
phenomena.

Still another current of thought very strong in Durkheim's day, and also one that he sought to negate as an influence or structural element of social science, was what can best be called here the philosophy of consciousness. This was an age in which the philosophies of Schopenhauer, who had died in 1860 but whose writings had become powerful in their influence a generation later, and of Eduard von Hartmann were widely read and discussed. In both, the elements of will, of consciousness and of the unconscious, of the reflexive character of the self, and of awareness played a large role. Preoccupation with self and consciousness was also a striking aspect of literature and art during this period, known as *fin de siècle* in the history of the poetry, drama, novel, and painting, and regarded as a subjectivist reaction against classical or objective tendencies in these areas.

We know that Durkheim tended to regard these movements in philosophy and art as signs of decadence, of malaise of the Western mind—he dealt with them in precisely these terms in his *Suicide,* toward the end where he is describing the larger currents of thought and behavior within which rising rates of suicide were to be seen—and we know also that he repudiated consciousness or its exploration as being in any way germane to the interests of social science as such. Much of the emphasis Durkheim gave throughout his life to external structures and events as the proper subject matter of sociology arose, surely, from personal opposition amounting almost to revulsion to currents of reflexive, self-drawn, and even narcissistic thought which were then, as in our own day, so common among intellectuals.

I have so far been describing the larger milieu of European thought within which Durkheim's distinctive ideas are to be seen. But no genuinely creative mind has ever lived in response to large milieu alone, no matter how powerful the themes and currents of that milieu may be. Always there is the smaller, more intimate milieu, which in Durkheim's case was the city of Paris in the late 19th century. Early in the century Goethe had declared Paris the most exciting, stimulating, and fertile city in the world. The mere fact, he told Eckermann, that a young man came of age in Paris meant that he was years in advance of his contemporaries elsewhere in Europe so far as learning, insight, and buoyancy of thought were involved.[6] Little of this had been changed by the time Durkheim first came to Paris to study, though of course there had been the devastating psychological blow to Frenchmen of their humiliating defeat by Prussia in 1870 and the dreadful aftermath in Paris with the Commune there and its fearful repression. Such events may have saddened Frenchmen of light and learning, preoccupied them, as was certainly the case with Durkheim, by thoughts of French national honor and greatness, but they did not dampen the creative ardor of one of the world's great intellectual and artistic capitals.

There is much in common, I think, between Paris in the 19th century and Athens of the 5th century B.C. Each city during its century of luster knew war and tragedy, victory and defeat. Each also knew the kind of effervescence of mind that is so often the result of persistence of traditions from the past which are attacked but not destroyed by intellectually revolutionary elements, making for that creative fusion between past and present, convention and revolt. In both cities we are struck by the number of those who came from small, remote, or distant regions, attracted by the luster of the great city, and who became accepted by kindred minds in the city. So many of the great Athenian creators of the 5th century B.C. had been born in obscurity, oftentimes at substantial distances from Athens, but who went to Athens, attracted by its fame as a haven for the vigorous mind, who were exhilarated by the swift-moving currents of thought, stimulated by the examples of the already-great, and who then in their varied ways added to the greatness of Athens.

Much of that was true of Paris in the 19th century, not least in the final decades of the century when Durkheim, along with so many others of like talent, left the place of his birth in the French hinterland to go to Paris, to study, work, and to become fired-up by the presences as well as the teachings and the works of authentically distinguished minds. Allow as we will for the inherent qualities of mind and spirit in creative minds, there appears to be nothing that substitutes for the energizing, shaping, and evocative influence of the city in history, the city that is in truth an open society, welcoming in effect all who come, but that also has managed to retain sufficient coherence and collective identity to attract and then motivate. The Paris Durkheim went to as a young man was in every essential respect a city, but it was a far cry from the huge, sprawling, amorphous aggregate of several millions of people we know today. The intense love that Paris aroused in the mind of Durkheim, that made him in a sense a Parisian from the moment he arrived, was to be found in the minds of just about all who went to that city.

As Paris was the immediate context, the fertile milieu, for Durkheim, the source of so many of his sociological and historical interests, so, in a manner of speaking, was the Jewish community into which he had been born. Or, rather, we should say the Jewish community set as it was in a country, especially in Paris itself, where anti-Semitism was singularly weak, if not entirely nonexistent. The Jews had been given full rights during the French Revolution, and although it would be absurd to imply that 19th-century France was without persisting prejudices toward the Jews —flaring up indeed on at least two occasions during Durkheim's years in Paris—there is no doubt that Jews of talent were accorded a far greater opportunity in France, and particularly in Paris, during the late nineteenth and early twentieth centuries than anywhere else in the Western world. The experience Durkeim knew of having been born in a close religious-cultural community, the Judaic community, and then liberating himself in substantial degree from the community of his birth and becoming assimilated in an open society like Paris was bound to have an exhilarating and also creative experience, given his intrinsic excellence of mind. There were more than a few French Jews in Durkheim's time who had known almost precisely the experience he had, or who would have that same experience still later, and it is no wonder that French Jews figure so prominently in the intellectual and artistic greatness of late-nineteenth-century Paris.

There is nothing at all bizarre in the thought that so many of

Durkheim's distinctive sociological interests were motivated in part by the kinds of experience he and other Jews in Paris knew so well: the release from childhood immurement within traditional community and dogma, the inevitable persistence of memory of such community, but, no doubt of still greater importance, the zestful experience of emergence of individuality in the setting of the city and modern legal state. I have already indicated the importance of the larger milieu in Western thought of biologism and individualism against which Durkheim reacted powerfully and creatively in his thinking. Not a little of his stress upon the social must have come too from personal experience in Paris. For in Paris, above any other capital in the Western world at that time, the concentrated essence of Western thought, spirit, and style was to be found, all set in a context that was, while large and open, yet small enough still, as cities go, for it to be assimilated and worked on by strong and vigorous minds such as Durkheim's. If, in sum, there is a great deal in Durkheim's sociology about community and structure and authority on the one hand, and about alienation, anomie, and disintegration on the other, we cannot overlook the milieu of Paris as an almost ideal one for the emergence and cultivation of these dominating interests.

For, if the metropolis was the context of individual achievement, it was also the context of individual loneliness, egoism, and occasional sense of estrangement from society and self. If it was the scene of intense and buoyant living, it was also the scene of the kind of malaise that always is the counterpart of that kind of living. And there is the fact too that it was precisely in such a city as Paris, wonderfully free by the standards of that age from limitations placed upon the accidents of birth, ethnicity, and locality of origin, that minds like Durkheim's should have become so sensitive to the power of the social in fixing the essential values of human life, and in providing the structural supports of human activity and thought.

Finally, there is the fact that Paris, I think above any other city in the latter part of the 19th century, was the microcosm of all the larger currents of thought, of all the clashes of principle, ideology, and aspiration, which made Western Europe as a whole so resplendent. In Paris the philosophical and political conservatism that had been generated early in the century by fierce reaction to the Revolution came to fruition, in sometimes warped and debased ways, in the works and activities of Charles Maurras and his *L'Action Française*. This movement, with its emphasis on social and national solidarity, on the intermediate groups, on absolute rejection of both individualism and national centralization, and on the mystique of the nation, could not have helped but arouse Durkheim's interest, however repugnant he inevitably found certain of its overt forms of reaction. At the opposite extreme was the almost millennialist socialist movement in France, led brilliantly by Durkheim's friend Jean Jaurès, relentless opponent of war, capitalism, and clericalism, separated from the Marxian socialism in other parts of Europe in part by nationalism, in part by greater emphasis upon historically developed ideals than was to be found in the works of Marx and his followers. In between these extremes lay a wide continuum of beliefs, all energetically and clamantly expressed in the dozens, even hundreds, of newspapers and journals which were their outlets. Paris was, without any question, the single most *political* of all settings in the Western world at that time. And, for good or ill, it seems to be a fact that the greater cultural ages in history are undergirded, or at least powerfully influenced, by the clash of political values.

But politics was only a small part of the total intellectual character of Paris. Innovation and experimentation of every kind were to be found in other spheres as well: music, painting, sculpture, literature, philosophy, and science. Moreover—and this is a crucial fact in cultural efflorescences—there was an astonishing degree of personal acquaintance, certainly personal awareness, among the principals of this age. They knew each other, often saw each other, and were stimulated by each other—whether positively or negatively—to a degree that is remarkable by contemporary standards. One need only run his eye down the listings of the intellectually, artistically, academically, and scientifically creative minds in Paris during the quarter-century leading up to World

War I that may be found in any textbook of modern French history to be made instantly aware of the field-impulses of mental character which formed Durkheim's day-to-day setting.

ANTECEDENTS

We shall limit ourselves here to those philosophers during the century preceding the commencement of Durkheim's labors whose influence on Durkheim is direct and clear. No worthwhile purpose is ever served, in examination of a scholar's works, by merely listing predecessors in which the claimed influence is either so general or so indirect as to lose effect. The best way of indicating Durkheim's intellectual antecedents is to take our departure from his own works, finding in these the scholars and philosophers whose effect upon him, whether positive or negative, was substantial.

MONTESQUIEU   He was the subject of one of the two dissertations (the other being the *Division of Labor*) Durkheim was obliged to write for his doctorate. Much of Durkheim's treatment of Montesquieu is critical, and it is critical precisely in terms of the very canons on which Montesquieu himself had built his great *The Spirit of the Laws*. For, unlike so many of the philosophers of the Enlightenment, Montesquieu had aimed at a work which would be as objective and dispassionate, as free of political or moral preconception as possible. For all the distinctive analytical power of Montesquieu's work, it falls short of these aspirations, and Durkheim realized it. Even so the merits of Montesquieu's comparative investigation of human polities and cultures overshadow the deficiencies. Almost certainly, it was from Montesquieu that Durkheim acquired the deep sense of analytical reasoning united with empirical observation that characterizes everything he ever wrote. The positivism that has so often been marked in Durkheim's philosophy and sociology has its roots more deeply in Montesquieu, I believe, so far as Durkheim's work is concerned than it does in such later writers as Comte who also influenced Durkheim.

ROUSSEAU   Early in his teaching career, Durkheim gave a course
on Rousseau, particularly his momentous *Social Contract,* and
we know that Rousseau's writings had formed in some degree a
major source of Durkheim's interest in the problem of association, in the nature of the social bond. Later Durkheim would
write a short study of Rousseau's *Social Contract,* drawn no
doubt from the lecture-notes of his course, and in due time his
monographs on Montesquieu and Rousseau would be posthumously brought together in a single volume, *Montesquieu and
Rousseau: Forerunners to Sociology.* But while Rousseau's own fascination with the nature of human association, and with the conditions of legitimacy of authority, very obviously generated much
of Durkheim's interest in these matters, there is one profound
difference between the conceptions of the matter we find in Rousseau and Durkheim. In the former, politics is the essence. Rousseau was a disciple of the political community, its fullness, totality, and immediacy to the individual, to a degree found nowhere
else in the history of thought save possibly in Plato. This assuredly cannot be said of Durkheim who, although keenly interested
in the political state, saw it as but one of the associative influences
on man, one indeed that must be limited in its claim and impact
by layers of intermediate authorities: the kind of intermediate
authorities that Rousseau had detested and specifically pro-
scribed. Even so, we cannot omit Rousseau from our list of those
whose central concerns had marked effect upon Durkheim. Political or no, Rousseau's *Social Contract* must have had substantial
effect on Durkheim's mind. The latter's monograph on Rousseau
makes that clear enough.

SAINT-SIMON   The context of Durkheim's direct interest in this
extraordinary figure, who wrote during the period immediately
following the Revolution in France, is chiefly socialism, a subject
in which Durkheim had a certain intellectual and even academic
interest. While still at the University of Bordeaux he gave a
course on the history of socialism in France, and Saint-Simon fig-
ured prominently in this. But without derogating from the so-

cialist effect, there is much reason for believing that Saint-Simon's larger influence on Durkheim was of a distinctly different kind. Unquestionably it was from reading Saint-Simon that Durkheim got his full measure of the effects on French thought generally of the political conservatives who flourished immediately after the French Revolution. Such men as Maistre, Bonald, François René de Chateaubriand, and Lamennais, all Catholics, all political conservatives, traditionalists to the core, had attacked the Revolution and its principles on every possible intellectual and moral ground. They objected, above all else, to the Revolution's individualism, its destructive effect upon traditional communities and systems of belief Saint-Simon was deeply impressed by the writings of the conservatives, as his references to them attest. And despite his quasi-religious interest in a new order, one that would spring from a new science, given moral structure by a new religion of humanity, there is a great deal in Saint-Simon's writings that can be explained only by his early fascination with the French conservatives. The same, as I have already made clear, is true of Durkheim himself. The intellectual, moral, and social conservatism in Durkheim's writings, in his envisagement of the problem of order, is a striking feature of his larger system of thought, in no way offset by Durkheim's political identification with the liberal left of his day—the Dreyfusards.

COMTE   It is difficult to be certain when Durkheim first read Comte, but there is no question of the effect on Durkheim's mind of Comte's positivism. No matter how much Comte may have taken from his early employer and master, Saint-Simon, he was himself a mind of learning and brilliance, much admired in his time, which was the first half of the nineteenth century. Far more systematically than Saint-Simon, Comte set forth visions and principles which were to powerfully enter the mind of Durkheim a half-century later. Among these were the very idea of a true science of society, called by Comte sociology, one that would be as determinedly positivist in its way as any of the other sciences, the absolute rejection of both individualism and critical rationalism,

the focusing of attention upon society, which for Comte was literally the *Grand Étre,* the subject of cult and worship before Comte
had died, upon the norms, groups, and statuses which compose
society, and, far from least, the conceptions of the social statics
and social dynamics which were Comte's two great divisions of
his social science. There can be no question that Durkheim, however much he may have improved upon, secularized, and system-
atized, drew substantially from Comte, even if he repudiated
Comte's almost religious emphasis upon the mission of science.
Comte too had been fascinated by the works of the conservatives
mentioned above, and Durkheim's reading of Comte represented
still another channel for the conservatism that so definitely influenced him.

SPENCER   Negative, for the most part, is the word here. But not
the less powerful. Spencer was, as we observed above, not merely
a sociologist—and without question the most noted of his day—
but also a philosophical utilitarian. Spencer tended to see everything social as either a direct emanation from individual nature
or as a highly intellectualized contract among human beings. Admittedly, Spencer was, or had been at one point in his life, be-
mused by the analogy of society to the organism. There is, in
short, slight ground at least for declaring Spencer, as many were
to declare Durkheim, though falsely, a social organicist. But the
overarching implications of Spencer's work flow directly from his
analytical individualism and his view of society as being fundamentally a manifestation of contract. Durkheim, in a large
number of contexts, bore down hard on Spencer and his views.
It is difficult to think of any single contemporary, or near-
contemporary, Tarde included, whom Durkheim attacked as systematically in his thought and writing as he did Spencer. And
their respective principles, or underlying premises, remain to this
day the principal polarity in the study of sociology.

FUSTEL DE COULANGES   He was, as was noted above, one of Durkheim's teachers, one of the very few indeed whom Durkheim ad-

mired deeply at the time when he was a student in college. Fustel de Coulanges was a historian, a widely admired historian, and was also one of the most learned men of his day. There is little doubt, I think, that from Fustel de Coulanges came a large measure of Durkheim's interest in the nature of consensus and in the roles of tradition and community in the larger structure of social order. Fustel's *The Ancient City,* published in 1864, is one of the most arresting treatments of the subject of consensus and community ever written: set in terms of a comparative study of the ancient Greek and Roman city states. Beyond the slightest doubt, Durkheim must have read and reread this work of his revered teacher. I think that much of Durkheim's interest in what he called "intermediate authorities" also came from Fustel de Coulanges—though it may well have been Tocqueville's great and widely known *Democracy in America,* in which intermediate associations are made the very substructure of political freedom. Fustel de Coulanges, however, was the author of a vastly learned history of French institutions, with especial emphasis on the Middle Ages and their plethora of associations in all spheres of life. So much of what Durkheim himself wrote on intermediate authorities and associations has a medieval background that we may justly assume, I think, that this work by his teacher was the prime source.

ERNEST RENAN   Here I deviate slightly from what I declared above would be the purpose of this brief treatment of antecedents —that is, citation solely of those predecessors whom Durkheim himself identified as strong influences on his thinking. We are told by the learned Henri Peyre that Durkheim had only distaste for Renan's writings, but, Professor Peyre continues, "Durkheim was influenced by them more than any historian of ideas has yet shown." Although evidence is hard to come by, I believe this to be true. Renan was one of the most celebrated figures in France, even Europe, during Durkheim's youth. His book *The Future of Science,* written in 1848, finally published in 1890, was an all-out, brilliantly conceived and written, defense of science and its applicability to man and society. His monumental studies of religion, *History of the Origins of Christianity* (1863–83) and *History of the People of Israel* (1887–93), are among the most neglected and underappreciated works of the 19th century at the present time. Immensely learned, rigorous in method, and concerned throughout with the social origins of the beliefs and rites dealt with, these books, appearing at the time they did, were bound to have had a great impact upon the young Durkheim. Renan's own nationalism, expressed in his famous essay of 1882 "What is a Nation?" is, almost syllable for syllable, Durkheim's own nationalism, expressed in later years. Tirelessly, Renan emphasized the necessity of explaining social phenomena by social factors—not by physical or biological ones. And Renan carried this specifically, as had Tocqueville before him, to the repudiation of race as proper explanation of mental and cultural phenomena. So too does Renan insist that the ethics of the future will derive basically from man's increasingly scientific command of self and environment. In sort, despite lack of favorable reference to Renan—whose elegance of personal style and cultivation of the limelight may have offended the young Durkheim as these did the young William James in America and many another serious young thinker of the time—we are obliged to agree with Professor Peyre, I think, and place Renan's profound works, with their cognate perspectives and interests, very definitely among the central influences on Durkheim. Durkheim could no more have escaped Renan than a young sociologist today could escape Talcott Parsons.

TÖNNIES   We shall be brief here. There is very little, if anything, in Durkheim's work that cannot be illuminated by sources to be found solely in France. Nevertheless it is a fact that Tönnies's *Gemeinschaft und Gesellschaft* was published six years before Durkheim's first major work, that Durkheim reviewed Tönnies's book a year after it was published, and that there is at least some affinity between the argument of Tönnies on the subject of types of solidarity and that to be found in Durkheim's the *Division of La-*

bor. There is also the fact, as we have seen, that Durkheim spent a full year in Germany just prior to publication of Tönnies's book and must surely have come in contact with issues which Tönnies dealt with.

BIBLIOGRAPHICAL

It will be useful if, before dealing with Durkheim's principal concepts as they pertain to contemporary sociology, we list and describe briefly his major books. I shall begin with his four major works, all published within his lifetime, describing each in a few short paragraphs, and then pass, with much more limited comment, to his posthumous publications.

THE DIVISION OF LABOR   This work, published in 1893, his first major one, written in the first instance as one of the two dissertations required for his doctorate at the *École* (the other will be noted below among Durkheim's posthumous works), is fundamental to any understanding of Durkheim's development as a mind. It is in a certain sense an unsuccessful book. That is, the book's announced thesis with respect to social solidarity is never demonstrated; further, Durkheim seems to have been well aware of his lack of success, and, it is worth noting, he never again employed the basic categories of this book, which are "mechanical solidarity" and "organic solidarity." Nevertheless, the careful reader will be able to see in this book, rich in insight and perspective, the essential materials of what would be his distinctive contribution to social science in all of his ensuing works.

The thesis of the *Division of Labor* may be stated succinctly. Society has evolved from a condition Durkheim characterizes as "mechanical solidarity" to one based upon the division of labor that he calls "organic solidarity." The first is primitive or folk in character, the second modern.

By mechanical solidarity Durkheim means a structure of society built in the first instance around "repressive law," that is, the law of crimes. Crime, we are told, is an act that offends the collective conscience. Punishment has its origins in the need of a society to purge itself, that is, its collective conscience, manifest in social codes, mores, and taboos, of the guilt created when one of its members violates this conscience. Mechanical solidarity is one of overwhelming likeness—social, legal, religious, and moral likeness. The pressure to conform is powerful and unremitting. Individuality, contract, will, and reason, as human qualities or relationships, are subordinated, as are tendencies toward differentiation of type. Kinship and religion are the dominant social ties.

Organic solidarity is the type of cohesion that rests upon division of labor, upon social differentiation, and individual specialization. Legally, Durkheim tells us, it is characterized, not by repressive-criminal sanctions but instead by those of a contractual or restitutive character, with the direct role of the collective conscience accordingly reduced. The function of division of labor is thus declared to be social: to be literally that of promoting a form of solidarity the elements of which in society have the same kind of complementary and symbiotic relation that the organs of the human body have to one another.

The *Division of Labor* concludes with Durkheim's recognition that, while the arc of development is indeed from mechanical to organic solidarity, certain historical factors in the West have prevented this development from occurring smoothly. "Abnormal forms" of social behavior are thus to be found in the West. These include spreading unhappiness of people, a mark of civilization, Durkheim argues, increases in the suicide rate, "anomic" division of labor characterized by industrial crises, "forced" division of labor resulting from class antagonisms, and so forth. The failure of division of labor, Durkheim concludes, is thus far to be seen in a lack of genuine moral consensus that will do for modern society what the collective conscience was able to do in primitive society.

This is the bare essence of the book. We shall come back to its details later. Here it will suffice to say that it was in the very process of seeking to establish the sufficiency of specialization and division of labor as the proper base of modern "organic" solidarity that Durkheim came upon the interests in social structure, in pathological behavior, in social psychology, in morality, and in religion which would last him the rest of his life. That is why the *Division of Labor* is so vital to any understanding of Durkheim. That the overall argument failed, could not be sustained—attested to sufficiently by the fact that Durkheim never again went back to it, never again made explicit use of the categories of mechanical and organic solidarity—and falls rather conventionally in an evolutionary framework that was so common in social science in the 19th century, is much less important than the fact that in the process of failing in a major attempt Durkheim arrived at insights which were to become constitutive not only in his own sociology but in that of the contemporary world.

THE RULES OF SOCIOLOGICAL METHOD This book, published in 1895 on the basis of articles which had appeared somewhat earlier, can be properly seen as a methodological and philosophical interlude in a life that was empirical to the core. Important, profound, and, by today's standards, unexceptionable though it is in very large part, it is yet unfortunate that this is the book that was for so many years Durkheim's main link with the rest of the Western sociological world. Here is where he makes explicit what had been implicit in much of the *Division of Labor,* and would be implicit in the later *Suicide* and *Elementary Forms of Religious Life:* a method, with elementary theory contained, for the study of human behavior in society that would dispense with biological, geographical, and related nonsocial explanations so prevalent in Durkheim's day and that would, equally, make unnecessary explorations of individual consciousness, feelings, and other internal states falling within the realm of psychology as then understood. The proper subject matter for the study of society, Durkheim writes in this small but far-reaching volume, are the constituent elements of society: social roles, statuses, norms, and the distinctive mechanisms of interaction these generate. Hence Durkheim's emphasis on the nature of social facts (in contrast to biological or psychological facts), the ways in which they can best be observed, the distinction—sociological distinction—between the normal and the pathological, the most useful methods of discovering social facts and then of explaining them. The book is a treatise on method as well as an essay in social theory; no profounder one has been written in sociology. Its principal contentions are today sunk deeply into the theory and empirical research of sociology. For all that, when Durkheim's little book appeared, such were the still ascendant idols of individualism, racialism, and instinctivism in the social science of his day, abroad as well as at home, such, I should say, was the reductionism of that day, the book was immediately characterized as a piece of social metaphysics composed of reifications and hypostatizations, the whole a variant of organicism.

Unhappily, that characterization has stuck in considerable degree even though during the past seventy-five years sociology has changed enormously in its theoretical and methodological substance, a great deal of the change the result precisely of assimilation of insights and axioms first to be found explicitly stated in *The Rules of Sociological Method*. As I shall make clear in the body of this book, there isn't more than a hair's breadth between Durkheim's view of the relation between society and the individual and the view that was later to be exposited in America by George Herbert Mead in his philosophy lectures at Chicago. The fact remains, to this moment, the view persists that whereas "the individual" exists as a reality in Mead's social psychology, with specific modes of interaction between individual and society made visible, neither "individual" nor modes of interaction are to be found in Durkheim. The view is, I believe, a wholly false one, but of its durability and momentum there can be no question.

I cannot help thinking that if *The Rules of Sociological Method* had remained unknown to Americans, if Durkheim's entry into the American scene had been accomplished entirely by *Suicide* and *The Elementary Forms of Religious Life*, works in which the same social psychology, the same method, and the same theory, are to be found that lie in *The Rules,* but are set in utterly empirical contexts, the kind of confusion I have been writing of would probably never have arisen in the first place.

SUICIDE   How many years exactly went into the research for this work we do not know for sure. It was published in 1897, only two years after publication of *The Rules,* four years after the *Division of Labor,* where Durkheim had first stressed the rising rates of suicide in modern society as well as the social character of the phenomenon. I do not mean that Durkheim was the first in France or in Europe to call attention either to the rise in rates under conditions of modernity or to the social-demographic character such rates have in a population. There had been earlier workers in social statistics who had done so, and in Tocqueville's *Democracy in America* there is a chapter emphasizing the relation between increases in suicide rates and patterns of social mobility in France. (In none of these works, however, was there an effort to explain, in social psychological terms, the relation.)

Suicide, Durkheim makes clear at the outset, has several objectives: not the least that of social policy research through which a reduction in rates of suicide in the population might be effected, with specific proposals offered toward the end of the volume. But along with this practical objective is to be found the strictly methodological objective of demonstrating *how* an act generally conceived as individualistic in essence can be studied and interpreted through use of the kinds of concepts that had been dealt with abstractly in *The Rules of Sociological Method;* how, in other words, suicide can be transferred, for explanation's sake, from the realms of the geographical, racial, psychiatric, and psychological to the sociological. And, finally, *Suicide* is a profound treatise in social psychology. I know of no other work in modern social science that precedes in time this book's analysis of the social nature of human personality and of the relation of personality to social structures. Not for more than a decade would the similar though fragmentary analyses of Charles H. Cooley and George Herbert Mead make their appearance in

America. The primary contribution of *Suicide,* or at least the most obvious, is its classification of suicides into the three broad types of "egoistic," "anomic," and "altruistic," classifications which have been refined in more recent sociological work but not seriously altered, much less dislodged. But in the process of elaborating upon these types and showing the empirical relevance of the types to the demographic data from which Durkheim worked, he was obliged to *explain* them. Discovery of the types was, in short, the first major step; explanation was the necessary second step. It is in Durkheim's explanation of the nature of "egoistic" and "anomic" suicide—the two types to which he gave greatest attention, "altruistic" suicide being relatively rare—that we find his brilliant exposition of the social roots of personality, of the dependence of personality upon social structure and social value, and of the predictable pathological effects upon personality of substantial dislocations of structure and value in a population. From this book above any other in sociological theory and research have come today's diversely fruitful principles and hypotheses in the study of deviance. But as we shall see, the importance of the book goes well beyond this field. Like many another first-rate study in sociology, including W. I. Thomas's *The Polish Peasant,* where theory, method, and fact are also united to such a fertile degree, *Suicide* is a book with numerous dimensions of meaning.

THE ELEMENTARY FORMS OF RELIGIOUS LIFE Not until 1912 did Durkheim publish this book, considered by many to be his masterpiece. We know that Durkheim's interest in the special form of social control embedded in religious rites and codes goes back at least to his treatment of mechanical solidarity in the *Division of Labor,* which had appeared in 1893. We know too that it was only shortly after that he taught his first course on religion, at Bordeaux, and from that time on religion never ceased to be in the very forefront of his sociological interests. Both the articles he himself wrote and those he accepted as editor for *L'Année* reveal an almost obsessive interest in the sociological nature of religion and its varied relationships to society and to human personality.

The book rests upon Durkheim's momentous distinction between the sacred and the profane. It is this distinction, he argues, and not belief in gods and spirits that is the universal and unfailing substance of religion. Agnostic though Durkheim himself was throughout his life, he nevertheless declared religion the source of the fundamental categories of the human mind—space, time, cause, etc.—and the origin too of all the fundamental institutions, including kinship, property, and law, which only late in evolutionary time became differentiated from their aboriginal source in man's sense of the sacred. For Durkheim indeed the sacred and the social bond are but two sides of the same coin. There can be, he argued, no durable social tie, no lasting moral value, apart from the cement provided by man's capacity for recognition of the sacred, that is, his awareness of meanings which transcend the merely utilitarian, pragmatic, and profane.

From his identification of the sacred as the original and lastingly residual element of religion, Durkheim moves to further identification of the social molecule of religion; this he finds in the *cult,* the smallest but hardest and most universal associative context of religion. In its origins the cult is totemistic, founded on the sacred community that primitive man had with some plant or animal as the quintessential manifestation of charisma—to use Weber's term, one that Durkheim did not use but that fits his treatment of the sacred and of the totemistic cult perfectly. Religion is a social thing in its foundation, with the cult the indestructible representation of the sacred. Associated with the cult there are found, in primitive as well as in advanced religion, the all-necessary *rites,* negative and positive, through which man is able by direct experience to participate in the sacred, to be cleansed of impurities (through the negative rites) and to be made a member (through positive rites) of that community, visible and invisible, which is founded everywhere on the sense of the sacred.

Throughout his book, Durkheim makes plain his repugnance for all merely rationalistic or utilitarian theories of religion and its origins. Not in superstition as such, not in animistic

belief, not indeed in any instinct or state of mind such as the rationalists of Durkheim's day, following the *philosophes* a century
earlier, hypothesized to account for religion, but through society
and its component elements does Durkheim seek to explain religion. That the intellectual character of religion and its regard
for the sacred—whether expressed in the aboriginal form of totemism or in belief in Judaic, Christian, or Muslim god—will
change from time to time, that the advance of science will always
have effect upon the varied cosmological and ethical beliefs to be
found in religions, all of this Durkheim allows for. But of the
eternality of religion, resting as it does upon man's differentiation of the sacred from the profane, there is not the slightest
doubt in Durkheim's mind. Durkheim may well have been atheist
and disbeliever. *The Elementary Forms of Religious Life* is, nevertheless, one of the most powerful statements of the functional indispensability of religion in society ever written.

POSTHUMOUS WORKS   The four books just described briefly are,
as I have noted, Durkheim's major works, the only major sociological works of book length published during his lifetime, and,
of course, the ones which have most deeply influenced modern social science. They are not, however, the only books which bear
his authorship. Durkheim was a prodigious worker, and during
his lifetime accumulated a considerable volume of articles published and unpublished, of lectures written but not put into
print, of manuscripts of varying subject and length, and a mass
of notes. That he would himself have converted these, or most of
them, into books is clear enough; his untimely death at age fifty-
nine prevented this, the more especially since his last few years
were given ardently to his beloved France in World War I.

Fortunately, his students, among them such distinguished social scientists in their own right as Marcel Mauss, Maurice Halbwachs—very possibly the greatest of Durkheim's students, whose
life ended in a German extermination camp in World War II—
Paul Fauconnet, and Georges Davy, saw to it that the abundant
materials Durkheim had left behind were put in book form.

Their work of finding, editing, and publishing Durkheim's rich manuscripts commenced in the early 1920s. I shall do little more than list these posthumous books here, reserving for later chapters the more detailed use they deserve. All have by now been translated into English, though this did not occur until three decades after they began to come forth in France. The date I give for each is the date of French publication.

Education and Sociology (1922) is an admirable expression of Durkheim's lifelong interest in the educational process and the relation of formal education to social structure and to the channels of socialization in society.

Sociology and Philosophy (1924) is an elaboration in many instances of philosophically oriented arguments found in *The Rules of Sociological Method* mainly, but also in other works. Durkheim had been keenly interested in philosophy while a student at the *École Normale*. The distinguished philosopher Emile Boutroux had been one of his most cherished teachers, and, it is interesting to know, one of Durkheim's classmates, Henri Bergson, was to become one of the most famous of 20th-century philosophers.

Moral Education (1925) is what its title would suggest, but it is also a profound study in social psychology, particularly of the socialization process, and clears up a good many of the questions raised in the minds of those whose conception of Durkheim's social psychology is limited to what can be found in *The Rules of Sociological Method*. We shall have much to say about this book in later chapters.

Socialism and Saint-Simon (1928) reveals Durkheim's lifelong interest in the ideology of socialism, its origins in the two revolutions of the early part of the 19th century, democratic and industrial, its relation to the rise of sociology in France, and its strengths and weaknesses as a prescription for social stability. Durkheim was an interested, in some ways affectionate student of socialism, but his writings and lectures on the subject reveal him to be generally skeptical of socialism as being much more than an indication of benevolent intentions in an individual or group.

Only in the very loosest and most tenuous sense was Durkheim himself socialist in political sympathies.

L'ÉVOLUTION PÉDAGOGIQUE EN FRANCE (1938)   This has not thus far been translated into English, which is a pity, for here is evidence enough of Durkheim's mastery of the main currents of European intellectual history as well as of the principles of research into this important area of historiography. As Maurice Halbwachs observes in his introduction, Durkheim may not have been a professional historian, but he had been an alert and knowledgeable student of history from the time he had studied at the *École* under Fustel de Coulanges. Originally offered as a course in 1904–1905, repeated each year until the outbreak of World War I, these valuable insights into intellectual and educational history in France were put in book form for publication in 1938, largely under the supervision of Halbwachs.

By any standard it is a first-rate study of the origins of French education in the early Middle Ages, and the development of both school and university through the high Middle Ages, the Renaissance, Reformation, Enlightenment, and Revolution, down to Durkheim's own day. Particularly good are the chapters on the medieval universities and on the long tradition of Jesuit education, both of which Durkheim admired. It is interesting to realize that Durkheim had a far sounder insight into the actual impact of the Renaissance than did many professional historians of his day. He recognized that for all the resplendence of this period, its contributions to philosophy and science were far less than what had begun in the medieval universities and, indeed, continued in the universities down to modern times. So too is there an interesting treatment of the affinity between Protestantism and the rise of practical, including scientific, work in the schools and universities.

PROFESSIONAL ETHICS AND CIVIC MORALS (1950)   is a treatise in political and legal sociology. There are some valuable chapters on the ritual origins of property, contract, and other legal insti-

tutions, and a substantial enlargement of views on the nature of
the state and on the necessity in modern society of organizations
intermediate to the individual and state which Durkheim had
first set forth in the final pages of *Suicide* and then expanded
somewhat in the preface to the second edition of his *Division of
Labor*. The book is indispensable to those interested in Durkheim's political sociology.

MONTESQUIEU AND ROUSSEAU: FORERUNNERS TO SOCIOLOGY (1953)
has for its first section the long essay on Montesquieu and his approach to a science of society that Durkheim had written and
published in Latin (1892) as one of the two dissertations required
for the doctorate at the *École Normale* (the other, as noted above,
being the *Division of Labor* which was published in French the
following year). The second section of the book is an essay on
Rousseau's *Social Contract* that Durkheim had prepared and that
was first published after his death as two articles in *Revue de
métaphysique et de la morale* (1918). The essay on Montesquieu
is much superior to the one on Rousseau.

SOCIOLOGY AND PRAGMATISM (1955) is based in large part on the
notes by students from lectures delivered by Durkheim on the
subject. There is unfortunately a fragmentary quality about
the work, but this does not prevent us from getting to the essence
of Durkheim's generally critical view of pragmatism, whether in its
putative European origins (Durkheim deals in the opening lec-
ture with the relation of Nietzsche to pragmatism's beginnings)
or in the full-blown works of Peirce, James, and Dewey.

Those are the principal posthumous works. To them should
be added the recently translated and published *Incest: The Nature and Origin of the Taboo* and *Primitive Classification,* both
published in this country in 1963, both translations of articles
Durkheim had written originally in *L'Année*. There is, finally,
Selected Writings, edited with an introduction by Anthony Gid-
dens (1972), the special merit of which is the number of excerpts
from book reviews and articles by Durkheim which have been

brought together in this volume, along with selections from major works, and organized topically.

In general, allowing only for rare exceptions, it can be said that all of the really fundamental ideas in Durkheim are to be found in the four major works he published during his lifetime. I do not detract from the clarification and frequently fascinating extension of these ideas in the posthumous works, as in *Professional Ethics and Civic Morals, Sociology and Philosophy,* and, of course, *Socialism and Saint-Simon,* which is wholly fresh, or the very real insight into mechanisms of socialization only hinted at in *The Rules* and *Suicide* that we get in *Moral Education.* Even so, the reader who wants to know the essential Durkheim can content himself with the four books he wrote and published during his lifetime.

1 The Scope and Method of Sociology

I shall be concerned in this chapter with three principal aspects of Durkheim's conception of sociology in the family of sciences: first, the boundaries of sociology; second, the proper data of sociology; and third, the nature of sociological explanation.

The reader must bear in mind that method, in the largest and truest sense, cannot be separated from the empirical and theoretical contexts in which we find it at its best. Taking sociology as a whole, the seminal treatments of method have proved to be such works as Max Weber's *Theory of Social and Economic Organization,* Georg Simmel's *Secret Society,* W. I. Thomas's *Polish Peasant,* the Robert Lynds' *Middletown,* and, far from least, Durkheim's *Suicide* and his *Elementary Forms of Religious Life.* None of these classics—and there are, of course, others—would be what it is in distinction were it not for the method of research set forth; but set forth in a way that binds it closely to the data worked with and the theories arrived at. I mention this important general point here simply to alert the reader that, while we shall certainly be concerned with aspects of method in this chapter, we shall continue to be concerned with such aspects in the substantive chapters which follow. Method and theory in the best and highest sense of each are inseparable, and both are to be seen in their richest colors when set in the contexts of the data being explained.

THE SCOPE OF SOCIOLOGY

Sociology was only just coming into existence as a distinctive discipline in Durkheim's lifetime. There was a great deal of self-consciousness and also jealousy to be found among the several disciplines making up the curriculum in European and American universities. The most ancient disciplines were, of course, the classics, which included the history as well as the literature of Greece and Rome, philosophy, law, and medicine. Only, really, in the 19th century did the fields of modern history and literature begin to enter the university curriculum, and the same is true, for that matter, of the sciences, physical, biological, and social. In the area of the study of society and social conduct, law was the nearest that many universities came to the social sciences at the beginning of the final quarter of the 19th century. Psychology was only gradually separating itself from philosophy. Economics, political science, anthropology, and sociology were all hardly more than names, what they covered only dimly and nebulously known, to the vast majority of educated people, including scholars in the universities, in the latter part of the century.

This is why we find so much explicit concern with the scope and nature of sociology, and also of social science generally, in the works of the major pioneers: Weber, Simmel, Durkheim, and Pareto in Europe, Cooley, Sumner, Giddings, and Park in the United States. The task was a double one. Not only did the claims of a social science have to be made to those in the physical sciences, philosophy, law, and other traditional areas of the academy; equally if not more difficult was the task of justifying sociology as a discipline against the emerging fields of economics, political science, anthropology, and, to the extent that it had emerged in a given university out of philosophy, of psychology. There were many who thought that whatever was important and enduring in a social science was already to be found in philosophy and law. And there were many more who, while accepting the idea of a social science, could not see the claims of sociology. Economics had business for a subject; political science had government; anthropology the cultures and races of the primitive areas of the earth's surface; and psychology the individual mind. What, it was often asked in European and American academic circles, did that leave for sociology?

It is in specific answer to this question that we are best able to appreciate the large amount of attention to the scope and boundaries of sociology we find in the works of the early sociologists. Durkheim was no exception. At the time he was a student at the *École Normale* there was not a single professorship in social science as such to be found in France. His own studies, as we have seen, were in philosophy and history. These were the areas in which he began his teaching in the *lycées*. Not until Durkheim went to the University of Bordeaux, which was his first major academic post, was a chair in social science created (for him), the first in France, by the French government. When, some years later, he accepted the call from the Sorbonne, it was in the beginning in the faculty of education. Only later did his title include the fact of his distinction as a social scientist and sociologist.

It is not strange therefore that Durkheim should have given much thought to the nature of social science and, in due time, to the specific character of sociology as one of the sciences. Even in his Latin dissertation on Montesquieu, published, as we have noted above, in 1892, we find his real interest not in this eminent philosopher as such but in the conditions and nature of a genuine social science. He chose Montesquieu as his subject because he believed that whatever may have been the deficiencies of that philosopher's work, *The Spirit of the Laws,* published in 1748, it nevertheless demonstrated irrefutably that a science of society— in contrast to philosophy or art—was possible.

In his study of Montesquieu, we find Durkheim setting forth the general conditions of establishment of a social science. These, as stated, may seem conventional enough to us today, but they had a rather striking significance in the milieu in which the young Durkheim was writing, and they are far from lacking in significance even now. As I have just noted, there were many at that time willing to argue that a social science was impossible or improbable, given the nature of the human will and the unique character of human events, and that what was really fundamental —and expressible—in the human sphere could be found in philosophy, history, and art. As no one needs reminding, that view of the matter has its exponents even in our time. It won't hurt, therefore, to summarize briefly Durkheim's propositions on the nature of a social science as these were set forth in his earliest writings. The point of view he states remained fundamental to his thinking about science and its relation to other areas of thought and action throughout his life.

In the first place, science is not coterminous with human knowledge or thought, nor should it be. Not every type of question the mind can formulate is amenable to science, nor does every perceived subject fall within the purview of science. It is possible for something to be the object of the philosopher or artist and not necessarily the stuff of science at all. What is unique or infinite in character must always remain the object of philosophical or artistic inquiry, not scientific.

"A discipline may be called a science only if it has a definite field to explore. Science is concerned with things, realities. If it does not have definite material to describe and interpret, it exists in a vacuum. . . . Before social science could begin to exist, it had to be assigned a definite subject matter."[1]

Now, if we look back on the history of Western thought, Durkheim writes, we find that, while philosophers have always been aware of "things" called laws, traditions, religions, and so forth, the reality of these was in large measure dissolved by philosophers' insistence upon dealing with these as but manifestations of human will. Inquiry was thus concentrated on the internal will or mind rather than upon the external bodies of data. Or, if these latter were dealt with as substantive things they were overwhelmingly considered in the conative, rather than cognitive, perspective; that is, what should be done with them, what their relation was to some arbitrarily adopted ideal, how congruent they were with human happiness. The idea of simply studying, with the view of explaining, social facts was, Durkheim tells us, virtually unknown in Western thought until the 19th century, and even then only imperfectly. Of the long line of social philosophers beginning with Plato, Durkheim writes:

> Whether they completely disregard reality or pay a certain amount of attention to it, they all have a single purpose: to correct or

transform it completely, rather than to know it. They take virtually no interest in the past and the present, but look to the future. And a discipline that looks to the future lacks a determinate subject matter and should therefore be called not a science but an art.[2]

That passage is well worth our serious respect today, living as we do in an age in which some of the wildest of flights of speculation concerning the future are given the trappings of science and called, in one of the latest of neologisms, "futurology." Durkheim would have said that preoccupation with the future is the proper subject of the novelist's or poet's art; it cannot possibly have underpinnings in science, in any reasonable use of that word. Later, in his *Rules,* Durkheim would make very explicit indeed his view that "prevision" of the temporal dimension we call the future is utterly impossible, save in speculative fancy, and all efforts to try to link causally past, present, and future are absurd. I shall have much more to say on that point in the chapter on social change.

Art and science, then, quite apart from possible common motivations and mechanisms of creative imagination between artist and science, are utterly different enterprises. Granted that they can interact in a given situation. The painter is not ignorant of the principles of light and perspective; the designer of a building must know the laws of structural engineering; the most utopian of minds in politics likes to offer reasons for his ideal system based as far as possible on experience or logic. So much is true. But, Durkheim emphasizes, the difference between art or action, on the one hand, and science on the other is vast. All efforts to fuse them in a single inquiry are fatal to either, especially so to science. When science becomes involved with art, its specific nature "is bound to be vitiated; it degenerates into something equivocal. Art is action; it is impelled by urgency, and whatever science it may contain is swept along in its headlong rush. True science does not admit of such haste."[3]

Clearly, Durkheim is using the word "art" here in its original meaning of doing and acting, with the conative uppermost. As I have mentioned above, Durkheim, while far from oblivious to the public scene and to social action, especially during his younger years, came increasingly to distrust the effects of ideology and social action upon the scientific consciousness. In very considerable degree Durkheim's conservatism of mind was buttressed by observation that the aims of science are more often put in jeopardy by radicals—inasmuch as most social action is radically motivated —than by conservatives, using the words "radical" and "conservative" here strictly in their political and social applications. Durkheim, like his great contemporary, Weber (who was somewhat more given, however, to political participation, and to more agonies of mind arising from this participation, than Durkheim), believed the vocation of science to be exemplary in its own right, among the very highest of all vocations, and susceptible only to corruption and disorganization when its distinctive aims were compromised by those emanating from religion, politics, or social action.

Not that Durkheim—or Weber—believed science to be something properly insulated from the world of action, policy—of art, as Durkheim epitomizes it.

> Quite the contrary. The sharper the distinction between science and art, the more useful science can be to art. What is more desirable for a human being than to be sound in mind and body? Only science can tell us what constitutes good mental and physical health. Social science, which classifies the various human societies, cannot fail to describe the normal form of social life in each type of society, for the simple reason that it describes the type itself; whatever pertains to the type is normal, and whatever is normal is healthy.[4]

In that passage Durkheim is anticipating themes which he would set forth in much more detail, and with greater cogency, three years later in *The Rules.* I shall defer until the chapter on deviance discussion of his use of the word "normal," which Durkheim strove to rest as firmly as possible on purely empirical and comparative foundations. Here I want to call attention to his word "type," for it is among the key criteria that Durkheim employed throughout his life in the identification of a genuine science. Either there are types or classes of subject matter or there is no possibility of a science, for there can be no science of the unique; only an art. If we were to insist, after the manner of the German philosophers, Windelband and Rickert, that each human datum is unique, that true types and classes of data do not exist in the social world, then, Durkheim concludes, there would be no alternative but "to treat such realities in the manner of poets and story tellers. . . ." In the precise spirit in which Aristotle had written, Durkheim tells us that "science cannot describe individuals, but only types. If human societies cannot be classified, they must remain inaccessible to scientific description."[5]

The next general criterion of a science, in contrast to art, is the susceptibility of a given subject matter to yielding general principles or, as Durkheim puts it in the fashion of his time, "laws." If societies "are not subject to laws, no social science is possible. . . . However, since the principle that all the phenomena of the universe are closely interrelated has been tested in the other domains of nature and has never proved to be false, it is also valid, in all likelihood, for human societies, which are a part of nature."[6] In such a passage it is clear that the influence of the doctrine of the continuity of the natural and the social worlds, a doctrine that was the very foundation of Saint-Simon's and Comte's theories of the organic filiation of the sciences, was powerful on Durkheim's mind.

This does not prevent him, however, from declaring the social as distinctive and autonomous a sphere of subject matter as either the biological and the physical. Durkheim is unyielding on the proposition that if there is no distinct universe of behavior, to wit, the social, of which customs, laws, traditions, and groups are the manifestations, and with its own distinctive set of laws to account for what the universe contains, then there is no possibility of a social science. It is interesting to observe that this proposition is stated as clearly and emphatically at the beginning of his career as it was when he came to write his great study of religion. The greatest single barrier, we are told, heretofore to a social science has been the propensity of philosophers as well as laymen to take recourse to human will and consciousness of lawgivers— that is, kings, statesmen, prophets, and generals—in the explanation of customs and traditions. Nothing "has no retarded social science as this point of view, which philosophers, whether consciously or unconsciously, have also accepted."[7]

There are two elements to be noted in Durkheim's discussion. In the first place, the accidental must be removed; in the second place, categories of human will and volition must be dispensed with. That there are indeed accidents—the purely fortuitous and random occurrences in history—Durkheim did not deny. Nor did he deny the existence of the human will and, within bounds, the freedom of the will. But, he declares, there can be no science of accidents (which is what Aristotle had written more than two millennia earlier) and the task of a social science is to concentrate on those uniformities and regularities in human behavior which are plainly not dominated by accident. And if it is indeed true that everything in society must be reduced to human volition, well enough. "But, as we have shown, such a science should be called psychology and not social science."

"If social science is really to exist, societies must be assumed to have a certain nature which results from the nature and arrangement of the elements composing them, and which is the source of social phenomena."[8]

There is, finally, the vital matter of a method. It is insufficient, Durkheim tells us, merely to have a subject matter that is "scientifically knowable." If we are to discern the uniformities and types, the laws, of society, "we must possess a method appropriate to the nature of the things studied and to the requirements of science."[9] We should not imagine that such a method "comes spontaneously to mind the moment we embark on a science. On the contrary, we find it only after much groping."

It is at this point, in the work from which I have been citing, that Durkheim then turns to an analysis of the works of Montesquieu, with major emphasis on *The Spirit of the Laws*. We shall not follow him in that analysis; it is irrelevant to our enterprise here. What is important is the fact that the criteria of a social science which Durkheim set forth at the beginning of this first published work remained to the end of his life the fundamental criteria of social science and the identifying attributes of the field he called sociology. I am aware that other interpreters, chiefly Talcott Parsons to whom we owe much for both introduction and clarification of Durkheim to American sociology, have argued a pronounced change in Durkheim's conception of the nature of a social science during his final years. Professor Parsons argues that a development took place in Durkheim's theory best described as one from strict positivism to an idealism of philosophical position which, "when combined with his doctrine of social types, would produce an impossible solipsistic skepticism."[10] The development would fit, of course, the pattern of development Parsons believed he had found, broadly speaking, in the works also of Alfred Marshall, Pareto, and Weber. I dare say something akin to this development did indeed exist in Durkheim's philosophy—and we should never forget that Durkheim considered himself as much philosopher as sociologist, concerned indubitably with some of philosophy's profoundest problems. The early rigorous positivism and almost relentless rationalism undoubtedly softened by the time World War I broke out. Even with the war against Germany as the incentive, it is hard to imagine Durkheim having written in his young manhood the almost mystical account of the French nation we get just a few years before his death.

Nevertheless, with all respect to this position regarding Durkheim's development toward a methodological idealism and voluntarism, I think it has to be rejected. Evidence for it is drawn by Professor Parsons chiefly from Durkheim's approach to religion in his final, great work on the subject. There, admittedly, we find Durkheim declaring that the true reality of religion must be seen from the religionary's own point of view; there, also admittedly, we find Durkheim repudiating the rationalist approaches to religion of his day. But the essential point, I believe, is that in each of these positions, there lies what proves to be a springboard to fresh espousal of the same fundamental objectivism, the same structuralism, the same insistence upon the priority of society and its forms to all internal subjective states that we have in the young Durkheim. I shall deal with this point in the chapter on religion. Here it suffices to say that in his final as in his first major work, Durkheim made institutions, rites, and social constraints prior to individual representations of religion.

THE DATA OF SOCIOLOGY

Sociology, Durkheim has told us, can exist only to the extent that there is a distinctive subject matter for it, one that is clearly distinguishable from subject matters of other disciplines. It is, as we have seen, particularly psychology and biology that Durkheim has in mind in this instance. For, if all explanations of social behavior are to be made upon what turn out to be at bottom biological or psychological data, then there is no need for a science other than biology and psychology so far as our understanding of human behavior is concerned. Are there, then, social data proper, and if so, what is their distinctive nature?

In his dissertation on Montesquieu, Durkheim had limited himself to rather vague references to "laws, customs, and traditions," and made no effort there to inquire into the specific character of the social. In the *Division of Labor,* published only a year after the dissertation on Montesquieu, Durkheim takes us a little farther, but, alas, down a road that proves to be a poor access to what he was in fact searching for. In that work he declares his subject to be "the facts of moral life" and his objective to be that of treating these "according to the method of the positive sciences." A little later he tells us that moral facts "are phenomena like others; they consist of rules of action recognizable by certain distinctive characteristics." Durkheim does not tell us in this work what these distinctive characteristics are, though we know that he was reflecting on them at the time, and he would cite them in his next book, *The Rules of Sociological Method.*

What Durkheim is most deeply interested in is identifying a

body of data which would be at one and the same time expressive of moral and social reality and also amenable to scientific treatment. He found this body of data in law—that is, prescriptive, legal enactments and codes. We cannot go to internal states of mind, he argues in the *Division of Labor;* consciousness, though real enough, will not serve the austere tests of scientific method. If we are to study moral phenomena in an objective fashion, we must substitute for the internal fact of consciousness "an external index which symbolizes it and study the former in the light of the latter." All social phenomena as such manifest themselves to the social scientist by "sensible indices" of which the "visible symbol is law." So insistent is Durkheim in this work on legal data alone as the proper subject matter of sociology that we find him even rejecting custom on the ground that "normally, custom is not opposed to law, but is, on the contrary, its basis."[11]

It is fortunate for us that Durkheim did not hold long to this excessively limited, and also deceptive, measure of social reality. It would appear that even before Durkheim had finished the *Division of Labor,* the fact had become clear to him that it is possible to deal objectively with other than strictly legal social data and still avoid the trap of mere impressionism. For a great deal of that seminal volume is concerned with material not the less external and social for its transcending of simple prescriptive law. One need but read the long section on mechanical solidarity in the early part of the book and the chapters on "forced" and "anomic" division of labor toward the end to see that Durkheim had, despite his opening remarks in the Preface, been obliged to go well beyond law, as such, to custom and tradition.

When we turn to *The Rules of Sociological Method,* published only two years after the *Division of Labor,* we find a much more expansive and resilient conception of the data of sociology. Bear in mind that this book is best seen as a kind of methodological interlude between two highly empirical works—the *Division of Labor* and *Suicide,* which would appear in print two years after *The Rules*—and can often seem overly sententious and also didactic. It is, nevertheless, making allowance for the milieu in which it was written, a remarkable treatise in the philosophy and method of social science, one that, as I shall stress, is a faithful compendium of principles he followed scrupulously in his empirical writings down through his *Elementary Forms of Religious Life*.

It is interesting and useful to read Durkheim's Preface to the first edition of *The Rules*. If there is to be a genuine social science, he argues, following up what we have already seen to be basic principles in his thought, "we shall expect it not merely to paraphrase the traditional prejudices of the common man but to give us a new and different view of them; for the aim of all science is to make discoveries, and every discovery more or less disturbs accepted ideas." Heretofore, he continues, it has been customary to think of social behavior as but the lineal product of ideal concepts in the human mind. What we must do, however, is give social behavior its own due. Durkheim acknowledges that this will expose him to charges of "materialism" and "positivism." Yet, he writes, it would be quite possible to see in the approach taken in *The Rules* an expression of a higher idealism. For, "just as idealists separate the psychological from the biological realm, so we separate the psychological from the social; like them we refuse to explain the complex in terms of the simple."

It is better, however, Durkheim continues, to abandon use of the terms "materialist" and "idealist." The principal objective of the book, he declares, is simply "to extend scientific rationalism to human behavior." Inasmuch as it can be shown that social behavior, when analyzed, is capable of statement in terms of cause and effect, then what we have learned from the past and present can be extended into policies for the future. "What our critics have called our 'positivism' is only one certain aspect of this rationalism." It will be noted that as early as 1895 when *The Rules* was published, Durkheim had already become sensitive to charges of positivism, a word that had then, as today, generally pejorative implications. Such sensitivity did not, however, drive Durkheim into the slightest abandonment of his fundamental stress upon the distinguishability and the external objectivity of social facts when set against biological and psychological data. We shall find Durkheim critical, in his *Elementary Forms of Religious Life,* seventeen years later, of the rationalist approach to the study of religion, but this, as I have just suggested above, does not at all bespeak any turn to idealistic emphasis upon individual, subjective, and volitional consciousness or will. On the contrary: no major work on religion is to be found in which stress is so continuing and precise throughout upon the objective, external, and structural aspects of religion—though Durkheim is far from lacking in awareness of the impact of these upon the individual mind.

In actuality, it would seem, the real purpose of *The Rules* is to demonstrate in every possible way the fallacy of reducing the social to the psychological. Precisely that form of reductionism had been involved in the philosophy of man and society ever since the early Greeks. In his own day, scholars as illustrious as Spencer in England and Gabriel Tarde in France continued to seek explanation of institutions and of collective ways of behavior in states or elements of individual consciousness. But this, Durkheim tirelessly insists, is false; as false as the reduction of the psychological to the biological, of the biological to the chemical or physical. In his Preface to the second edition of *The Rules,* Durkheim, who by then had the advantage of the critical attacks on the book he had predicted in kind and intensity, wrote: "Social facts do not differ from psychological facts in quality only; *they have a different substratum;* they evolve in a different milieu; and they depend on different conditions." This does not mean, he continues, "that they are not also mental after a fashion since they all consist of ways of thinking and behaving." So, he could have added, are they physiological and even geological, if one has reference to total composition and setting. The point, however, lies in *explanation.* On this point he writes:

> That the substance of social life cannot be explained by purely psychological factors, i.e., by the states of the individual consciousness, seems to us to be most evident. . . . The group differs from the individual in its constitution, and the things that affect it are therefore of a different nature. . . . To understand the way in

which a society thinks of itself and of its environment one must consider the nature of the society and not that of the individuals. Even the symbols which express these conceptions change according to the type of society.[12]

We shall come back briefly to that insistence upon the fallacy of psychological explanations of social data in the next section of this chapter. For the moment I want only to stress that Durkheim, living in an age when psychological explanations of this type could seem possessed of common sense as well as scholarly gravity, felt obliged to iterate and reiterate propositions such as that just quoted in order to give base to his effort to arrive at a just conception of social data. Durkheim is not arguing that individuals do not exist, that they do not eat, drink, sleep, reason, and associate, that they do not provide the visible units of any group or community. (He is simply arguing that once groups and communities are formed, once customs, traditions, and codes come into existence to help shape, educate, and socialize individuals, a sphere of data is opened up that is as evident and as real as what one finds in the individual human being, taken separately.) There is not an iota of that argument that would not have been fully acceptable to the minds of Mead, Cooley, and Ross in America who, a decade later, were in their own way and milieu doing precisely what Durkheim had done: demonstrating the reality of the social in contrast to the individual. One can find, easily enough, in works such as Mead's *Mind, Self, and Society,* Cooley's *Social Organization* and his *Human Nature and the Social Order,* and in Ross's *Social Control* statements if anything more extreme than Durkheim's on the priority of the social to the individual, above all on the separability of the social and the individual. Mead's preeminent objective in his famous lectures on social psychology at the University of Chicago was not that of rescuing the individual from the social, conceptually speaking, but rather that of rescuing the social from the individual—which was exactly Durkheim's earlier objective.

The chief characteristic of social facts, Durkheim tells us, is, along with their incontestable externality and objectivity, the *constraint* they may be seen to exert upon individuals at all stages of their lives. Durkheim concedes that to define the social in terms of constraint and coercion is to "risk shocking the zealous partisans of absolute individualism." These feel that the individual is diminished by reference to the contexts of his milieu and of his interaction with values, symbols, and codes which long preceded his own arrival in the world. But, Durkheim asks, how can these social elements "become part of us except by imposing themselves upon us?"

To confirm the coerciveness of social facts in their effects on individuals, one need but look at education's effort "to impose on the child ways of seeing, feeling, and acting which he could not have arrived at spontaneously." The very essence of education is "precisely the socialization of the human being; the process of education therefore gives us in a nutshell the historical fashion in which the social being is constituted." It is the character of every social milieu to seek to fashion the individual in its own image, and, in this process, "parents and teachers are merely the representatives and intermediaries."[13]

Durkheim stresses that the clue to social facts does not lie in their universality. "A thought which we find in every individual consciousness, a movement repeated by all individuals, is not thereby a social fact." What is vital to sociality is the corporate or "collective aspects of the beliefs, tendencies, and practices of a group that characterize truly social phenomena." Clearly, Durkheim is using the word "social" here in almost exactly the same way that the ethnologists of his day, beginning with E. B. Tylor, in his important *Primitive Culture,* were using the word "culture." We today generally distinguish, in sociology and social anthropology, between the two words and what they are made to denote. Neither Tylor, writing about culture, nor Durkheim, writing about society and the social made this distinction. For each what was crucial to the concept he emphasized was the set of values, ideas, techniques, and symbols which are transmitted, not through germ plasm, but through the collective, associative means of education, taking that word in the large sense of socialization.[14]

The ultimate, essential characteristic, however, of social data is, in Durkheim's view, the *constraints* which they represent upon human behavior. Durkheim has been often criticized for this emphasis, and no doubt it would have been possible to have found a more neutral word for a quality about social norms and roles that all who have ever dealt with the socialization process have been obliged to stress. It is worth noting that Durkheim's great contemporary, Freud, also saw constraint to be a vital element of the social and cultural milieu. Pathological behavior arises, Freud argued, in large part out of the conflicts between ego and culture which are generated by this coercive or constraining quality. As we shall see, Durkheim works through a different route to arrive at an explanation of the pathologies of human behavior, one that is, predictably enough, wholly social.[15]

So too did Mead emphasize the importance of social constraint or, in his phrase, "social control." Apart from social control—the kind of coercion that springs initially from the customs and codes of the community in which the individual is born and the unremitting efforts of others to impress these upon the individual from infancy on—there cannot be, Mead argued, the kind of individual control we commonly refer to as "self-criticism." It is Mead, not Durkheim, who writes that "self-criticism is essentially social criticism, and behavior controlled by self-criticism is essentially behavior controlled socially." Such constraint or control, Mead goes on, "so far from tending to crush out the human individual or to obliterate his self-conscious individuality, is, on the contrary, actually constitutive of and inextricably associated with that individuality; for the individual is what he is, as a conscious and individual personality, just in as far as he is a member of society."[16]

Clearly, Mead, in that passage and indeed throughout his whole work in social psychology, *Mind, Self, and Society*, just as evidently premises a society distinguishable from the individual, a society constraining in its impact upon the individual, as Durk-

heim does. For Mead, as for Durkheim, the essence of the socialization process is the priority of the social to the individual
and the conceptual autonomy of social facts. The same is precisely true of Cooley, who is so often contrasted today with Durkheim in the imagined light of greater dependence upon the individual in his sociology and social psychology. It is Cooley, not
Durkheim, who tells us that human nature is "group nature,"
that individual personality is a "primary phase of society," a
"general condition of the social mind." It is Cooley who, in giving
stress to the priority of the "We" to the "I" in the development
of individual thought and to the indissoluble bond between the
individual and all of those external values, ideas, and traditions
that Durkheim had epitomized in the phrase "collective representations," writes: "All innovation is based on conformity, all
heterodoxy on orthodoxy, all individuality on solidarity." Again,
we are forced to say: Durkheim could not have expressed himself
more characteristically. Differences between Durkheim and either
Mead or Cooley are, of course, very real, as they tend to be among
all creative minds. It would be foolish to question the differences
of emphasis that exist, for example, with respect to specific processes of socialization. We shall come to some of these later. But it
is nevertheless important to stress that the differences to be found
between Durkheim and Mead or Durkheim and Cooley are set
against a very large common background of premises regarding
the nature of society and its priority in the development of individual mind, self, and consciousness.

The data of social science, or more particularly sociology
which is Durkheim's primary concern from the writing of *The
Rules* onward, are, then, the phenomena of social groups, customs, traditions, laws, values, and other elements of the social order which may be seen to have constraining and even coercing effect upon individuals during the process of socialization. These
data are, quite evidently, as external and objective from the vantage point of the social scientist as are the data worked with by
chemists and biologists. That each of us has attitudes toward
these, feels himself a part of some of them, feels them as parts of

himself, Durkheim is well aware of and makes reference to. Such circumstances merely highlight the need, in social as well as physical science, for a method that will facilitate dealing with social phenomena in a way as free as possible from personal feelings.

> We thus arrive at the point where we can formulate and delimit in a precise way the domain of sociology. It comprises only a limited group of phenomena. A social fact is to be recognized by the power of external coercion which it exercises or is capable of exercising over individuals, and the presence of this power may be recognized in its turn either by the existence of some specific sanction or by the resistance offered against every individual effort that tends to violate it.[17]

Although Durkheim did not again occupy himself so directly with definitional matters in sociology, or with method as such, we can see to the very end of his scholarly labors full concurrence of his empirical work with that statement. As I have said, *The Rules* is best seen as a kind of methodological interlude, a means of making explicit what would henceforth be implicit. If we turn to *Suicide,* his next work, we find an identical emphasis upon the external, objective, and also constraining qualities of social facts. Suicide is a *social,* as well as individual fact: That is, in a sense, the great theme of the book. It can be dealt with as a social fact, as generated by social facts, and in light of its impact upon other social facts. That suicide is also an affair of individual motivation Durkheim never questioned, anymore than he questioned the fact that in medicine epidemiology was both possible and desirable even though no two individual manifestations of a disease are ever exactly alike.

So too with *The Elementary Forms of Religious Life.* There are those who regard this work as marking the passage of Durkheim's mind to a more idealistic, or at any rate less positivistic, stage of thought. I am obliged to confess that I cannot find this. The entire purpose of the book is that of demonstrating the social character of religion, of using the social facts of cult and rite rather than the mental facts of belief and attitude to illuminate this character, and, not least, to show in the context of religion how the constraining effect of social facts is so great as to produce even the essential categories of the human mind. With all its faults, however many these may be, *The Elementary Forms* is in very large degree a remarkable, a very successful exemplification of methodological principles set down abstractly in *The Rules of Sociological Method.*

Before concluding this section on Durkheim's conception of the data of sociology, something should be said about his idea of "collective representations" on which so much criticism of Durkheim has rested, ranging from ascription to him of materialism to organicism. Little, if anything, is to be found on this concept in *The Rules of Sociological Method,* though, to be sure, Durkheim comes close to the phrasing in his treatment of the collective character of social facts and in his account of the latter as being the result of collective association.[18] It was three years after publication of *The Rules,* in an article entitled "Individual and Collective Representations" in *Revue de Métaphysique et de Morale*[19] before Durkheim addressed himself head-on to the concept of collective representations, and it is as the result of this piece rather than from anything in *The Rules* that the heaviest criticisms of Durkheim have come.

In some ways the article was useful, in other ways not. What is good about it is the continuation of emphasis from *The Rules* upon the collective nature of social facts, their occupation of a sphere of reality capable of scientific study that cannot properly be studied through other disciplines, and Durkheim's insistence that concentration upon social facts conceived as external to the individual and distinct from individual consciousness in no way diminishes the stature of man. Collective representations, as Durkheim makes very clear indeed in this essay, are but the customs, traditions, ideas, values, and other elements of society which take shape historically in human culture and form the milieu in which the individual is socialized and educated. "Despite its metaphysical appearance, this word (collective representations) designates nothing more than a body of natural facts which are explained by natural causes."[20] And, as we read this essay carefully, we are obliged to agree with Durkheim that it is indeed the case and also, I think, conclude that there is nothing in the phrase or the description of what is contained in it that would have been unacceptable to either Mead or Cooley, each of whom used words more loaded in metaphysical implication than Durkheim's "collective representation."

What is less useful and undoubtedly suspect on any ground is the argument in the essay that takes up its greater part to the effect that the relation between collective representations and society is the same as the relation between individual representations, or ideas, and the neural structure of the brain. No doubt there are, even in the light of contemporary neural psychology, some suggestive as well as valid insights here, but one can only conclude that Durkheim did not really help his case very much for the reality and externality of social facts. Clearly, Durkheim had been stung by reviews and other criticisms of *The Rules* which had appeared during the three years preceding this essay.

THE NATURE OF SOCIOLOGICAL EXPLANATION

All science rests on, first, discovery of data and, second, the explanation of the data. I do not mean to imply that the two processes are in any way separated from one another. They are in operation but two aspects of the same thing. The discovery of data often carries with it strong implications of explanation. Similarly, the effort to explain a given phenomenon often carries with it the need for discovery of new data. By reading Durkheim carefully on the nature of social facts we cannot help but acquire a leading sense of Durkheim's larger method for the explanation of these facts. Thus, in his insistence upon the social character—that is, the collective or corporate nature—of such phenomena as customs, traditions, laws, and communities, we can hardly fail to see the germ of equally firm insistence upon the social character of explanations of these phenomena.

This is, indeed, the very first point to be made about Durkheimian explanation: the necessity, in sociology, of social explanations of social facts. In Chapter 5 of *The Rules,* which is concerned with the nature of sociological explanations, we find Durkheim once again drawing sharply the line between individual and society, and along with this, the line between psychology and sociology. Again it is useful to stress that at no time did Durkheim repudiate—as Comte, for one, had—the discipline of psychology or the value of psychological explanations of appropriate phenomena. That man is a thinking, feeling, consciousness-implicated being, Durkheim did not doubt. What Durkheim does repudiate are all efforts to derive social phenomena from nonsocial states, that is, from the states of mind and body to be found in the individual alone. Or, for that matter, from what may be found, or hypothesized to exist, in race or geographic environment.

Much later, the English social anthropologist A. R. Radcliffe-Brown, himself profoundly influenced by Durkheim and also one of the founders of modern social anthropology, wrote: "No amount of investigation can explain the characteristics of society by simple reference to the nature of human beings; but by an investigation of human beings *arranged in a certain order,* yes. The social scientist is studying the structural arrangement of the units and takes the internal structure of the units for granted."[21]

Durkheim, it goes without emphasis here, would have agreed with every word of that. So has the mainstream of creative social science in all areas been fundamentally in accord with the Durkheimian principle that when social phenomena (which include, of course, political, moral, economic, and other institutional phenomena) are to be explained, explanations must be cast in the terms of the phenomena themselves. Granted that, as Durkheim writes, "nothing collective can be produced if individual consciousness is not assumed. . . ." But while the existence of individual consciousness is necessary, it is "by itself insufficient." If we begin with the individual as such, then there is no possibility of understanding what can exist only in terms of aggregates of individuals and the socially derived and transmitted structures of functions, authorities, norms, and roles which have their locus outside any single individual.

"In a word, there is between psychology and sociology the same break in continuity as between biology and the physico-chemical sciences. Consequently, every time that a social phenomenon is directly explained by a psychological phenomenon, we may be sure that the explanation is false."[22]

We are thus now in a position to understand Durkheim's famous statement, which he offers as the first rule for the observation of social facts, that "social facts are things." They do not have to be, they cannot be considered as mere extensions of individuality, as shadows cast by the individual. Social facts are as real and distinct as are physical facts. The great problem is, Durkheim tells us, that social facts, instead of being dealt with as things, as concrete realities worthy of direct attention and study, have been dealt with in the light of concepts or notions. Heretofore social science, or social philosophy, has "dealt more or less exclusively with concepts and not with things." Thus, Durkheim writes, the unhappy abundance in social science, so-called, of concepts which rest historically upon personal dispositions or notions and which may or may not have anything substantive behind them. "We ridicule today the strange polemics built up by the doctors of the Middle Ages upon the basis of their concept of cold, warm, humid, dry, etc., and we do not realize that we continue to apply that same method to that very order of phenomena which, because of its extreme complexity, admits it less than any other."[23]

Social facts, then, are things in precisely the sense that physical facts are—having exteriority and objective assessability—and they cannot be understood scientifically in terms other than of themselves. What is the next step in explanation? We shall omit here an elaboration of his statement "All preconceptions must be eradicated"[24] simply because, as Durkheim himself says, this follows from everything else that has been said and is in any event a preliminary to use of the scientific method anywhere. The importance of the statement is nevertheless evident, and however difficult it may be to follow, scientific work in any proper sense of the term is unthinkable without such eradication—or at very least *awareness* of one's preconceptions. Not the least important aspect of science of any kind is its effort, through method and technique carefully arrived at and kept under observation, to reduce at least to a minimum the effects of the prejudices and distortions of view that, as Francis Bacon wrote three centuries ago, so easily become "idols" of the mind.

Next, Durkheim tells us, "the subject matter of every sociological study should comprise a group of phenomena defined in advance by certain common external characteristics, and all phenomena so defined should be included within this group."[25] Here, too, we can be brief. Without a body of data that are given unity by the question asked or problem posed, a body of data sufficiently objective and "external" as to make possible equivalent studies for confirming or corrective purposes by other investigators, *science,* in contrast to ordinary impressionism or unverifiable supposition, is simply impossible. By groups or classes of phenomena Durkheim is referring merely to such manifest orderings as kinship, law, government, and economy: each a term of aggregation we use to cover types of far-flung, variable, and empirical forms of social behavior, or social facts, which take on sufficient degrees of likeness through common function to make possible comparative studies and hypotheses. Here too in no small degree Durkheim is seeking a way in which we can become liberated as far as possible from parochialisms and distortions which we acquire from our limited social milieus.

Durkheim then comes to one of the most important points that is to be found in *The Rules* or in any other of his works, one that I shall mention very briefly here but give extended treatment to in the chapter on deviance. This is his distinction between "normal" and "pathological" in social behavior. He deemed the matter important enough to warrant a full chapter, and indeed it is. It would be hard to find anywhere in the scientific literature of the late 19th century any chapter of greater long-run importance to the study of social behavior. As he points out, the scientific study of man has been held back in large degree by the tendency of so many writers to deal with as "pathological" forms of behavior which are merely different from those we ourselves follow. For countless centuries man has insisted upon subjecting all human behavior to the imperious word "ought." The result, as he points out, has been to take forms of kinship and law just as "good" and "normal" in their ways, in the light of the norms which prevail in the surrounding cultures of these forms, as any to be found among ourselves and declare these "wrong" or "barbaric" or, in the most general category, "pathological." But, writes Durkheim:

"A social fact is normal, in relation to a given social type at a given phase of its development, when it is present in the average society of that species at the corresponding phase of its evolution."[26] Thus, Durkheim suggests, our conventional treatment of crime. We term all crime as "pathological." But, Durkheim goes on, while we are indeed entitled to refer to any given crime as wrong, immoral, and a flouting of values we believe in, it is nonsense from any scientific point of view to declare crime as such abnormal or the product of some incorrigible wickedness in man. In the first place, he argues, *some* degree of crime is inevitable in any culture at any time by virtue of the same continuum of behavior that has at opposite end "good" or "normal" behavior. In the second place, if there were not occasional deviances, floutings of norms, there would be no change in human behavior and, equally important, no opportunities through which a given social order can either reaffirm the norms which provide cement to a culture or else reassess such behavior and modify the norm itself.

We shall come back to this matter later. My only interest here is to indicate that, irrespective of all other derivations from his thesis on the normal and the pathological, he emphasizes, as a point in scientific method, the utter necessity of the sociologist's abandonment of conventional terminology and thinking. What is "normal" and "pathological" in human behavior, Durkheim tells us, can only be ascertained through criteria which are not those of inherited morality, of parochial outlook, but instead those of recognition of the generality of the supposedly pathological behavior, its relation to milieu, time, and social structure. Thus, suicide may be regarded as "wrong" if one likes, working from a set of values that makes preservation of life absolute, but, as Durkheim showed in his great study of the subject, it can hardly be called pathological or abnormal, given certain suicidogenic currents in society, and the kinds of conditions which exist for large numbers of persons in modern society where the social contexts of personality have been eroded and where the taking of one's own life is merely the ultimate expression of an egoism that flows from "the cult of personality." From the sociologist's point of view, in short, suicide, crime, and war can be, given appropriate causal conditions present, far more "normal" than opposite types of behavior.

We come now to what is perhaps the major Durkheimian methodological proposition: that pertaining to *function*. It is from this that so much of modern functionalism in sociology and anthropology has flowed. We cannot hope to understand or describe adequately any form of social behavior, Durkheim declares, simply by describing its manifest form or use. Such limited description would be only that and would result in a kind of descriptive atomism that would be the very opposite of explanation. The sociology of Durkheim's day, and also the anthropology, was all too full of this kind of descriptive atomism, with social and cultural data set forth in either evolutionary or diffusionist schemes which were often little more than huge receptacles for "facts" widely drawn, their identities resting solely on loose accounts of their individual structures and the immediate uses to which they were put. Hence, the growing disenchantment by the end of the 19th century with both kinds of scheme, diffusionist and evolutionary. Hence too, in both sociology and anthropology the growing recognition of the need for better explanatory procedure. In this, Durkheim was, of course, a key figure.

"When, then, the explanation of a social phenomenon is undertaken, we must seek separately the efficient cause which produces it and the function it fulfils."[27] Durkheim uses the example of punishment. What is the "cause" of punishment? One's immediate answer is "crime," that is, the specific offense that elicits punishment. But this, Durkheim argues, tells us nothing of the larger *function* of punishment which is, he observes, to be understood only in the relation punishment has, not to a given offense that activates punishment, but to the larger social order of which punishment is a part. The function of punishment is structural; that is, it participates in the processes that have the effect of shoring-up a given social order. Its *use* may be that of seeking to deter crime. But, in the larger sense the institution of punishment is directed toward social stability, with vital offshoots extending to many parts of the social order and to the whole socialization process. And if crime "causes" punishment, it is equally true that punishment, by its very existence, "causes" crime.

In his *Division of Labor,* published two years before *The Rules,* Durkheim had argued that the function of division of labor in society is that of the promotion of social solidarity. The "use" may be what is ordinarily implied by the words "division of labor," that is, a differentiating and specializing of labor to the end of greater production and greater skill. The function, however, is social, Durkheim tells us in that work and related to the "organic solidarity" that had succeeded "mechanical solidarity" and that, in his view, represented a higher order of social life than the earlier. It is true, as I have already stressed, that Durkheim, knowing as he proceeded the weakness of his developmental typology, abandoned it, never to pick it up again, but what he did not abandon was the idea of function.

No idea has been more fruitful in modern sociology and social anthropology than the idea of function. It has had the effect of turning attention from the surface aspects of form and use to the deeper aspects of the relation of a given custom, tradition, structure, or habit to the larger social order. As Robert Merton demonstrated in a now historic essay on political machines, the uses, which were concerned strictly with political ends, tended for a long time to conceal the functions these entities had in the assimilation of many minorities—Irish most notably, but by no means exclusively—to American society. The real strength of the big urban political machines for so many years, despite all that political reformers were able to prove about them in the way of corruption, lay in the fact that their function went far beyond politics to the very roots of the individual's relation to community and culture. The function, as Merton points out and as Durkheim would have agreed fully, thus is social, not political or technical.

Despite charges sometimes made that by reference to function Durkheim is carrying us into a form of teleological reasoning, the reverse is true. If by "teleology" one is arguing that all social behavior must be seen in terms of a design formed by certain ends which are antecedent to the behavior, thus making for the kind of symmetry much prized by 17th-century rationalists, Durkheimian empiricism is its own answer to the charge. No more naturalistic social science is to be found. All that Durkheim is arguing is that we have not exhausted the nature of a social fact until we have found the function it serves with respect to the rest of society. It may be a fact repugnant to our conscience, irrational and superstitious in the extreme. No matter. If it persists in time, we can best understand this persistence by turning to the function it serves—serves for the individuals engaging or believing in it and serves for the community that tolerates the fact. It was Durkheim's demonstration of the function of religion in his *Elementary Forms,* a function that is, as he stressed, social, not philosophical or creedal, least of all cosmological, that, more than any other single part of his work, turned modern attention to the functional aspects of all social phenomena.[28]

With function as with each other aspect of his methodology, Durkheim is careful to stress that the ultimate referent is social, not psychological. He writes: "The determining cause of a social fact should be sought among the social facts preceding it and not among the states of the individual consciousness." And, a few lines later, he adds to this: "The function of a social fact ought always to be sought in its relation to some social end."[29] This is in no way to declare that social facts have no psychological functions so far as participating individuals are concerned. The psychological function of membership in a political machine may be that of instilling in the individual a sense of confidence or even of zest for life and politics. The psychological function of ethnic hatred may be that of creating in the individual concerned a sense of his personal superiority. Durkheim is not ruling out psychological functions anymore than he is ruling out the existence of psychological data. It is *sociology,* not the field of individual psychology, that must be concerned with social functions, that must be aware that social facts have social functions and contexts. Until we have ascertained the function that a given custom or tradition has to the larger social order, we have not provided adequate explanation. Mere formal or utilitarian qualities the social fact may possess do not suffice. We shall come back to Durkheim's treatment of function in the chapter on social change, though we shall, of course, be dealing with the concept implicitly in almost everything treated in this book. Functional analysis is to be found in one degree or another in just about all of Durkheim's work.

The final point to be made about Durkheim's logic of explanation is his stress upon the *comparative* nature of social science. He is not impressed by what experimentalism offers to causal analysis. The only way we are going to reach understanding of the causal process in any given relationship is through its comparison with like or unlike processes in other, cognate relationships. It is evident from Durkheim's discussion in the final chapter of *The Rules* that he was well aware of the spurious quality of what so often was called "the comparative method" in his day, which, as in the works of Comte and Spencer, turned out to be only a device for reaching great unilinear patterns of mankind's development, with the West invariably shown to be at the vanguard of this development.

For Durkheim the comparative method must be precisely that, one in which there are no overtones of cosmic implication, one in which the prime purpose is simply that of ascertaining through comparative observation and analysis what the crucial or causal factors are in some social process. Only through com-

parative analysis, Durkheim tells us, is it possible to avoid the
fallacy of reasoning that connects causally two states when, in
fact, both states are the results of some third state or factor. For
example, he writes, we can establish easily enough that the tendency to suicide varies directly with education. But comparative
analysis leads us to seek out a third condition which has both education and tendency to suicide as its consequences.[30] Durkheim,
following Mill's *Logic* refers appreciatively to "the method of
concomitant variations," calling it indeed "the instrument par
excellence of sociological research." But, as Hanan Selvin has told
us in a penetrating analysis of the method Durkheim used in *Suicide*—an analysis in which Professor Selvin, without glossing over
the technical imperfections in Durkheim's use of the method,
brings out the lasting and still valid elements—what Durkheim
was really employing was what we today call multivariate analysis: "the study and interpretation of complex interrelationships
among a multiplicity of characteristics."[31] Durkheim was by no
means the first to employ this kind of analysis, but there have
been few who have used it with greater and more fruitful effect.

This is a suitable place in which to refer to Durkheim's sharp
criticism of a certain form of comparison of social facts which was
then very common in both anthropology and sociology and which
was known indeed as The Comparative Method to minds such as
Comte, Spencer, Tylor, and Frazer. That method consisted at bottom of seeking as many instances as possible of a given trait—belief, technique, artifact, as the case might be—declaring these all
to be the same, irrespective of the utterly different function that
might be served from one people to another in whom the trait
had allegedly been found, or the utterly different context of
meaning ascribed to the trait, thus wrenching the trait from the
social organization in which, as Durkheim points out, it alone
had the distinctive significance it deserved to have from any
proper analytical point of view. Durkheim's words on this common practice are valuable to this very moment when, unfortunately, exponents of social evolution in the grand manner are re-
viving the very practice Durkheim properly condemned.

In the first place, for the sociologist as for the historian, social facts vary with the social system of which they form a part; they cannot be understood when detached from it. This is why two facts which come from two different societies cannot be profitably compared merely because they seem to resemble each other; it is necessary that these societies themselves resemble each other, that is to say that they be only varieties of the same species. The comparative method would be impossible, if social types did not exist, and it cannot be usefully applied except within a single type. What errors have not been committed for having neglected this precept? It is thus that facts have been unduly connected with each other which, in spite of exterior resemblances, really have neither the same sense nor the same importance: the primitive democracy and that of to-day, the collectivism of inferior societies and actual socialistic tendencies, the monogamy which is frequent in Australian tribes and that sanctioned by our laws, etc.[32]

In sum, the comparative method, properly understood, is the very framework of the science of society, but it must be comparative of structures and processes which are, in Durkheim's wording, legitimate "social types"; that is, modes of behavior in which function, contextual significance, and meaning, as well as mere overt form, are duly taken into consideration. Taken in this sense, rather than that found so extravagantly in the works of the evolutionary ethnologists of Durkheim's day, the comparative method is inseparable from a scientific sociology.

"Comparative sociology is not a particular branch of sociology; it is sociology itself, insofar as it ceases to be purely descriptive and aspires to account for facts."[33]

With this we can terminate the discussion of Durkheimian methodology. I am well aware that what has been set forth here is at best the skeleton of the matter, but, then, that is precisely how Durkheim saw *The Rules of Sociological Method*: as a skeletal statement, set forth in terms of abstract definition and shorthand, of what can only be gained in full from detailed study of such works as *Suicide* and the *Elementary Forms of Religious Life*. We shall be concerned throughout this book, as I have already emphasized, with Durkheim's conceptions of the scope of sociology, the nature of social facts, and the nature of sociological explanation.

One important word before ending this chapter. No one who has looked carefully into the statements about their work that have come from the greatest scientists, those at least willing to describe their thought processes and perceived contexts of discovery, can suppose for a moment that there is no more to scientific explanation than what can be set forth in terms of abstract method, its rules and techniques. We have but to look at what scientists of the stature of Newton, Darwin, Maxwell, Planck, Einstein, and many others have said about such matters as dreams, fantasy, pure intuition, luck, not to mention sustained concentration of attention, often in a degree beyond the capacity of most of us, to realize that method alone will never be enough to carry us to creative result. There is a good deal in common between science and art, and the greatest scientists have known this and have been properly more sensitive to the roles in their work of sheer imagination and superlative intuition than to such matters as the nature of data, hypothesis, structure of explanation, and other elements of so-called scientific method.[34] We can respect this and agree with it. Method has never yet lifted a mediocre imagination to more than mediocre result in science. But this is just as true in art— which, after all, has its own techniques and methods—where we so often naïvely suppose imagination to reign unfettered by demands of experience and verisimilitude. That a Durkheim has nothing to say about the whole realm of creative imagination and its prime contribution does not mean that he was unaware of this. He took it for granted for purposes of *The Rules of Sociological Method* in the same way that an Einstein, in describing the vital role of intuition in reaching his historic theory of relativity, took for granted that listeners would realize that no intuition in science can be altogether free of requirements of evidence and verification, requirements which when summarized are, basically, what we mean by method.

2 Social Structure

Of all contributions that sociology has made to contemporary thought none is greater than, if indeed as great as, its envisagement of human behavior in terms of social structure. I am not, of course, suggesting that the capacity to see human life and thought in terms of wholes—systems, organizations, ecological relationships, institutions, structures, call them what we will—is unique to sociology. Structural analysis is very much to be seen in other social sciences, particularly social anthropology and economics. Nor do I suggest that attention to structure, however we define it, had to await the rise of the systematic social sciences in the nineteenth century. From the ancient Greek philosophers down through the greater medieval and modern thinkers we can find occasionally remarkable interpretations of actions, events, and changes in terms of some kind of structure: often either of an organic or equilibrial kind.

Nevertheless, these preliminary remarks made, it remains true that sociology is the discipline in which the most characteristic and sustained effort is made to subject the events, interactions, motives, attitudes, and other elements of social behavior around us to structural analysis: that is, to throw light on these elements by discerning the patterns of norm, role, function, and meaning in which the elements are in fact to be found. In innumerable studies of population processes, of deviant behavior, political and social attitudes, psychological motivation and performance, as well as of many other aspects of human behavior we have become used to the concept of structure and its capacity for lifting this behavior out of the realm of the atomistic, discrete, and supposedly unique and placing it securely within structural relationships which are themselves vital elements of the explanations we seek. One need only contrast early studies of "social problems" with the kind of analyses we are more likely to get today of social deviance to see instantly the role that structural analysis occupies in contemporary sociology. And it is through this type of analysis that we are able to see the social basis of a great deal of behavior and thought that conventional thought once ascribed to biological, psychological, and even supernatural forces.

Durkheim is without question the preeminent sociologist of social structure. From his first major work, the *Division of Labor*, with its typology of mechanical and organic solidarity, through his treatment of crime in *The Rules*, of suicide in his classic work of that title, down to his final great study, *The Elementary Forms of Religious Life*, we see an unremitting effort to utilize the idea of patterned social behavior, of structure, in the explanation of human ideas and acts. Education, morality, mental illness, the nature of personality and mind, quite literally everything Durkheim ever undertook to explain in depth came in for analysis in terms of social structure.

It is the idea of structure indeed, above any other single aspect of his teaching, that Durkheim transmitted to his followers. What gives special character to the works of the ethnologists, geographers, jurists, historians, and others who were influenced by him is their profound interest in structures, in whatever sphere, by which the ostensible discreteness and atomicity of life in time and in space is brought under explanatory consideration. I have already mentioned Marc Bloch, Lucien Febvre, and Fernand Braudel, all very young historians or historical geographers at the time Durkheim's *L'Année Sociologique* flourished. If there is a single overarching theme behind the work of the *Annales* school that these three gifted historians established, it is the idea of structure: of substantial, patterned modes of behavior through time which an older, more orthodox form of history, with its emphasis on genealogical strings of events and on discrete personages, acts, and changes, tended so often to overlook. One need but read Braudel's classic *The Mediterranean* to see how powerful the idea of structure in historiography can become.

We shall be concerned throughout this book with Durkheim's structural analysis, for there is no subject he touched that did not rest basically on this analysis. What I wish to do in this chapter, however, by way of noting the boldness and thrust of Durkheim's structural approach is to high-light it through brief examination of a few of his lesser-known analyses along this line: specifically, contract, property, the nature of mind and thought, and the role of incest.

CONTRACT

It will help in our appreciation of Durkheim's structural approach to contract, in our appreciation indeed of the brilliance of his approach, if we recall that the idea of contract as the aboriginal relationship in society had been a strong one in European thought ever since the seventeenth century. In point of fact there are indications of a belief in contract in certain writers in ancient Greece, among the more philosophically minded of the Roman Lawyers, and even the Middle Ages in discussions of the origin of institutions. But, whatever the importance of the idea in earlier times it was as nothing compared to the monumental influence of the idea in the seventeenth and eighteenth centuries. Such was the hostility of natural law philosophers towards all explanations resting on either revelation or conventional history, upon tradition or religion in any form, that they sought to explain not merely all concrete relationships but whole societies, the whole of society indeed, by reference to the contractual relation. There was method in this on the part of many philosophers, for, by declaring society the product of contract in the first instance—among individuals or between a group of individuals and a ruler—it became possible to use contract as the touchstone of legitimacy for government. Thus the daring declaration of a number of philosophers, with Rousseau the most notable, that when the ruler seems to be contravening the terms of the original contract the people are justified in overthrowing him.

There are few, if any, social contract theories in the 19th century. Basically, the idea had died with the French Revolution. But there were numerous spawn of the social contract ideology, among them the thesis that—leaving absolute social origins out of the question entirely—the source of all social relationships is to be found in the idea of exchange. This was basically the economists' view of man's behavior, and consequently classical economics rested in large degree upon the view of the individual as the profit-maximizing, interest-actuated participant in incessant exchange with other individuals similarly driven. The characteristic social relation for the economists was thus that of tacit contract, with one person giving another individual something—whether labor, capital, love, protection or what—but only on the basis of the other individual's giving something—wages, interest, answering love, obedience or what—in return.

Herbert Spencer made much use of the idea of contract, or, as we would say today, exchange, as the most basic mechanism in social relationships, whether kinship, political, educational, economic, or religious, premising this mechanism upon the assumption of the individual as being fundamentally driven by desire for gain and avoidance of pain—the so-called hedonistic psychology of Jeremy Bentham and the utilitarians.

The fallacy of the idea of contract—or exchange—as the prime motivational mechanism in human relations lies, Durkheim tells us succinctly, in the fact that there is no observable contractual relation in human society that does not rest upon non- or precontractual foundations. In a brief phrase, there is more to any contract than the contractual. Spencer and the utilitarians generally envisaged the whole social order as "a vast system of particular contracts which link individuals as a unique basis." From this envisagement the utilitarians see social solidarity as "nothing else than the spontaneous accord of individual interests, an accord of which contracts are the natural expression." Given this overview, "the typical social relation would be the economic, stripped of all regulation and resulting entirely from the free initiative of the parties."[1] But, Durkheim writes, there is no instance to be found in human society of such an exchange relationship except as it is buttressed, given sanction and meaning, by a prior system of social constraint. The very efficacy of a given contract between two individuals depends upon the anterior notion that there is something transcontractual involved, something that is at once antecedent and superior to the contract itself and to the separate interests of the two contracting individuals.

Moreover, Durkheim tells us, there is nothing in the element of individual interest that can bind two or more individuals more than briefly and transiently. "For if interest relates men, it is never for more than some few moments. . . . There is nothing less constant than interest. Today, it unites me to you; tomorrow it will make me your enemy."[2]

Now, this is doubtless extreme. Durkheim's animadversion to the utilitarian principle of egoistic priority takes him a little too far. There are certainly relationships in which distinct personal interest on each side can be seen extending for long periods of time, and where it is not necessary to see antagonism as the inevitable reversal of relationships founded upon self-interest and exchange. We are entitled to say that this criticism is both premature and somewhat shallow.

What is neither premature nor shallow, however, is Durkheim's demonstration that in every specifiable contract known to us, there are and there have to be noncontractual foundations resting in the constraint of morality, of religion, or of law—or all of these. Consider, Durkheim asks us, the moral and legal codes of the peoples known to us through the reasonable detailed records left behind in history. Contracts are to be found mentioned in all of them. But invariably in these contractual relationships are to be found injunctions and prohibitions which emanate from supra- or extracontractual sources. There is an element of contract to be found in all relationships. Durkheim concedes this. So too may it be said that the number of contractual relationships increases with the evolution of society. But it is not possible to reduce contract merely to the interests of the two contracting parties; no more possible than to reduce a social structure of any kind merely to the individuals involved in the structure.

> In sum, a contract is not sufficient unto itself, but is possible only thanks to a regulation of the contract which is originally social. It is implied, first, because it has for its function much less the creation of new rules than the diversification in particular cases of pre-established rules; then, because it has and can have the power to bind only under certain conditions which it is necessary to define.[3]

In his *Professional Ethics and Civic Morals* he carries his analysis a great deal further, supplying in detail social roots for contract that he drew from his studies of comparative religion. In the *Division of Labor* Durkheim makes clear that it is the persisting influence of the kind of constraint to be found in what he calls mechanical solidarity that alone makes possible the contractual and restitutive relationships of modern society founded upon division of labor and characterized by organic solidarity. What we find in Durkheim's later thinking is ever more explicit derivation of contract—and also of other modern, essentially rationalist-utilitarian conceptions—from the ritual ties of ancient religion. Here, plainly, Durkheim reveals the influence on his thinking of his early teacher at the *École,* Fustel de Coulanges whose *The Ancient City,* published a third of a century before Durkheim's the *Division of Labor,* had shown the foundations of early Greek and Roman society in the ritual bonds of religion. But the influence of Sir Henry Maine's classic, *Ancient Law,* published only three years before Fustel de Coulanges' work, is also to be seen. Precisely as Maine found that all individualistic and contractual relationships were preceded developmentally by relationships founded upon ascriptive status, so does Durkheim find this to be the case in his chapter on contract in the *Professional Ethics.* There he traces the idea of contract back to the aboriginal relationship between a people and its god, back to the overriding, overpowering condition Durkheim calls the *sacred.*

Hence the prevalence of oaths and other declarations of absolute
obedience to some god or sacred thing that is deemed antecedent
to and in control of the contracting parties.

In ritual, that is, in man's aboriginal compact with the gods,
themselves but manifestations of the sacred essence of society, lies
the origin of contract, conceived as a binding tie between human
beings.

> It is the solemn ritual nature of the undertaking that gives it
> this characteristic, by sanctifying it and by making of it something
> that no longer depends on myself, although proceeding from me.
> The other party is thus justified in counting on my word—and vice
> versa, if the contract imposes mutual obligations. He has morally
> and legally the right to consider the promise as inevitably about to
> be kept. If, then, I fail in this, I am transgressing two duties at
> once: (1) I am committing sacrilege, because I am breaking an oath,
> I am profaning a sacred thing, I am committing an act forbidden
> by religion, and I am trespassing on the region of sacred things;
> (2) I am disturbing another in his possession, just as if I were a
> neighbor on his land; I am injuring him, or there is danger in it.[4]

In the beginning, in short, the only contract worthy of the
name was that represented by ritual, the covenant, so to speak,
between man and the sacred realm. When, gradually, agreements
between men came into existence, whether with respect to human
beings, as in marriage, or things, as with property, or war and
peace, as in treaties, the only secure basis these agreements could
have, if fluctuating self-interest were not to be feared with its possible consequences of betrayal of agreement, lay in the domain of
the sacred, which was, as Durkheim stresses, no more than the
power of society raised to hyperintensity. In the course of social
evolution, with the gradual secularization of more and more areas
of social and economic life, the civil law replaced sacred ritual as
the basis of contract. But at no time, Durkheim emphasizes, has
contract ever been simply a matter between two or more private
parties operating from individual self-interest. Always, whether
in sacred or secular form, there has been the structure of human
society to give contract its binding force.

PROPERTY

Durkheim supplies precisely the same kind of analysis for the origin of property in human society and for the continuing respect for property we find in all societies, however differently property may be defined from one society to another. Neither the origin nor the continuing respect springs from any instinct in many, from any rationalist sense of reciprocity, or from any utilitarian notion that what one mixes his labor or cunning with is manifestly his. Durkheim has little to say about property in his *Division of Labor,* but there is an excellent section on the subject in the *Professional Ethics.* Here too we can see structural analysis at its finest.

"Property is property only if it is respected, that is to say, held sacred." So begins Durkheim's essay on property. We might think, he writes, that this respect springs from the respect that an individual has for himself, transferred to the object that the individual has tilled and worked. "In this case the property would have no moral value except that lent to it by human personality: this would be the value which, by entering into a relation with things and by making them its own, would confer a certain dignity on them by extension, as it were."[5] This kind of explanation was the common one in the Age of Reason, widely used by natural law theorists such as Locke; and it continued well into the 19th century where, in a host of philosophies and ideologies, the idea of the sanctity of property was deemed a projection of the individual's inbred sense of the sanctity of self.

 But, Durkheim writes, neither the individual's sense of personal value nor the value that the individual sets upon his property, nor the sanctity he places upon other persons and other pieces of property, springs from the self—either the instinctivist self or the rationalist self. Always we find these senses and values preceded and then reinforced by relationships and values which are in no way individualistic or material. This is, at one and the same time, the *collective* and the *sacred.*

These two qualities, the collective and the sacred, are for Durkheim but two sides of the same coin. "The gods are no other *dream of self primitive interpretation is that of spiritual being.*

than collective forces personified and hypostasized in material form." Precisely as individuals became prized in the first instance by virtue of sacred essences conceived to lie within them, essences drawn from gods or spirits representative of the wholeness of the community, so, in time, did certain things—plots of ground, streams, lakes, trees, hill tops, and so forth—become prized by members of the community; prized in a way alien to their relationships to things in general.

In this, the priority of the social, of the collective, is fundamental. Man is himself regarded as sacred in the first instance because "there is a god within him and indeed several." But the god or gods held to lie in man are but reflections of the communal and of the superiority of the community to all else including the individuals which form it. And community cannot exist save upon some piece of the earth's surface, and this too becomes invested with sacredness. "If, then, there are gods in things and especially in the soil, it is because things, and especially the soil, are associated with the intimate life of the group just as much as human beings are. This is because they are believed to live the life of the community."[6]

The notion, therefore, of certain areas or things closed save by special permission to man's free use, the notion in short that lies at the heart of the institution of private property, arose in the first instance in connection with the sacred community. Collective appropriation thus precedes private appropriation. Only the notion of possession by the totality of the community, possession which made trespass and theft offenses of gravest import inasmuch as they violated the religio-sacred, could give rise in time to the derivative notion of possession—that is, property—as being in itself sacred.

Long before there was any clear idea of individual property, there was the idea of property held in trust, as it were, by families and by clans. Even this was a concession, Durkheim tells us, by the larger collectivity, the tribe or people. Since the sacredness of the collectivity was held to pass into the ground on which they lived, hunted, tilled, and harvested, endowments of this ground, and the water and other resources that went with it, could be by permission only of the larger group. These endowments went, not to individuals, but smaller groups, the component kinship groups. "This is why the coming of agriculture undoubtedly gave to family groups smaller than the clan a cohesion and stability they had not known before."[7] Henceforth these groups possessed a double identity: that springing from descent and that rising from the land that was in their trust.

As Durkheim shrewdly notes, it is this indissoluble relation between sacred essences and sacred things that explains why, throughout the history of civilization, "people are possessed by things at least as much as things are possessed by people." Durkheim calls our attention to the fact that in both ancient Greek and Latin the word for family was held to include not only persons, not only servants and slaves as well as those of consanguineal descent, but also *things:* the livestock, the buildings, the surrounding land, and all the implements and weapons by which life was maintained. Everything we know from both comparative law and comparative religion reinforces the Durkheimian argument that property in the beginning had no existence save as an undifferentiated element of the social, of the social structure that was invested with the idea of the sacred.

How, then, Durkheim asks, does property in time lose its collective roots and become something individual? "How is it that individuals thus grouped together, attached to an identical group of things, came to acquire separate rights over separate things?"[8] To ask this question is by implication to ask a prior one: Under what circumstances did certain individuals attain such identity and force of personality that the sacred notion of property could be transferred, so to speak, from the collectivity to the single individual? The answer Durkheim gives is connected with the rise of patriarchalism in primitive kinship. With this momentous change in the history of kinship the "head of the family became a high moral and sacred power: this is because the whole life of the group was absorbed in this head, and thus he came to have the same transcendence over each of its members as the collectivity itself. He was the family entity personified."[9]

This is true enough up to a point, but what Durkheim fails to emphasize is the fact that long after patriarchalism arose, with the father the transcendent figure by virtue of the *patria potestas* he wielded (the power of life and death over all members of the family and of management of everything belonging to the family), property was still regarded in ancient Greek and Roman law as a possession *of the family*. The patriarch was the trustee. Under no circumstances, for a very long time, could property be alienated from the family. What was to become known much later as the law of entail—making impossible any individual's selling or giving off of land belonging to a family line—was a cardinal feature of the early patriarchal family. In both Greece and Rome, it was, more than anything else, warfare and, with it, the rise of the military chief, the general, and also the rise of armies in the field, with service becoming ever longer, that had the effect of a gradual individualization of property. Durkheim might have gotten this insight from Maine's *Ancient Law,* a work that he much admired and clearly knew well. We know that one of the ways generals were able to keep soldiers at war was by promising them the right to keep for themselves booty which they had acquired in battle.

Nevertheless it must be granted Durkheim that he deals with the individualization of property sociologically, that is, by showing how it, as well as the prior collectivization of property, sprang basically from structural considerations. What gave the individual—first the patriarch, then the sons to whom the property passed—in due time a direct relation to things was nothing inherent in the individual himself but, rather, in his relation to the community. When it could be said that *his* eminence was the reflected eminence of the *group,* then the conception of things belonging to his eminence, to him, became an ever clearer one.

The second main cause in the rise of an individualized notion of property was no less social or structural. It is to be found in the increasing trade in personal or movable property. Personal property, Durkheim tells us, probably never had even in the beginning the degree of sacredness attaching to it that land did, but whatever sacredness it did have tended to become lost once communities began to exchange it by barter and, then, through use of money. Clearly, that which can be separated from one's self in return for new things cannot be as sacred as, say, the land one lives on and that contains the spirits of all the departed. In the beginning personal property may have been as immovable in fact as landed. And certainly such property could never have been regarded as being as important as landed property.

> With time, however, and with the progress of trade and industry, the personal or moveable property took on greater importance; it then cut away from this landed property of which it was only an adjunct; it played a social role of its own different from landed property, and became an autonomous factor in economic life. Thus a fresh nucleus of property was made outside real estate, and so did not of course have its distinctive features.[10]

Thus, in sum, we are able to see how it was landed property in the beginning that established the bond between communities and things, for it was in land that the same sacred essence could be found, had to be found, that inhered in the community living on the land. Far from being, as individualists and utilitarians conceived it, something inhering in the individual, property is inseparable from social structure. It was the community that formed the idea of property, that gave material things some of the same distinctiveness and sacredness that was first found only in the community itself. And, in due time, it was a series of structural processes—chiefly those pertaining to nature of economy and its changed relation to family and local community—that led to transfer to the individual many of the values originally inhering in the community alone. In short, with respect to property as to other modes of ostensibly individual behavior and possession, we are obliged to see all of these as relatively late manifestations of normative systems inseparable from society.

THE CATEGORIES OF THE MIND

By general assent Durkheim's effort to demonstrate the social sources of what he called the "categories" of the human mind is less successful than most of his other utilizations of the structural approach. The effort is nevertheless of sufficient interest to warrant account of it here. And even if his analysis fails in certain epistemological respects—which it surely does—the analysis is a valuable one for the sociology of knowledge: that is, the relation of externally manifest ideas of space, time, force, cause, and the like in a given culture to the type of social organization within which we find that culture and its dominant ideas. Quite apart from ultimate origins of ideas or of thought, no one will question that human thinking operates within and is strongly influenced by social structures and processes, even when man's profoundest ideas are involved.

Durkheim's analysis of ideas is to be found in his *Elementary Forms of Religious Life.* The analysis must be seen as a by-product of the larger treatment of the nature of religion, also a structural treatment, to which we shall come later in this book, and of the anteriority of religion to all other forms of intellectual life in man's history. It is doubtful that Durkheim had epistemological objectives in mind when first he turned to the phenomenon of religion, but such, he came to believe, was the overpowering influence of the sacred in mankind's early condition that he concluded it must have affected the very structure of the human mind.

> At the roots of all our judgments there are a certain number of essential ideas which dominate all our intellectual life; they are what philosophers since Aristotle have called the categories of the understanding: ideas of space, class, number, cause, substance, personality, etc. They correspond to the most universal properties of things. They are like the solid frame which encloses all thought. . . . They are like the framework of intelligence.[11]

In this manner Durkheim sets forth the nature of his intellectual problem. For what he wishes to do is show the origins of these master-ideas in the human mind by reference to religious-social processes. The problem was one of great interest in Durkheim's day—it continues to be in our own; witness the works of Lévi-Strauss, Noam Chomsky, and others, who deal with the problem, of course, in a very different way, Chomsky especially, from

Durkheim—and whatever else we may think of Durkheim's results, they are radical in nature.

Heretofore, Durkheim tells us, philosophers have tended to follow either David Hume or Immanuel Kant in their explanation of these mental categories. Hume, the arch-empiricist, concerned solely with the experiential life of the individual and the transfer to the mind of this experience, found the origins of the categories in repetitive experiences of the individual from infancy on. Thus, with respect to the idea of causation, the individual gradually acquires this general, constitutive idea as the result of a large number of personal experiences: experiences in which one condition may be seen as "causing" another. Beyond the cumulation of such experiences and their perception as being in habitual succession in time, given a certain motivating condition, there is, Hume concluded, no idea of cause. Kant, however, reacting specifically to Hume's radical empiricism, declared that no amount of mere sensory experience would ever result for the individual in an idea as imperative, as binding, and as authoritative in one's thinking, as the idea of cause. We can account for the distinctive role this idea—and, of course, other equally constitutive ideas—holds in our thinking only by assuming that the categories are inseparable from the mind; that is, they are essentially innate and to be regarded as aspects of the very structure of the individual mind.

From Durkheim's stringently sociological and structural point of view, both answers to the question of the origins of the categories were unsatisfactory. Hume's insufficiency springs basically, Durkheim tells us, from the fact that no mere addition of experiences in the individual's sensory life could ever add up to something as coherent and, above all, as authoritative as, say, the idea of cause. There is, Durkheim correctly notes, a universe of difference between the act of thought which declares A to be the cause of B and any of the large number of lesser acts of thought, feeling, or perception which are clearly the product of individual experience. No amount of strictly individual sensory experience would ever result, in a single individual's lifetime, in the commanding position in our thinking that certain ideas, such as time, space, and cause have.

But Kant is no more satisfactory, Durkheim thinks; that is, apart from Kant's correct appreciation of the utter inadequacy of individual experience alone as the basis of our possession of the categories of thought. Kant and the apriorists have indeed seen that the mind is capable of transcending experience and of adding "to that which is given to it directly." But "of this singular power they give neither explanation nor justification. For it is no explanation to say that it is inherent in the human intellect. It is necessary to show whence we hold this surprising prerogative and how it comes that we can see certain relations in things. . . ."[12]

Now, we can honor Durkheim in wishing to go beyond the explanation of "inherency," for all too many fallacies in the history of human thought have taken essentially that form, but even so, most philologists and psychologists today would not rule out categorically the very strong possibility that in the very structure of the human mind, wherever we find it, certain fundamental patterns are to be found of a neuropsychological kind which make thought and language alike possible. In sum, while all explanations based on inherency should be looked at carefully and critically, it would be wrong to presume in advance that all are probably false.

Nevertheless we have here the background of Durkheim's social-structural examination of the primary and constitutive ideas of human thought. It is acknowledgedly in his repudiation of both Hume's empiricism and Kant's apriorism that his own analysis takes its beginning. If the categories of the mind cannot be explained either through cumulative individual experience or apriorism, how, then, are they to be accounted for? The answer Durkheim gives, imperfections and inadequacies to one side, is one of the boldest in all sociology—the origins are to be found in the authority of society.

> Society is a reality *sui generis;* it has its own peculiar character-
> istics, which are not found elsewhere and which are not met again
> in the same form in all the rest of the universe. The representations

which express it have a wholly different content from purely in-dividual ones and we may rest assured in advance that the first add something to the second.[13]

There is nothing mysterious about the action of these "collective representations"—which is but a phrase for what most of us call more commonly traditions, codes, and themes in culture—for, Durkheim notes, "man is double." That is, man is not merely a biopsychological being; he is also a social and cultural being.

> There are two beings in him: an individual being which has its foundation in the organism and the circle of whose activities is therefore strictly limited, and a social being which represents the highest reality in the intellectual and moral order that we can know by observation—I mean society. This duality of our nature has as its consequence in the practical order, the irreducibility of a moral ideal to a utilitarian motive, and in the order of thought, the irreducibility of reason to individual experience. In so far as he belongs to society, the individual transcends himself, both when he thinks and when he acts.[14]

We shall have more to say about that passage and a number of related ones concerning the nature of personality in the next chapter. For the moment we must pass over the analysis it deserves, for our concern here is with the problem of the mind and its categories. I have, in the passage just cited, sought only to show the means whereby Durkheim moves to a sociological explanation of such ideas as cause, time, and mass. There is nothing supernal, given Durkheim's social psychology, in his declaration that the source of these ideas lies in society, for it is fundamental to Durkheim's social psychology that society is but one of the two aspects of man himself. Man is dual, and the social is as vital a part of his mental nature as is the biological.

It is this social aspect of the mind, this *social half,* that gives society and reason alike the exceptional authority each possesses in human life.

> This seems to be the origin of the exceptional authority which is inherent in the reason and which makes us accept its suggestions

with confidence. It is the very authority of society, transferring itself to a certain manner of thought which is the indispensable condition of all common action. The necessity with which the categories are imposed upon us is not the effect of simple habits whose
yoke we could easily throw off with little effort; nor is it a physical
or metaphysical necessity, since the categories change in different
places and times; it is a sort of moral necessity which is to the intellectual life what moral obligation is to the will.[15]

"Since the categories change in different places and times . . ."
In these words, drawn from the preceding quotation, we have the
really fundamental observation behind Durkheim's structural
form of analysis. There is no single conception of cause, or of
time, or of space, or of any other major realm of experience
known to man. There is, on the contrary, a great diversity of such
conceptions, and what we find, Durkheim argues, is that such
diversity is matched almost perfectly to the diversity of social
milieus in which individuals live and form their intellectual representations. This, Durkheim argues, is where both Hume and
Kant erred: in thinking there is some single, more or less uniform,
set of categories of the mind. Such, however, is not the case. There
is wide variation between the actual representations of fundamental ideas in the human mind, and this variation proceeds in
terms of social structures, of cultures, and societies.

Consider the idea or category of cause—more accurately, of
the process of causation. No idea is more basic, Durkheim notes,
to the structure of human reason. Where did it arise in the first
instance in man's consciousness? Wherever the prior idea of force
and of impact resulting from force arose. And, Durkheim argues,
it is logical—and also supportable by the comparative evidence of
prehistory and of contemporary primitive peoples—to suppose
that man's first clear notion of force and, later, cause was expressed in religious terms, which are, in Durkheim's view, social
terms.

Our analysis of facts has already enabled us to see that the prototype of the idea of force was the mana, wakan, orenda, the
totemic principle or any of the various names given to the collec-

tive force objectified and projected into things. The first power which men have thought of as such seems to have been that exercised by humanity over its members.[16]

Once again, in short, we are brought to a social, a structural explanation of something others had declared to be individual or racial in origin. Primitive man's experience of the awesome power of the entire community, sovereign in all things, was the basis of his gradually evolved notion of force, that is, of any power sufficient to bring about a given effect. Closely bound to the idea of force, Durkheim observes, is that of ascendancy or mastership or domination. "It is society which classifies beings into superiors and inferiors, into commanding masters and obeying servants; it is society which confers upon the former the singular power which makes the command efficacious and which makes *power*."[17] And it is through society's impact upon the primitive mind, an impact manifest in socialization extending over countless generations in the primitive experience of the human race, that man's culture, and then man's very social-cultural nature, acquired the idea of force—abstract force, but force nevertheless conceived in essential social and religious terms for a very long time.

But there is, Durkheim notes, more to the idea of causality than simple force. There is also the vital idea of connection— *necessary* connection between cause and effect. "The mind posits this connection without having any proofs of it . . . ; it postulates it, as they say, *a priori*."[18] Whence, then, the more complex and sophisticated idea of cause? Individual, empirical experience would never, Durkheim tells us again, yield the idea of necessary cause, of necessary relation between a given act or event and a succeeding one to which we give the label of "effect." Again, then, we must turn to society and the sacred sense of its superiority to the individual in all matters. Specifically, we must turn, Durkheim says, to certain types of religious rite where the constant repetition of calculated, sacred acts, followed by foreseen results, is the social basis of what in time becomes the more abstract and generalized notion of cause and effect. From the sacred character of the ritual act and its effect springs the notion of obligation or, more accurately, *necessity*. The crux of the idea of cause in the human mind, Durkheim has already told us, is necessity: the belief that there is a necessary relation between cause and effect. Such necessity, as an idea, could only have come in the first instance from the experience of cause and effect in the imitative rite.

> To prescribe that one must imitate an animal or plant to make them reproduce, is equivalent to stating it as an axiom which is above all doubt, that like produces like. Opinion cannot allow men to deny this principle in theory without also allowing them to violate it in their conduct. So society imposes it, along with the practices which are derived from it, and thus the ritual precept is doubled by a logical precept which is only the intellectual aspect of the former.[19]

Thus the origin of the human category of thought we call causality. Precisely the same type of explanation is given, though more briefly, to the other categories: time, space, and so forth. Thus the idea of time, of temporality, arose, Durkheim suggests, from the observation by primitive man of the regular practice of the sacred, life-giving ceremonies, the very regularity, in accord with solar and lunar rhythms perhaps, creating the notions of periodicity, duration, and temporality. Similarly, the conception of space was suggested by the very patterns of habitation practiced by the tribe; that is, square, rectangular, or circular patterns of housing and of cultural life in general. Thus, Durkheim tells us, the Australian aborigines live in circular compounds, concentric in character, and their notion of all space is similarly circular and concentric in character.[20]

Too many critics of Durkheim's theory of the origin of the mental categories have failed to credit Durkheim with the spirit of tentativeness, of provisional hypothesis, in which his ideas were set forth. On the idea of causality, Durkheim concludes his observations with these words:

> It is to be borne in mind, moreover, that we have never dreamed of offering the preceding observations as a complete theory of the con-

cept of causality. The question is too complex to be resolved thus. . . . The views which we have set forth should be regarded as mere indications, which must be controlled and completed.[21]

Durkheim was not, of course, the first to deal with the categories of thought from a social point of view. Throughout the 19th century, beginning indeed in the works of some of the French religious conservatives, especially in those of Gabriel de Bonald, we find a continuing line of such interest. It was an interest fed in part by philosophical reaction to the strict individualism of the Enlightenment, in part by sociological currents of which Durkheim was a major part, and in part by the constant widening of interest in the types of culture—and with these types of mentality—to be found in the primitive areas of human society. The profound emphasis on the idea of culture in 19th-century ethnology, especially after publication of Edward B. Tylor's *Primitive Culture* in 1871, was fit companion to the equally profound emphasis in French circles on the idea of society. From both emerged a steadily growing interest in the social or cultural components of human thought.

As I noted at the beginning of this section, there are not many today among those working with the problem of the origin of the mind and its categories of cause, space, time, and so forth, who find Durkheim's conclusions satisfactory. Even by his own standards, those, for instance, of his analysis of religion, the account of the origin of the categories is unsatisfactory in many respects. But this is true only if we are thinking of the matter of ultimate psychological beginnings in man, that is, in human and social evolution. Very different is the reaction we must have if we think of Durkheim's work regarding the categories of thought in the light of comparative social or cultural psychology rather than in the light of human evolution. Considered in the latter light, his account is certainly deficient in many respects, as the work today of the linguistic philosophers and philologists makes clear enough. But if we see Durkheim's propositions as concerned at bottom with the close relation individual modes of thinking

have to the social and cultural settings in which these modes
have their development, we cannot help but regard Durkheim's
thought as significantly contributory to the sociology and ethnology of knowledge. Different as the contributions of Mauss, Halbwachs, Granet, and Lévi-Strauss assuredly are to this whole subject, different and also more sophisticated, their continuity with
Durkheim's seminal thinking is evident.

CLASSIFICATION AND CONCEPT

Closely related to the foregoing, but well worthy of separate treatment, however brief, is Durkheim's approach to the nature of
logical thought—that is, thought that proceeds in terms of reference to certain impersonal, widely accepted norms of internal
rigor, clarity, and deductive relation. We speak of logical thought
foremost perhaps when we have such a field as geometry in mind
with its rigorous derivations of a constantly ascending generality
of truth from what is in the beginning simple and self-evident.
Logical thought is the opposite of merely random or associative
thought, and also of what we tend to call intuitive thought,
though this, as we know, can lend itself to perfectly logical expression.

Here too Durkheim gives us a stringently sociological analysis. The origins of logical thought, he believes, are to be found
in the capacity of the human mind to arrange things in terms of
classes, each reflecting some dominant attribute of a thing; that
is, the redness of a given bird seen as falling within the "class" of
red things, the feathers within the "class" of feathery things, and
so on. Beyond doubt logical thought, even in this simple sense, is
relatively late in man's intellectual evolution. How did it come
into being in the first instance? Durkheim's answer is as relent-
lessly sociological as it is in his account of the categories of
thought.

> Far from it being the case, as Frazer seems to think, that the
> social relations of men are based on logical relations between

things, in reality it is the former which have provided the prototype for the latter. . . . The first logical categories were social categories; the first classes of things were classes of men, into which these things were integrated. It was because men were grouped, and thought of themselves in the form of groups, that in their ideas they grouped other things. . . .[22]

Only when things were thought to be constitutive elements of society, Durkheim argues, did things become constitutive elements of thought, and the process of thinking about things tended, he argues further, to follow the structure of society. "It is a fact of current observation that the things which they (genera) comprise are generally imagined as situated in a sort of ideational milieu, with a more or less clearly delimited spatial circumscription."[23] Might it not have been, therefore, the form of *social* groups and classes within social space that first determined the mental and logical groups in which things were placed by human thought?

Not only are the logical classes in all probability evolutionary derivations of social structures, but it is also probable, Durkheim argues, that "the relations uniting them" are also social in origin. The manner in which social groups "fit into" one another—subclan into clan, clan into society, etc.—suggest the ways that things may be seen as fitting into one another through the classes in which they are located. "Thus logical hierarchy is only another aspect of social hierarchy, and the unity of knowledge is nothing else than the very unity of the collectivity, extended to the universe."[24]

The dependence of human thought upon social structure had been deeply thought out in Durkheim's *Suicide,* published a number of years before his essay on classification and also his full-length study of religion in which he deals with the categories of the mind. There, however, it could be assumed by the reader that his only intent was to demonstrate the close relation between social structure and stability of personality, though, as we shall see, there is in *Suicide* a full-blown social psychology. In *Primitive Classification,* on the other hand, the intent is nothing less than declaration that the very structure of the human mind—that is, the logical structure, the capacity to reason in terms of concepts and classes of concepts—is an emergent of social structure.

So radical a hypothesis is not likely to be accepted today in the form in which Durkheim stated it anymore than it was in his own time, for here, as in his treatment of the categories, there is the almost insurmountable problem of distinguishing between the things that are social, and hence the products of postnatal socialization, and the things that are indeed bred into the genetic structure of the mind as this has come into existence through processes of *natural,* rather than social, selection. And, in all fairness, Durkheim himself recognized that his theory was, and had to be, only provisional and tentative. "At least", he wrote, "this is a new way which deserves to be tried."[25]

It must be conceded that Durkheim's way is a step forward from the conventional analyses of his time in terms of anthropocentrism. The center is not man, as man, Durkheim shrewdly realized; it is man-in-society. "The centre of the first schemes of nature is not the individual; it is society. It is this that is objectified, not man."[26] In short, we must take a *sociocentric* view of the matter inasmuch, Durkheim tells us, as it was the structure of society, its classes, associations, and roles, that first formed the model for human understanding of experience and nature.

Logical classification is, of course, classification of *concepts.* In many respects, the heart of Durkheim's theory of the nature of logical thought, and of its sociocentric origin, lies in his treatment of concepts. We find this in both his *Primitive Classification* and the *Elementary Forms of Religious Life.* A concept, Durkheim writes, is the notion of a clearly determined group of things. The boundaries of a concept, as such, are more or less clearly evident to us. Very different is an emotion, which is "fluid and inconsistent." An emotion or affective state "spreads far beyond its point of origin, extending to everything about it, so that it is not possible to say where its power of propagation ends."[27] What we find in the history of mankind is a progressive detachment of the conceptual from the affective, of the logical and cognitive from the emotional. "Thus the history of scientific classification is, in the last analysis, the history of the stages by which this element of social affectivity has progressively weakened, leaving more and more room for the reflective thought of individuals."[28] In that statement, it is interesting to note, we have an expression strikingly akin to Simmel's better known theory of "autonomization" in which he pointed to the successive liberations of thought—in the beginning indistinguishable from the religious, the affective, the social, and utilitarian—from the contexts in which for so long it had been confined. Durkheim's primary concern is with classification and concepts, but the thrust of his position is essentially the same.

Durkheim is, of course, correct in his contention that ultimately the problem of the relation between society and logical thought becomes the problem of the relation between society—or, rather, of social forms—and of concepts. And he is also correct in his view that what is basic in the concept is its presumed immutability, its supra-individual character, its universality. For me to speak of *goodness* is clearly a very different thing than for me to speak of *my feeling* about goodness. What is abstract, Durkheim implies, was in the first instance general; it sprang from the generality of the social, not from the specificity of the individual feeling, emotion, or impulse, though no one would question the often-noted observation that our definitions of the abstract have a striking relation to our perceptions of what we are involved in.

The concept is the key unit of human communication.

> It is impossible [Durkheim writes] for me to make a sensation pass from my consciousness into that of another; it holds closely to my organism and personality and cannot be detached from them. . . . On the other hand, conversation and all intellectual communication between men is an exchange of concepts. The concept is an essentially impersonal representation; it is through it that human intelligences communicate.[29]

Thus, Durkheim continues, the ultimately social or communal origin of the concept. Its very universality, its capacity for exchange from one person to another, its crystallization of meaning, thus permitting human beings generation after generation to draw from this fund of more or less constant meaning, all suggest an origin in the social group. If the concept has more stability of meaning from person to person or age to age than the simple sensation or direct feeling, this is the result, Durkheim writes, of the interpersonal and eventually impersonal foundation of the concept.

> Every time that we are in the presence of a *type* of thought or action which is imposed uniformly upon particular wills or intelligences, this pressure exercised over the individual betrays the intervention of the group. . . . What it expresses is the manner in which society as a whole represents the facts of experience. The ideas which correspond to the diverse elements of language are thus collective representations.[30]

It is surely too simple to locate the origins of the human capacity for classification and for conceptual thought—that is, the ultimate origins—in society alone. Present day studies suggest that we are obliged to go more deeply into the nature of the human mind and into those early, complex, still unrecovered—perhaps unrecoverable—processes of neural evolution out of which human thinking, as we know it, emerged. If there is indeed a universality of certain fundamental linguistic structures, as our contemporary explorers tell us, there is every reason to believe that this universality is inseparable from man's organic evolution. And certainly the relation between abstract or conceptual thought and language is an unbreakable relation, neither possible without the other, in whatever form. The imperative quality Durkheim finds in logical thought and in logical classification cannot, it would seem, be derived solely from society, cannot, in all probability, be separated from the very psychoneural origins of thinking and language.

But Durkheim does not err in giving to society vast influence upon the configurations which thought—and logic and concept—assume in human experience. If we think of Durkheim's contributions as being to the sociology of knowledge and of culture, they take on immediate relevance and power. For it would be absurd to deny the immense weight of society upon the individual's specific expressions of logic and concept or upon the varied patterns in which these appear in the innumerable languages of the world. And if we focus attention upon the socialization of the young in any society, we can hardly be blind to the reinforcing influence of social norms upon whatever may exist preculturally in the individual mind so far as the mental categories are concerned. The incontestable fact is that a very great deal of culture is made up of collective representations of time, space, cause, and of modes of classification and of conceptualized thought. It is not possible to say with Durkheim that the social classifications of clan, moiety, and tribe are the *causes* of classificatory thinking in the individual, but it is assuredly possible to agree that such social classifications, in primitive and advanced society, exert great influence upon the ways individuals think.

INCEST

Our final example of Durkheim's use of social structure to account for human behavior will be drawn from his *Incest: The Nature and Origin of the Incest Taboo.* No principle of morality is more universal than the prohibition of sexual mating within specified kinship relations. We are today prone to think of such mating as being between parent and child or brother and sister. We do not ordinarily regard—in the West at least and in areas culturally shaped by the West—mating of cousins as incestuous, though we once did. There have been, and still are, though the number diminishes in our world today, peoples where the mating of relatives within a dozen degrees of relationship would be deemed incestuous and subject, therefore, to the full effects of stringent taboo and sanction. In traditional China it was thought incestuous to marry when the clan name of two individuals was the same, even though a given clan could number millions of persons spread out over large areas.

The common repugnance that is felt when we learn of an incestuous act between brother and sister or parent and child, the almost instantaneous aversion the overwhelming majority of us have at the thought of sexual encounters of this category for ourselves, together with the universal existence of incest taboos, however diverse these may be, has suggested to many persons that there is some biological, some instinctual basis for such repugnance and aversion. There is even a belief, still ascendant in many quarters but without scientific foundation, that such mating of close blood-relatives is biologically injurious to the genetic strain.

No such biological basis can, however, be established, and were it not for the symbolic properties religion long ago gave to blood and to the ties of blood within consanguineal relations, it is highly unlikely that any supposition of this sort would ever have come into being. In the first place, some of the most powerful of incest taboos have prevailed in kinship categories where the biological or consanguineal factor has been utterly absent; where the category has been agnatic, formed solely by legal or customary consideration. Kinship is, after all, a social-legal, not a biological thing. And, in the second place, history is not without instances of sexual relationships duly permitted by religious tradition between even brothers and sisters—as in the royal lineages of ancient Egypt and premodern Hawaii. Here, and also among other peoples, marriages were not only permitted but enjoined that would be declared incestuous in fullest degree ordinarily. Nor can we be oblivious to the prevalance of themes of incest in world literature. We need but think of the great tragedies of Aeschylus and Sophocles in ancient Greece and of the strong suggestion of incestuous attraction between Hamlet and his mother. True, the context of such themes in literature has been almost invariably one of horror and, eventually, retribution. Even so, there has been a certain fascination with incest that would be difficult to account for if the roots of our taboos on the subject were entirely biological.

Durkheim was one of the very first to deal with the origin of incest taboos in the structural terms of the kinship system. Specifically, he locates the roots of the taboo in the principle of exogamy: the organization of society in terms of groups the original bond of which was totemic, that is collective subordination of members of the exogamic group to the sacred essence represented by the totemic plant or animal. In exogamy, Durkheim tells us, society in the true sense was founded, and the purpose of the incest taboo from the beginning was to prevent any profanation of the totem of the exogamic group by any form of uncleanness, whether pertaining to sex or to food and drink. By virtue of the sacred character of the totemic group, relationships within it were no less sacred among individuals: relationships of elders to the young, as well as of the sexes to each other and also of peers within sexes. Indiscriminate sexual intercourse among males and females of this sacred exogamic group would have been as much a flouting of the sacred as indiscriminate eating and drinking.

Given the prior sanctity of the exogamic relation, then, arrangements for marriage and for any kind of sexual union had to be made elsewhere—though always within some prescribed collectivity. As the principle of exogamy directed that marriages be *outside* a given group, endogamy prescribed that they be *within* a given group—tribe, people, area, as the case might be. Not, in sum, in biological aversion but in aversion to profanation of the totem and its collective manifestation in clan or similar group, did the incest taboo arise and early become one of the most powerful of all human commandments and prohibitions.

> It is repugnant to us [Durkheim writes] to admit that a principle of our contemporary morality, one of those most strongly internalized within us, can be traced to a dependence, even a long time ago, on absurd prejudices from which humanity has long since freed itself.
>
> However, there is no doubt but that the dispositions of our codes relative to marriages between relatives are linked to the exogamic practices by a continuous series of intermediaries, even as our current domestic structure is linked to that of the clan.[31]

Only, he continues, on the assumption that original horror of incest, however defined specifically by a group, sprang from horror of offending the spirit, the sacred essence that alone gave human beings their identity and their protection in this world and the next, can we understand the extent to which the incest taboo has prevailed among all human beings throughout the history of mankind. To assume, Durkheim writes, that sexual attraction would not spring up between individuals of the two sexes—given the propinquity and maximum of temptation—apart from some supervening obligation of duty is to suppose nonsense. Always the possibility of sexual union was present, between parent and child and between brothers and sisters, *and still is present,* and the only possible barrier to this can be a principle of morality so deeply rooted in believed conditions of survival as to invoke horror and instant punishment upon those who deviate.

The structural principle behind the incest taboo is no less clear when we turn from primitive exogamic group to the family as we know it today. There is, Durkheim notes, a nearly absolute incompatibility between the conjugal and the kinship functions. The first, which is that of sexual relation between husband and wife, is based—in some degree at least everywhere, "marriages of convenience" notwithstanding—upon personal attraction and love. Whatever duty arises grows from these affectional roots. Very different, Durkheim argues, is the relation within the kinship group proper. Relationships of affection may or may not exist between parent and child, between siblings. Here what is uppermost, and has been for countless ages, is the *duty* that is owed by individuals to the several relationships, norms, and roles comprising the family.

> Everything concerning the life of the family is dominated by the idea of duty. Our contacts with brothers, our sisters, our parents, are strictly regulated by morality; . . . Assuredly, sympathy and special inclinations are far from being banished; however, the domestic affections always have the distinctive propriety that the sentiment of love is strongly colored with respect. Love in this instance is not simply a spontaneous movement of personal sensitivity; it is, in part, a duty. . . .[32]

Kinship, in sum, demands that its participants be united even though there may be no love. For duty, respect, and dependence are crucial in kinship, and they have been perforce since the time kinship was man's exclusive form of protection from the elements of nature. Precisely because of the fundamental idea of duty in relations between brothers and sisters, between parents and children, not to mention the several other degrees of kinship relations, it has been necessary from earliest times to prevent these relationships from being corrupted, polluted, or even confused as they assuredly would be if sexual unions were permitted, with issue that would have, necessarily, a hopelessly disintegrative effect upon the kinship relations and its nomenclature. One need but think of the confusion introduced into this nomenclature by the presence of a child within the kinship group that was the issue of the father and one of the daughters or, for that matter, of brother and sister, or any other such sexual union. The sheer magnitude of the classificatory problem thus generated is, when expanded to include a large number of such unions, enough to boggle the mind.

But to look at the problem as but one of taxonomy is hardly enough. For from earliest times the kinship relations have been steeped in the values of religion. No relationships more sacred than those arising from the family are to be found, not even those of communicant to God. If parricide and fratricide were the most heinous of crimes in ancient times, incest must be placed with them, for it too is a profanation of the sacred ties of the family. The aversion, then, to incest springs historically from what its effects would be to the structure of the family and its all-important roles.

But even today, Durkheim writes, long after the ancient regard for the sanctity of the family has become significantly moderated, the incompatibility between the two types of relationship, kinship and conjugal, remains; and in sufficient degree for us to continue to be psychologically repelled by the thought of incestuous union. For even in our time, the relationships of parent-child, of brother to brother, of sister to sister, and brother to sister, remain strong and respected relationships. There may or may not be close affection, but few of us wish explicitly to corrupt or damage in any way these relationships.

> . . . The dignity of the relationship which unites us with close kin thus excludes any other link which would not have the same value. One cannot court a person to whom one owes and who in turn owes you a respectful affection, without this latter feeling being corrupted or vanishing in one way or another. In a word, *given our present ideas,* a man cannot make a wife of his sister without her ceasing to be his sister. This is what makes us disapprove so strongly of incest.[33]

So much is true, but the foundation of Durkheim's argument concerning the *origin* of the incest taboo is developmental. That is, it must be seen as having first come into existence in mankind long before there were kinship relations as we know them with their complex taxonomies of consanguineal and collateral connection. Very probably, Durkheim suggests, incest existed for a long time after *Homo sapiens* was evolved biologically. But from the time that human beings began to form themselves exogamically, totemistically, with the sacred spirit emanating from plant or animal deemed to be their sole security in this and the next world, then and then only did a tampering with, a confusion of, the relations within an exogamic unity come to seem a profanation, a risk of existence itself, not to mention identity, and thus to arouse deepest horror—and necessary taboos.

> Without the beliefs derived from exogamy, nothing enables us to be sure that we would have our present ideas of marriage, nor that incest would be prohibited by our codes. In making this hypothesis, we do not mean to say that exogamy has been a contingent accident. It is too closely linked with totemism and to the clan, which are universal phenomena, for one to be able to stop at such a supposition. One should rather see in our formula only a process of exposition, aimed at isolating the variable of each factor.
>
> No doubt the eternal antithesis between passion and duty would have always found a means of demonstrating itself; but it would have taken on another form. It is not in the heart of the

sexual life that passion would have established, so to speak, its center of action. Passion and love between the sexes would not have become synonymous.[34]

We shall be able to see in even larger context Durkheim's residual explanation of the prohibition of incest when we come to the chapter on morality. With respect to morality generally and incest specifically, the heart of Durkheim's analysis lies in the structural elements he provides: duty, discipline, ordered arrangement of roles, and the ineradicably sacred character these have in primitive life.

3 Social Psychology

Durkheim was not, in the strict sense of today's usage, a social psychologist; nor did he claim to be. He is nevertheless securely among those minds at the turn of the century whose perspectives regarding the formation of the self in social context are the foundation stones of modern social psychology. In the same way that Durkheim derived, as we have just seen, the categories of the mind from the structures, symbols, myths, and other constraints of society, so did he derive the human self, personality, from society and its mechanisms of socialization. Granted that Durkheim's principal interests lay in the realm of social organization, we find neverthelesss a fascination with the social nature of man that goes back at the very least to the *Division of Labor.* In that work he makes emphatic indeed the proposition that we cannot derive society from the ego, that we are obliged instead to derive the ego from society.

It is apparent in Durkheim's essay "Individual and Collective Representations" (to which brief reference was made above in Chapter 1 in the discussion of the nature of social facts) that he was tantalized by the idea of a social psychology. That essay, published in 1898, only three years after *The Rules of Sociological Method* had appeared and been so roundly attacked by individualistically oriented minds, is clearly an effort to establish operational connection between social facts and the individual consciousness—also the individual unconscious on which there are some suggestive words. In the essay there is, first, a theory of the relation between the individual mind and the neural structure of mentality and, second, an analogous theory of the relation between individual mind and the social order: manifest in the symbols and values which Durkheim categorized as "collective representations." What Durkheim had in mind for a social psychology may perhaps be inferred from the following passage of the essay:

> When we said elsewhere that social facts are in a sense inde-pendent of individuals and exterior to individual minds, we only affirmed of the social world what we have just established for the psychic world. Society has for its substratum the mass of associated individuals. The system which they form by uniting together, and which varies according to their geographical disposition and the nature and number of their channels of communication, is the base from which social life is raised. The representations which form the network of social life arise from the relations between the individ-uals thus combined or the secondary groups that are between the individuals and the total society. If there is nothing extraordinary in the fact that individual representations, produced by the action and reaction between neural elements, are not inherent in these elements, there is nothing surprising in th fact that collective repre-sentations, produced by the action and reaction between individual minds that form the society, do not derive directly from the latter and consequently surpass them. The conception of the relationship which unites the social substratum and the social life is at every point analogous to that which undeniably exists between the physi-ological substratum and the psychic life of individuals, if, that is, one is not going to deny the existence of psychology in the proper sense of the word.[1]

Clearly, what Durkheim is pointing toward here, but does not in fact reach in the essay, is a branch of science concerned with the precise ways in which social facts—"religious beliefs and practices, the rules of morality, and the innumerable precepts of law—that is to say, all the most characteristic manifestations of collective life"—become internalized in the conscious and uncon-scious minds of the individual.

Three years after publication of this essay, the second edition of *The Rules of Sociological Method* appeared (1901), and in the Preface written specially for this edition we find Durkheim still preoccupied by the attraction of a social psychology, a discipline that would be as different in its way from sociology as individual psychology is from neurology. Durkheim does not, however, believe that sufficient knowledge has as yet been acquired and assimilated to make possible such a discipline. Proper principles or laws are lacking.

> Social psychology, whose task it is to determine these laws, is scarcely more than a name, without a definite subject matter, and including all sorts of generalities, diverse and inexact. We need to investigate, by comparison of mythical themes, popular legends, traditions, and languages, the manner in which social representations adhere to and repel one another, how they fuse or separate from one another, etc.[2]

Here, obviously, what Durkheim is writing about has more to do with the mechanisms and patterns of interaction of "social representations" among themselves in a given society than with the channels by which such representations become internalized in the individual. And yet, as he perceived, the two aspects of social psychology are very closely related. A great deal of Durkheim's concern with what he called "moral education" (dealt with in Chapter 6 below) is at bottom concern with the means whereby the constraints and symbols of the social order become assimilated by the individual in the forms of conscience and consciousness alike.

Durkheim's largest objective was the scientific study of the varied structures of human society; he was first and last a sociologist. But he could not have written as brilliantly and eloquently on the nature of these structures, on their vital importance in the understanding of behavior, ostensibly individual behavior, had he not had a very clear, if generalized, notion of the genesis of mind, ego, and self in social circumstances. It is this aspect of Durkheim that puts him in the company of those such as William James (whose *Principles of Psychology* with its notable chapter on the social self had appeared in 1890 and was obviously important in Durkheim's thinking) and George H. Mead whom we are more likely today to think of among the founders of modern social psychology.

THE REVOLT AGAINST DUALISM

It is not possible to appreciate the almost revolutionary character of what we find in Durkheim, Mead, Cooley, and others at the turn of the century regarding the human self and its relation to society if we do not remind ourselves of the compelling atmosphere of individualism in this age and of the dualism that went with this individualism. From at least the age of Descartes this dualism had been a powerful force in European thinking about man and society. What it contained was the image of the individual mind, separate and aloof from, basically undirected by social structures and mechanisms. When Descartes uttered his celebrated "I think: therefore I am," he was in effect making man, not God, not society, master of his own identity.

Through the 17th, 18th, and the 19th centuries was carried the essence of this Cartesian dualism, with man's mind or personality the primary fact, all else—society, culture, institutions—secondary and derivative from what lay at birth in the individual. The associationist psychology of the 18th century, which flowered during the French Englihtenment, may have stressed the importance of what education and environment generally might write on the *tabula rasa* that was the individual mind at birth. But this had to do only with content, not structure of the mind. There was no more question among the philosophes about the fundamental stability of this structure and about its absolute priority to social experience than there had been among the more immediate followers of Descartes. At best, society, through education, wrote on the mind; it assuredly did not create it or, for that matter, self and character.

This was pretty much the conception of mind and self that reached the final decade of the 19th century. True, from Hegel and also from some of the French philosophical conservatives such as Bonald and Chateaubriand in the early part of the century there had come intimations of what a psychology might be if it proceeded from society as the primary fact rather than from the individual. The careful student will find in the fruitful studies of language, not least those of speculative and general cast in Bonald's writings where he makes both society and language prior to individual personality and mind, but also in the works of the German philologists such as the Grimm brothers, a very clear adumbration of the idea of human personality constructed in large degree of socially inherited myths, symbols, and other external constraints. Throughout the 19th century in Germany there was too the whole interest in *Volkerpsychologie,* the kinds of collective mind that it was thought lay with different peoples, that was a part of biological as well as social inheritance, that could be seen, as Wundt argued so persuasively from classroom and laboratory, in the contrasting structures of language and myth.

None of this is to be denied. Even so, however, if we look to the mainstream of thought on the nature of the individual and the self in 19th-century philosophy and psychology we find a view of man that is not very different from that which Cartesian philosophy had set forth more than two centuries earlier. The dualism of man and society persisted well into the 20th century, as is attested by the works attacking this dualism written as late as the 1920s by John Dewey, by Graham Wallas, and by the American school of cultural anthropologists. The idea of the reality of the human self considered prior to and separately from society was a very common one.

Nevertheless, the revolt against this dualism and its implied conception of the discrete self is one of the principal facts of the intellectual history of the late 19th century. And in this revolt the writings and teachings of Durkheim must be seen today as having played a prominent role.

The essence of the revolt consisted precisely in making the human personality an aspect of, a representation of, an extension of society and, arising from the structures and authorities of society, the process of socialization. It is impossible to understand,

even to envisage properly, the human self save in terms of its incessant interaction with the symbols and structures of society, all
of which, of course, precede the life of any given individual. I am
stating the matter perhaps more clearly, or distinctly at least, than
the actual writings of the time might support. But no one who
has ever read the superb chapter on the social self in William
James's *Principles of Psychology,* published in 1890, will need to
be told that it was possible to find, and in one of the authentically
great styles of American writing, in the final decade of the century a very clear idea indeed of the interaction of personality and
society and the dependence of one's sense of self upon the net-
work of relations with others. And William James was one of the
most carefully read American writers in Europe at that time. We
know that Durkheim had great admiration for James's work,
though it is not entirely clear just when Durkheim first read him.

The point here is not, of course, priorities of discovery; it is,
rather, the fact that in Europe and in America there is to be seen
during the final years of the 19th century the definite beginnings
of that abandonment of Cartesian dualism that would flower in
the social theories of mind, self, attitudes, and personality which
are the background, the indispensable background, of the social
psychology, strictly defined, we know today. It would be absurd
to claim for Durkheim—or James, Mead, or anyone else at the
turn of the century—the kind of subtlety and precision of conception of the individual's relation to the social process that we find
today. Even Mead, in his lectures at the University of Chicago
beginning in the first decade of the 20th century, whose keen interest in symbols and their assimilation and internalization by
the individual in the social context brings him closer to the
present in more ways than can be said of his contemporaries, was
first and foremost the philosopher, not the social psychologist.
And as philosopher, it was *society* that Mead was primarily concerned with; in this respect he was exactly like Durkheim.

I am aware that much of the writing about Mead at the present time chooses to stress not society but the self in Mead's work
and to set Mead as often in the company of philosophers of in-

dividual consciousness and of phenomenological awareness as in the company of those philosophers with whom Mead would most certainly have preferred to be identified. During the last decade or two in America, with the efflorescence of ideas of subjectivism and reflexiveness and consciousness generally, there have been many efforts to put Mead's ideas in this overall pattern. But no one who has pored over Mead's *Mind, Self and Society,* his *Movements of Thought in the Nineteenth Century,* and also his *The Philosophy of the Act,* and who has noted the sheer volume of references to society in these works and the obvious sense of elation in Mead at what he regarded as the emergence and triumph of the idea of society in his age, will doubt that if Mead had had to choose between being labelled a "social determinist" and any one of the labellings which rise today from reflexive, consciousness-oriented sociology and philosophy, Mead gladly would have chosen the former.

"Social determinist" is, to be sure, an inaccurate label for Mead, and it has been badly overworked for Durkheim. But what is not inaccurate, either for Mead or Durkheim, is ascription of a view of the self that begins basically in society and its symbols. What is called Mead's "symbolic interactionism" (and the phrase is a proper one) must always be understood by the reader of Mead against the background Mead tirelessly constructed in his lectures and writings of a society that pre-existed the individual's evolutionary acquisition of mind and thought. Over and over, Mead, like Durkheim, insists upon the priority of society and its social and symbolic structures to anything which might be found in or deduced from the individual mind.

Consider the following quotations, half of them from Durkheim, half from Mead, all of them fully representative of their authors' larger philosophies of man and society:

> 1. Indeed, any psychological or philosophical treatment of human nature involves the assumption that the human individual belongs to an organized social community, and derives his human nature from his social interactions and relations with that community as a whole and with other individual members of it.

2. If the idea of society were extinguished in individual minds and the beliefs, traditions and aspirations of the group were no longer felt and shared by individuals, society would die. We can say of it what we just said about the divinity: it is real only insofar as it has a place in human consciousnesses. . . . Society cannot do without individuals any more than these can do without society.

3. Certainly society is greater than, and goes beyond, us, for it is infinitely more vast than our individual being; but at the same time it enters into every part of us. It is outside us and envelops us, but it is also in us and is everywhere an aspect of our nature.

4. The community speaks to him with an identical voice, but each speaks from a different standpoint, and yet these standpoints are inter-related within the co-operative social activity, and the individual in assuming the attitude of one finds himself by the character of the response implicated in the responses of the others. In this fashion the individual attains the universality of the community response. . . .

5. This mental process, then, is one which has evolved in the social process of which it is a part. And it belongs to the different organisms that lie inside of this larger social process.

6. The psychologist who restricts himself to the ego cannot emerge to find the nonego. Collective life is not born from individual life, but it is, on the contrary, the second which is born of the first.

The first, fourth, and fifth of the quotations are taken from Mead;[3] the second, third, and sixth from Durkheim.[4] Needless to say, in each instance the quotations are fully reflective of the larger thrust of both Durkheim's and Mead's writing on the relation between self and society. Despite current insistence, as I write, upon the radical difference between Durkheim and Mead on this problem, neither, I am confident, would have himself recognized any such difference between them. Again, it is useful to stress that Durkheim was preeminently the sociologist, Mead the philosopher-social psychologist. At no point, not even in his *Moral Education,* did Durkheim ever deal with the matter of internal assimilation by the individual of the symbols of morality and society with anything like the subtlety and direct concern with the processes of formation of the self that Mead did. We find little in Durkheim anywhere to suggest the kind of thinking in

Mead that bore fruit in his treatment of the "I" and "Me," the concrete process of interaction among individuals, the roots of the self in perception of the "generalized other," and so on. None of this can be taken away from Mead or ascribed in any degree of specificity to Durkheim.

Again, however, allowing for inevitable differences between two creative and differently constituted minds, it is well not to lose the forest for the trees, and to remind ourselves of what Mead, as well as Durkheim, considered to be the major thrust of his work. This thrust is, as I say, the revolt against traditional dualism and the elevation of society as sovereign in the understanding of human thought and feeling as well as of human behavior. It is only today, with consciousness-, self-, and reflexive-sociology all around us, if only transiently, as I believe, that the individualistic and consciousness elements of Mead's work are consecrated. One need only read the following passage from Mead to sense how appalled he would be by some of the uses being made at the present time of his philosophy:

> Human society, we have insisted, does not merely stamp the pattern of its organized social behavior upon any one of its individual members, so that this pattern becomes likewise the pattern of the individual's self; it also, at the same time, gives him a mind, as the means or ability of consciously conversing with himself in terms of the social attitudes which constitute the structure of his self and which embody the pattern of human society's organized behavior as reflected in that structure. And his mind enables him in turn to stamp the pattern of his further developing self (further development through mental activity) upon the structure or organization of human society, and thus in a degree to reconstruct and modify in terms of his self the general pattern of social or group behavior in terms of which his self was originally constituted.[5]

There isn't a word or implication in that passage from Mead that Durkheim could not have accepted, that does not indeed find a clear counterpart in Durkheim's writing, especially in the study of moral education where he deals at length with, not only the processes of "attachment to the group" but also those of "individual autonomy" in the formation of individual conscience.[6]

PERSONALITY AND SOCIAL STRUCTURE

Durkheim's view of the nature of man follows rigorously and clearly from his conception of the nature of society. Society may be *sui generis* but it is not external to man; indeed, it is inseparable from man and his mind, character, and role. Man and society are fused. Durkheim's theory of personality is first set forth in the *Division of Labor,* in his general attack on utilitarianism and its effort to derive society from presocial individuals:

> The psychologist who restricts himself to the ego cannot emerge to find the nonego. Collective life is not born from individual life, but it is, on the contrary, the second which is born of the first.[7]

What one sees, in rising emphasis throughout the rest of Durkheim's life, is the further argument that, when attention is restricted to the ego, not only cannot the social be discovered but even the nature of the ego will remain hidden. Man, Durkheim declares, has a dual nature:

> There are two beings in him: an individual being which has its foundation in the organism and the circle of whose activities is therefore strictly limited, and a social being which represents the highest reality in the intellectual and moral order that we can know by observation. This duality of our nature has as its consequence in the practical order, the irreducibility of a moral ideal to a utilitarian motive, and in the order of thought, the irreducibility of reason to individual experience.[8]

Unquestionably the severest criticism of Durkheim, and the most general, relates to the supposed obliteration of the individual and the ascription to society of a mind and existence independent of individuals. It is easy to draw this conclusion if one limits his reading to those few paragraphs—scattered throughout Durkheim's main works—in which his emphasis upon society becomes virtual apostrophe. Even Durkheim's defenders have found themselves, for the most part, going to merely casual or polemical pieces for evidence of his actual recognition of individuals in society and of the sanctity of their political rights. By friend and foe alike, Durkheim's envisagement of the human being has generally been regarded as tenuous, to say the least.

What is the truth in the matter? What, in fact, is Durkheim's actual view of the relation between society and man? It is—and this must be emphasized—not very different from the view that is today taken for granted in sociological studies of human behavior. It has close affinity with the conception of personality that has come to characterize the social sciences within the past two or three decades. Certainly, it would be difficult to find fault with the statement quoted above. Quite apart from its contemporary acceptability, it has roots in a great deal of the Western tradition. What Durkheim did was to expunge the utilitarian image of man —an image that drew heavily upon the rather narrow view of man as a self-sufficing, discrete, and self-stabilizing being.

Did Durkheim deny the existence of specific creative human beings?—individuals who, by special combination of biological and cultural qualities, towered above their kind? Certainly not. Did he deny the historical importance of such human beings in politics, religion, and philosophy?—again, certainly not. Durkheim was by no means ignorant of or insensitive to history. He had, after all, studied under Fustel de Coulanges. He was certainly not blind to those processes which, at certain times, result in the widespread release of individual minds from tradition, to the consequent enrichment of culture. His posthumously published lectures on education and on citizenship reveal this clearly.

Admittedly, one might wish that Durkheim had given more attention to the specific mechanisms by which collective representations in society are translated, in distinctively individual and often creative ways, into the individual representations that reflect man's relationship to society. But, again, it must be remembered that Durkheim was waging a war against a psychological and biological determinism that it is now all too easy to forget existed. He lived in an age when emphasis on discrete individuals, at the expense of contexts and processes, was very common.

Attention to those parts of his work where he is concerned specifically and pointedly with the nature of the bond between society and man reveals a conception of individuality that is familiar enough. Consider, for example, *Moral Education,* which is a treatise not only on morality, but also on social psychology as this field is today understood. Here, especially in the final sections, Durkheim treats in detail the processes through which individuality is formed.

There is no question in Durkheim's mind of the priority of society in these processes. For Durkheim, it must be remembered, *society* includes all that is today more commonly contained under *culture.* It is fundamental and prior but it is neither in conflict with individuality nor external to the individual.

> Individual and society are certainly beings with different natures. But far from there being some inexpressible kind of antagonism between the two, far from its being the case that the individual can identify himself with society only at the risk of renouncing his own nature either wholly or in part, the fact is that he is not truly himself, he does not fully realize his own nature, except on the condition that he is involved in society.[9]

Nor is society something that lies outside man's developed individuality. In each of us lies, Durkheim writes,

> . . . a host of states which something other than ourselves—that is to say, society—expresses in, or through, us. Certainly society is greater than, and goes beyond, us, for it is infinitely more vast than our individual being; but at the same time it enters into every part of us. It is outside us and envelops us, but it is also in us and is everywhere an aspect of our nature. We are fused with it. Just as our physical organism gets its nourishment outside itself, so our mental organism feeds itself on ideas, sentiments, and practices that come to us from society.[10]

But the mental organism feeds itself in unequal ways. Not all individuals assimilate and internalize society's codes in the same way. Conflicts among norms can result in tensions within individuals. Different values are set by society on individuals, and the consequence of this is a tension between individualism and the moral authority of society that is eternal.

Durkheim was well aware of the tension created in society by individual deviation from social norms. Indeed, he recognizes individualism as endemic in all civilizations. In the *Division of Labor* he wrote:

> Individualism, free thought, dates neither from our own time nor from 1789, nor from the Reformation, nor from scholasticism, nor from the decline of Graeco-Latin polytheism or oriental theocracies. It is a phenomenon which begins in no certain part, but that develops without cessation all through history.[11]

Durkheim distinguishes "two extreme and opposed types" of personality in the history of society. On the one hand are those individuals who are notably sensitive to tradition, to rules, and authority. Such personalities "do their duty as they see it, completely and without hesitation, simply because it is their duty and without any particular appeal to their hearts. These are the men of substantial intellect and strong will—Kant is an ideal example —but among whom the emotional faculties are much less developed than those of the intellect."[12]

The opposite personality type is revealed in those individuals characterized "not by self-control and a tendency to withdraw, but by a love of spending themselves, by an outward expansiveness." These Durkheim calls "the loving hearts, the ardent and general souls." If they are capable of great deeds, of flights of brilliance, they yet find it hard to restrict themselves to mundane obligations. One is less sure of these men, Durkheim remarks, for passions, "even the most noble, blow successively hot and cold under the influence of chance circumstances and in the most erratic ways."[13]

The two personality types reflect two types of morality in human history—persisting, universal types—and both personality and moral types are illustrated successively in the various ages of the history of culture. There are the classic ages, such as those of Augustus and of Louis XIV, in which general love of form, rule, and standard brings to the fore discipline and restraint as sovereign values. At such times, the first personality type flourishes. There are, on the other hand, ages—and Durkheim characterizes his own as one—in which standards, rules, and forms become attenuated and flux reigns. In such ages the second personality type becomes more expressive, when there is search for objectives to which men can commit themselves.[14]

It is hard to avoid feeling that Durkheim strongly prefers the first type of personality, morality, and age; but rarely has the second type been portrayed with more sympathy and insight by anyone of this preference.*

It would be hard, even by contemporary standards, to find a more exemplary statement of the relation between culture and personality than the following, buried in his notable treatment of the elements of religious sacrifice:

> On the one hand, the individual gets from society the best part of himself, all that gives him a distinct character and a special place among other beings, his intellectual and moral culture. If we should withdraw from men their language, sciences, arts, and moral beliefs, they would drop to the rank of animals. So the characteristic attributes of human nature come from society. But, on the other hand, society exists and lives only in and through individuals. If the idea of society were extinguished in individual minds and the beliefs, traditions and aspirations of the group were no longer felt and shared by the individuals, society would die. We can say of it what we just said of the divinity: it is real only insofar as it has a place in human consciousnesses, and this place is whatever one we may give it. . . . [S]ociety cannot do without individuals any more than these can do without society.[15]

In tradition and in community, then, lie the essential moral and social sources of what is known as individuality. The utilitarians and critical rationalists had sought to trace what is creative and free in man almost exclusively to processes of separation from institutions and traditions. In release rather than member-

---

* See Chapter 6 below for a fuller account of these two personality types.

ship, they argued, lie the crucial sources of individuality. There is something in this, of course—more, indeed, than Durkheim was willing to emphasize. But creativeness and innovation cannot be separated from tradition, as every great age in the history of culture witnesses and confirms. The great man of thought and action, however radical, works with materials he has inherited, through ways that are normatively given, and toward ends that are firmly planted in his culture. That the creator rearranges and redirects these, and applies to them energies of uncommon dimension, does not detract from the role of tradition and community.

Plainly, it is personality that Durkheim is concerned with. Reading his works less from the point of view of what he says about the "individual" and more from that of what he says (in *Moral Education,* for example) about the "person," one finds a theory of human nature not different in its essentials from that of Cooley, Mead, and Dewey.

Those who ascribe to Durkheim a purely passive view of the individual in relation to society have not read him carefully. Always he premises the notion of an active, *acting* person. It is well to remember at this point Durkheim's treatment of autonomy as one of the three cardinal elements of morality. Autonomy is, as has been noted, a process by which society's norms and incentives become internalized in the individual, giving rise to self-awareness and self-discipline. The whole idea of personality presupposes for Durkheim what he calls a "self-mastery that we can achieve only in the school of moral discipline."

But the distinction achieved by Durkheim's treatment of the self and self-mastery in the history of social thought lies in its insistent emphasis upon the medium within which the self realizes itself:

> A person is not only a being who disciplines himself, he is also a system of ideas, of feelings, of habits and tendencies, a consciousness that has a content; and one is all the more a person as this content is enriched. For this reason, is not the civilized man a person in greater measure than the primitive; the adult than the child? Morality, in drawing us outside ourselves, and thrusting us into the

> nourishing milieu of society, puts us precisely in the position of developing our personalities.[16]

Only in society is the individual to be discovered; only in the behavior of individuals is society to be known.

Does all of this mean that the creative activity of specific human beings does not vary from age to age? Does the omnipresence of society's collective conscience assure uniformity? Far from it. Durkheim, as has just been noted, is keenly aware of contrasts among personality types, and he is equally aware that morality is, so to speak, creatively incomplete in some persons whose very obduracy before a given moral code or belief makes them, on occasion, creators of new moral codes and beliefs:

> We have contended that the erratic, the undisciplined, are morally incomplete. Do they not, nevertheless, play a morally useful part in society? Was not Christ such a deviant, as well as Socrates? And is it not thus with all historical figures whose names we associate with the great moral revolutions through which humanity has passed? Had their feeling of respect for the moral rules characteristic of the day been too lively, they would not have undertaken to alter them. To dare to shake off the yoke of traditional discipline, one should not feel authority too strongly. Nothing could be clearer.[17]

But it does not follow from this that an entire moral order may be constructed on the basis of ways of thought and behavior peculiar to the exceptional—to the "erratic, the undisciplined, the morally incomplete." Theories that celebrate the beneficence of unrestricted freedom are, Durkheim says boldly, "apologies for a diseased state." It is only through the practice of moral rules that man develops the capacity to govern himself—that is, to be free.

It is important, Durkheim argues, to keep separate two very different feelings: "the need to substitute a new regulation for an old one; and the impatience with all rules, the abhorrence of all discipline." The former is a normal and natural feeling, one on which the progress of order—as well as freedom—depends. The latter is, however, always abnormal "since it prompts us to alienate ourselves from the basic conditions of life":

> Doubtless, with some of the great moral innovators, a legitimate need for change has degenerated into something like anarchy. Because the rules prevailing in their time offended them deeply, their sense of the evil led them to blame, not this or that particular and transient form of moral discipline, but the principle itself of all discipline. But it is precisely this that always vitiated their efforts; it is this that rendered so many revolutions fruitless, not yielding results corresponding to the effort expended. At the point when one is rising against the rules, their necessity must be felt more keenly than ever. It is just at the moment when one challenges them that he should always bear in mind that he cannot dispense with rules.[18]

There are ages of tradition and there are ages of individualism. Both are equally "social." The ascendancy of individualism in the history of a society indicates that the society has in some way transferred to values of revolt and liberation the esteem previously accorded values of tradition. Man becomes, through social processes, the heir of what was formerly vested in tradition.

But such ages have their inevitable termination, for in the very process of transferring society's honor from institution to man, Durkheim writes, there arises a false conception of individualism—one in which society's attributes become conceptually transferred to man's biological nature:

> In societies where the dignity of the person is supreme, where man is a God to mankind, the individual is readily inclined to consider the man in himself as a God and to regard himself as the object of his own cult. When morality consists primarily in giving one a very high idea of one's self, certain combinations of circumstances readily suffice to make man unable to perceive anything above himself. Individualism is, of course, not necessarily egoism, but it comes close to it; the one cannot be stimulated without the other being enlarged.[19]

Durkheim's treatment of the relation between individualism and egoism is reminiscent of Tocqueville, who had also put the two in common focus. Egoism, wrote Tocqueville, "is a passionate and exaggerated love of self which leads a man to connect everything with himself and to prefer himself to everything in the world." Individualism, on the other hand, is a mature and calm quality which disposes each member of the community to separate himself from the mass of his fellows. Egoism originates in instinct; individualism proceeds from erroneous judgment—from deficiencies of mind rather than from perversity of heart: "Egoism blights the germ of all virtue; individualism, at first, only saps the virtues of public life; but in the long run it attacks and destroys all others and is at length absorbed in downright egoism.[20]

Tocqueville, too, had been struck by the tendency of the individualistic characteristics of democracies—the drive for wealth, equality, status, and so on—to produce a general malaise and the paradox of men increasingly miserable even in the midst of relative abundance. The essence of the process, for Tocqueville, was the gnawing sense of despair men felt at their inability to reach the heights that were progressively opened to them, new heights that appeared maddeningly on the foundations of what they *were* able to achieve. Tocqueville believed that the frustration caused by constantly receding goals, coupled with the separation from statuses and norms which—however binding they may have been —had at least offered certainty and repose, made democracy and capitalism increasingly traumatic to human sensibility.

Durkheim's view does not differ, basically, from Tocqueville's:

> Social man necessarily presupposes a society which he expresses and serves. If this dissolves, if we no longer feel it in existence and action about and above us, whatever is social in us is deprived of all objective foundation. All that remains is an artificial combination of illusory images, a phantasmagoria vanishing at the least reflection; that is, nothing which can be a goal for our action. Yet this social man is the essence of civilized man; he is the masterpiece of existence. Thus, we are bereft of reasons for existence, for the only life to which we could cling no longer corresponds to anything actual, the only existence still based upon reality no longer meets our needs.[21]

There were others in the nineteenth century—artists, humanists, social philosophers—who could have written those words:

Balzac, Nietzsche, Burckhardt, and Simmel, among others. But it is hard to imagine such a passage having been written by anyone in the Enlightenment or by any one of the utilitarian heirs of the Enlightenment in the nineteenth century.

Durkheim refers in this passage to the necessity of "a goal for our action." He then goes on to expand upon this point, with special reference to religious goals. It is not true, he writes, that men must have supramundane ends to give meaning and direction to human life. But there is this much truth in the religious position: social man, in contrast to physical man, requires something that both transcends and reinforces his being. Physically, "man can act reasonably without thought of transcendental purposes. Insofar as he has no other needs, he is therefore self-sufficient and can live happily with no other objective than living."[22] This is not the case with social man, civilized man. He has numberless ideas, feelings, and practices utterly unrelated to organic needs. The function of art, morality, religion, and science is not "to repair organic exhaustion or to provide sound functioning of the organs," and any effort to so reduce them is deceptive. The function is to create sentiments that bind us to others and to expand our social roles: "To play our social role we have striven to extend our intelligence and it is still society that has supplied us with tools for this development by transmitting to us its trust fund of knowledge."[23]

It is interesting to note an apparent contradiction in Durkheim's concept of individualism. At times individualism is made to appear as nonsociety, as the mode of behavior or thought that ensues when man is divorced from society. It is, in this view, the very opposite of the social. But there is another view of the matter, one that arises from his sweeping insistence that everything above the level of physiology derives from society. And in this second view individualism becomes, along with the collective conscience itself, something social in origin. Individualism, Durkheim maintains, is—quite as much as religion itself—the result of society: of society's substitution of what he calls *the cult of the individual* for the traditional religious cult leading to an attribution to man of qualities that were formerly vested in religion. It is the second view that is more consistently Durkheimian—that is, consistent not only with his premises but also with the full body of his work.

Social man is thus, for Durkheim, a precarious unity of two opposed but vital tendencies in history: the collective conscience of society, and individualism. There is even a history of personality to be seen in Durkheim, one represented by an alternation of intensity of these two tendencies. In primitive or folk society, collective conscience is strong; individualism, weak—though not nonexistent. Durkheim does not, like Freud, derive the individualistic, aggressive force from biology, with culture acting as the repressant on this force. For Durkheim, the individualistic element is as "social" as the collective conscience, but its sociality is different, reflecting unlikeness rather than likeness, differentiation rather than homogeneity. Over a long period of time the individualistic element has become stronger as the collective conscience has grown weaker. And this, for Durkheim, is as it should be: it is the basis of freedom. The difficulty lies, however, in the fact that in recent times a disequilibrium has appeared—one in which, under the sway of the cult of the individual, the individualistic element in personality has become relatively hypertrophied, the communal element atrophied. The balance must be somehow redressed by deliberate reinforcements of the collective conscience, but in ways that will not jeopardize either freedom or the democratic nation: hence, his proposal for professional associations.

All of this is a far cry from the total obliteration of the individual and of individual freedom with which Durkheim has so often been charged. It was not personality—not individuality—that Durkheim sought to drive out of sociological consideration; it was, rather, the artificial, abstracted conception of individuality that had come into existence at a time when European philosophers took for granted the massive stability of the social order, seeing in man's biological nature qualities that should have been referred to the institutional and moral order that had been shaped by history. Once one grasps this point, he will find it difficult to charge Durkheim with the annihilation of the individual and deification of society!

But two critical observations must be made, both reflecting Durkheim's failure to carry analysis further. First, he sets his view of individualism more often within its negative or pathological effects (as suicide, divorce, and mental alienation) than within the equally credible, and actual, processes of creativeness in culture. He does not do in any detail what some of his followers—notably Gustave Glotz, Maurice Halbwachs, and Marcel Granet—did: carry the identical perspective into an analysis of historical processes of cultural and intellectual efflorescence.

The second point of criticism relates to the actual mechanisms by which individuality is formed through interaction between what Durkheim repeatedly refers to as "the two natures of man": the biological and the social. He provides some promising leads in *Moral Education*—especially the second part, in which he deals with the child in the context of school and related social influences—but little more. Not much can be gleaned from his use of the concepts of collective representations and individual representations: both are descriptive, rather than analytical, concepts and serve to emphasize the role of society and its codes rather than to clarify interactive processes. Nor is there anywhere in Durkheim's writing the kind of analysis of personality in its social elements and states that marks so much of Simmel's microscopic treatment of human nature. Durkheim, in this respect at least, does not even rival Weber. There is in Durkheim a certain reticence about carrying analysis deep into the nature of man. Whether this was the result of personal limitation or a choice dictated by the special mode of positivism to which he dedicated himself is far from clear.

The point is not in any event an important one. What is important about Durkheim in the history of social psychology is his early and continuing emphasis upon the inseparability of personality and society. A full decade before Mead and Cooley began their lectures and writings in America on the social origins of personality Durkheim, in his *Division of Labor,* had suggested very clearly and fruitfully the utter impossibility of deriving either society or what is social in the individual personality from either the individual as such or from contractual or cooperative relations predicated upon the basis of discrete individuals. In that work, written at the beginning of the last decade of the nineteenth century, Durkheim sets forth the essential fallacy of the utilitarian and individualistic position. This fallacy consists "in deducing society from the individual." But, Durkheim argues,

> nothing we know authorizes us to believe in the possibility of such spontaneous generation. . . . With autonomous individualities, as are imagined, nothing can emerge save what is individual, and, consequently, co-operation itself, which is a social fact, submissive to social rules, cannot arise. Thus, the psychologist who starts by restricting himself to the ego cannot emerge to find the non-ego.[24]

That thesis is carried through by Durkheim in everything he ever wrote on the subject of personality and individuality. It becomes indeed an ever-enlarging, ever more fully articulated part of his general social theory, a foundation stone of his epochal study of suicide in 1896 and a vital aspect of his interpretation of religion, the subject to which we turn next in this book. It is precisely that thesis, too, on which—more surely I believe than can be said of any other single thinker in the final years of the nineteenth century—the structure of modern social psychology rests. There is no better way of indicating the measure to which Durkheim broke away from both the individualist-instinctivist manifestation of "social psychology" in the late nineteenth century, but also, and equally, the social mind manifestation, so common in what the Germans of the day called *völkerpsychologie,* than by the following brief passage:

> . . . (S)ocial action does not confine itself to demanding sacrifices, privations, and efforts from us. For the collective force is not entirely outside of us; it does not act upon us wholly from without; but, rather, since society cannot exist except in and through indi-

vidual consciousnesses, this force must also penetrate us and organize itself within us; it thus becomes an integral part of our being and by that very fact this is elevated and magnified.[25]

There isn't an atom of difference between the social psychology represented by that statement and the inspiriting themes of such works as Mead's *Mind, Self, and Society,* Cooley's *Social Organization,* and John Dewey's *Human Nature and Conduct.*

4 Political Sociology

We are not as likely to think of Durkheim in relation to the sociology of political organization as we are of Weber, and for sufficient reason. No one among the classical writers in sociology can challenge the sweep of Weber's mind when it comes to the nature of the state, law, and government, and, above all, the character of bureaucracy and its relation to history. Nevertheless, there is a very clear and important theory of politics and power to be found in Durkheim, one that is to be found within his larger and more encompassing consideration of types of authority and their roots in social development and history.

Let us begin with Durkheim's famous distinction between mechanical and organic solidarity, to be found in his first major work, the *Division of Labor*. As I pointed out above in my brief description of this book, Durkheim never, in any of his later work, chose to go back to this distinction or to the typology involved. Clearly, he had come to regard the distinction as being without great merit, as being indeed fallacious in many respects. For, despite the initial attractiveness of the mechanical-repressive thesis for primitive and folk peoples, with its declaration that all law is of the criminal and repressive type, flowing from the collective conscience, the fact is that everything we know about primitive social organization teaches us to the contrary. And, similarly, despite the plausibility at first glance of the restitutive sanctions of contract forming the essence of the social bond in modern society, given articulation, Durkheim argues, in organic-functional form by division of labor, the facts suggest a constantly rising body of genuinely criminal law, or repressive law in all forms, criminal, administrative, or civil, with the organized state serving through government and judiciary as the instrument.

Durkheim writes: "In lower societies, law, as we shall see, is almost exclusively penal; it is likewise very stationary. Generally religious law is always repressive; it is essentially conservative. The fixity of penal law evinces the resistive force of the collective sentiments to which it corresponds."[1]

Now, the facts, as contained in most contemporary social anthropology, are quite the reverse. The greater part of law in societies of primitive or folk nature is not penal but more nearly in the character of what we today call tort law. Offenses which are indeed criminal, which are defined as crimes, as offenses against the state, in modern society are often considered as falling within the realm of private law among peoples even as highly developed as the ancient Romans under the Republic or the Chinese down until very recent times. Such offenses as theft, trespass, assault, even murder, are considered within the realm of negotiatory processes between two or more families or clans. One would never guess from Durkheim's several references to the Greeks prior to the time of Cleisthenes, to the Romans of the Republican stage of their political history, or to various other peoples used as illustrations of Durkheim's thesis, that there was in fact a minimum of criminal-repressive law among these peoples so far as the greater number of offenses were concerned. A few offenses such as clandestine murder, conspiracy, incest, and treason were dealt with as crimes, in our sense of the word, and thus to be met by acts of punishment exercised by the whole assembly or by the council of elders representing the assembly—the Roman Senate being the best example of the latter. But for the vast majority of offenses against the public weal, as we today would consider them, the common mode of disposition was through one or another variant of the blood feud: that is, opposition among the kinship groups directly involved through the offense of a given member. True, as such peoples developed in time, there was a stake held by the entire community in restitution of peace among the affected kinship groups, and the good offices of one or other representative of the whole community would be available for quickest possible settlement. But prior to about the 1st century B.C. in Rome there was little, if any, doubt as to where the center of gravity of the legal system lay. And this was in the *patria potestas,* the unchallengeable right of the household to deal directly, through force or, as became increasingly common, negotiation, with offenses by individuals against it or any of its members.

The striking point here is that Durkheim gave far too little regard to the role of restitution and of restitutive sanctions in the early history of the European—and *a fortiori* other—peoples. As the result of his initial acceptance of the criminal-repressive structure of law and punishment for premodern peoples, and correspondingly of his acceptance of the contractual-restitutive structure for modern peoples organized around the principle of division of labor, he came very close to getting the realities of the matter reversed. For, as the chief studies of both social anthropology and comparative legal history have made clear, there is a very great deal of the restitutive-contractual in all societies where kinship and local ties are strong and where central authority tends by contrast to be rather weak or at least very limited in its uses.

I am inclined to think that Durkheim's mistake here springs from a work by his great teacher, Fustel de Coulanges, *The Ancient City.* This book is still a classic, and properly so, for it is unexcelled in its detailed accounts of the kinship and religious organization of both the early Romans and the Greeks. But, as Gustave Glotz—who himself was closely acquainted with Durkheim's teaching—much later pointed out in his remarkable studies of, first, the early Greek kinship system and, then, the Greek city state, Fustel de Coulanges, for all the wealth of valuable insight in his work, had completely misunderstood the relation of household and clan to central authority in the early Greek—and also Roman—community. Fustel had argued absolute power over individuals in *both* the Greek family and the surrounding Greek community, with decline of both in later times proceeding equally and functionally. However, as Glotz had no difficulty in demonstrating, this was not the case. In early times it was the household and clan that possessed the greater authority over individuals, and it could claim this only because the central authority was weak: made weak by tradition that distrusted such authority and that found legitimate authority to lie principally in the household or one of its related kinship structures. In both Greece and Rome what we find in their histories is, on the one hand, a constant decline in the authority of the kinship group—together with the structure of decentralized, private law proceeding from it— and, on the other, a constant increase in the intensity of central authority. In Athens it was the famous reforms of Cleisthenes that signalized the final dominance of the central authority over clan and household, and these took place relatively late in Athenian history, at the very end of the 6th century B.C. In Rome such centralization did not take place in any significant degree prior to the 1st century B.C.[2]

Nor can one gain a clear idea from Durkheim's treatment of modern society in his *Division of Labor* of the actual intensity of criminal-repressive law in the very circumstances of division of labor and of what he chose to call organic solidarity. Almost all of Durkheim's illustrations of social modernity in that book are Western European. Western Europe and its social crisis is indeed the prime subject of the book. But, as any social and political history written in either the nineteenth or twentieth century stresses, what characterizes political modernity above all else is the relentless development in every Western nation of the allied forces of centralization of power, nationalism, and of collectivism in one degree or another. Parallelling this development, very much indeed functionally a part of it, is the shift of the center of gravity in the legal system from kinship, village community, guild, and church—from the plurality of groups, each claiming autonomy in its sphere of operation and from the diffuse pluralism necessarily involved—to the newly ascendant power of the national state. To compare, in sum, the amounts of criminal-repressive law to be found in any modern European state, or in any developed state in antiquity, with the amounts to be found in earlier times in these same areas is to be treated to a heavy preponderance on the modern, or developed, side.

Durkheim seems to have been basically unaware of this when he set himself to the writing of the *Division of Labor*. And yet in this respect, as in so many others, the very effort of seeking to establish what could not really be established led him to much more fertile fields. In the act of attempting, he failed, but in the act of failing he derived insights into the nature of political history and of the role of the state in modern society, and the relation of the state to other forms of association, which were to direct his thinking thereafter.[3]

THE STATE AND SOCIAL ATOMIZATION

The first clear conception we get of the political state in Durkheim's major writings is toward the end of *Suicide* where he is writing of possible ways available to European nations for the arresting or reversal of high suicide rates in modern society. Suicide rates are reflections, in Durkheim's view, of progressive deterioration of the social bonds which normally unite and give psychological support to individual personalities. We shall come to this in the chapter on deviance, but for the moment it will be enough to note that Durkheim sees two major types of suicide in modern society: egoistic and anomic. The first is a direct consequence of the disintegration of social groups under the forces of industrialism, ethical individualism, and other elements of modernity, leaving individuals ever more precariously exposed to the exigencies of life. The second type, the anomic, is closely related but distinguishable; it is the result of the breakdown of stable patterns of values under much the same set of forces in modern society. The problem Durkheim sets for himself at the end of his study of the causes of suicide is, what counteractive social means are within our reach? He considers successively family, religion, and education, finding each of these, as such, inadequate to the demands of significant restoration of the sense of community in modern society, and then turns to the possible uses of the state, of the strengthening of political government and law in human lives. Durkheim finds the state quite as inadequate to the problem as he does each of the other associations mentioned above, and it is in the process of explaining this inadequacy that we are given a glimpse, a first glimpse in point of the development of Durkheim's mind through his published works, into the nature of the political state and into the historical relation between state and society. The question he asks is, "what groups are best calculated constantly to reimpress on man this salutary sentiment of solidarity?" Here is his answer:

> Not political society. Especially today, in our great modern States, it is too far removed from the individual to affect him uninterruptedly and with sufficient force. Whatever connection there may be between our daily tasks and the whole of public life, it is too indirect for us to feel it keenly and constantly. Only when matters of serious import are at stake do we feel our dependence on the body politic strongly. . . . Such unusual circumstances as a great national or political crisis are necessary for it to assume primary importance, invade the consciences of men, and become the guiding motive of action.[4]

In that paragraph is to be found the first statement, so far as I am aware, by Durkheim on modern political organization that puts him in the company of Tocqueville, Weber, Simmel, and others in the century who also saw remoteness and impersonality as the dominant characteristics of the political arm of society. A little farther along in the same chapter, Durkheim goes on to say of the state: "It is a cumbersome machine, made only for general and clearcut tasks. Its ever uniform action cannot adapt and adjust itself to the infinite variety of special circumstances. It is therefore necessarily compressive and levelling in its action."[5]

Compressive and levelling in its action. Such a view of the political state is drawn very clearly from a general state of mind to be found in 19th-century Europe, especially France where the political centralization and collectivism of first the Revolution and then the Napoleonic regime had become obsessive issues for many liberals and conservatives. From the time of the conservative reaction to the Revolution and to Napoleon in early 19th century France, there had been a growing body of thought—social Catholic at one extreme and secular anarchist at the other—in which the political state, democratic or other, was seen as one of the chief forces at work in the dislocation of the smaller social unities and in the creation of a bureaucracy, centralized and omnicompetent, that made difficult the work of creating new forms of social association. If the conservatives, chiefly Bonald and Maistre and Chateaubriand, were the first in France to perceive the potentially destructive effects of the political state upon society, their work was taken up far more creatively and impressively by those such as Lamennais and Tocqueville among liberals and by Proudhon among radicals who saw, not simply a problem of order in the state's inroads into the social sphere, but, more importantly, a problem of freedom. Tocqueville thought the greatest problem of freedom confronting Western society was precisely the set of centralized, collective, and bureaucratized powers that had reached their heights in the democratic nation. To Tocqueville's seminal writings on the subject should be added those of the historian and polemist, Hippolyte Taine, whose strictures on centralized and militarized bureaucracy, resting on the phenomenon of the mass state, were among the most eloquent in the nineteenth century and surely very well known to Durkheim as they were to other literate Frenchmen.

Although, as I have indicated elsewhere,[6] I think the evidence is clear regarding the basically conservative character of Durkheim's mind, it would be mistaken to seek roots for his view of the political state among conservative writers alone. Granted that the peculiar quality of French—chiefly Catholic—conservatism lay in its sharp distinction between state and society and in its dedication to shoring-up the foundations of nonpolitical society, so did the peculiar quality of French radicalism, the kind of radicalism to be seen best in Proudhon, lie also in this distinction and, with it, the determination to build a society upon, not the political nation and its centralized powers, but upon a plurality

of local and voluntary associations whose freedom from nationalism and centralization would be the measure of their claim upon
allegiances of their members. By conservatives, liberals, and radicals alike, in short, there was a profound sense of the limitations
of the political state so far as both order and freedom were concerned and an equally profound sense of the necessity of reinforcing or else establishing *intermediate* groups and associations; that
is, groups and associations—whether kinship, religious, local, or
occupational—which would lie intermediate to individual and
the political state. One of the major sources of antagonism between French and German radicalism in the late nineteenth century stemmed precisely from this French interest in the importance of localism, voluntary association, and decentralization of
both function and power in society. There is little, if any, appreciation of these values to be found in the writings of Karl Marx
and Friedrich Engels who became, by the last two decades of the
century, the dominant radical voices outside France and those
areas such as Spain which also followed, both in conservative and
radical thought, a decentralist, localist, and functionalist philosophy.

It is almost as though we were reading Tocqueville—or Taine
or Proudhon or many a liberal-social Catholic of the century—
when we read Durkheim's analysis of the effects of political modernity on society. The thrust of modernity, he writes, "is to have
swept away cleanly all the older forms of social organization. One
after another they have disappeared either through the slow erosion of time or through great disturbances."[7] Inevitably the individual has become ever more precariously exposed to the tempests
of change and the storms of revolution in social and moral spheres.

> Only one collective form survived the tempest: the State. By
> the nature of things this therefore tended to absorb all forms of
> activity which had a social character, and was henceforth con-
> fronted by nothing but an unstable flux of individuals. . . . It has
> often been said that the State is as intrusive as it is impotent. It
> makes a sickly attempt to extend itself over all sorts of things which
> do not belong to it, or which it grasps only by doing them violence.

Thence the expenditure of energy with which the State is re-proached and which is truly out of proportion with the results ob-tained.[8]

THE THEORY OF INTERMEDIATE ASSOCIATION

It is, then, in this light of a fundamentally antipolitical tendency of mind—antipolitical, that is, in the sense of use of the political structure for any and all social and moral problems—that we can best understand Durkheim's now famous proposal for the intro-duction of new occupational associations or corporations into so-ciety. For a long time this proposal was only imperfectly under-stood by sociologists and others unacquainted with the currents of political and ideological thought in Durkheim's France—and Europe. It was sometimes thought to be a rather eccentric lapse into reformism; it was even, much later, rather darkly thought to be tinged with "fascism" inasmuch as Mussolini had introduced nominally similar associations into Italy in the 1920s. But, in truth, Durkheim's proposals for the establishment of occupa-tional groups of national dimension in France, or in any Western country, emerge from precisely the tradition in French thought that regarded centralization and bureaucratization of power and nationalization of all functions and authorities as the major ene-mies of freedom and community alike. Durkheim is one with Tocqueville and with Weber in his analysis of both the power and the impotence of the state in the social and moral sec-tors of society. It would be impossible, I think, to find a mind more deeply dedicated to freedom and justice than Durkheim's— he was, after all, let it be remembered, an active Dreyfusard and, for a time, loosely linked with democratic socialists, though the increasingly collectivist character of socialism came to repel him. There is a close kinship between Durkheim's proposals and those of some of the anarchists and the guild socialists of the time and also, it should be pointed out, of the social Catholics and their es-sentially syndicalist conception of social reform. One can find the theme of intermediate association, of the need for reinforcing or establishing this kind of association in economy and society, in short, in radical, liberal, and conservative—even reactionary—thought in the French nineteenth century. Those who have tried to label Durkheim reactionary in the light of his proposal are simply uninformed as to the larger contexts. Pluralism and decentralism, happily, are cabin'd, cribb'd, and confin'd by no single ideology.

It is pluralism and decentralization that Durkheim sees as a crowning necessity for the West of his time. The question is, what are the social units to be around which a pluralist-decentralist society can be achieved with consequent gain to political freedom and to social integration? The day is long since past, Durkheim writes, when kindreds and clans can serve as these vital units; and equally obsolete, so far as contemporary industrial-mass society is concerned, are the kinds of territorial units which in mankind's early history succeeded kinship groupings: the villages and city states of antiquity. Education is useless because, Durkheim argues, any educational system will tend to be little more, at bottom, than a reflection of the society it serves. And religion is at once too specialized and spiritual an activity in modern society to serve in this respect.

> The only decentralization which would make possible the multiplication of the centers of communal life without weakening national unity is what might be called *occupational decentralization*. For, as each of these centers would be only the focus of a special, limited activity, they would be inseparable from one another and the individual could thus form attachments there without becoming less solidary with the whole. . . . It (the occupational association) can fulfill its destined role only if, in place of being a creature of convention, it becomes a definite institution, a collective personality, with its customs and traditions, its rights and duties, its unity. The great difficulty is not to decree that the representatives shall be selected by occupation and what each occupation's share shall be, but to make each corporation become a moral individuality. Otherwise only another external and artificial subdivision will be added to the existing ones which we wish to supplant.[9]

That, in a nutshell, is Durkheim's theory of occupational association, his response to, at one and the same time, the problems of alienation and anomie in the social sphere and the problem of political centralization, with its atomizing effects upon society, on the other. He did not, however, leave the proposal in the brief form in which it is to be found in the final pages of *Suicide.* When it came time to bring out a second edition of the *Division of Labor* in 1902, nearly a decade after initial publication of this book and five years after publication of *Suicide,* Durkheim wrote a special, quite detailed, preface to this new edition for the express purpose of elaborating his theory of intermediate association. He gives the preface the title "Some Notes on Occupational Groups." There is no need to repeat the basic theory, for it remains essentially what it is in the earlier *Suicide.* Suffice it to say that the view of the centralizing, atomizing, and collectivizing properties of political power remains the same, as does the view of need for new, intermediate associations, based upon occupation, in which human beings may regain the reinforcing sense of membership in society —lost, as Durkheim had argued so forcefully in *Suicide,* through the acids of modernity.[10]

There are, however, two points of interest in this preface to the second edition. In the first place, Durkheim seeks to unite the thesis to what he had written originally in the *Division of Labor.* He refers in the preface to "an idea undeveloped in the first edition which it will be useful to bring to light" and says further that if "originally we came into contact with the problem only by allusion, that is because we expected to consider it again in a special study."[11] As one inspects the "allusions,"[12] however, there is not very much to suggest that Durkheim did in fact have very much of a glimmering of the idea of intermediate association when he wrote the *Division of Labor.* True, he indicates the relative lack of "regulative centers" in modern society, but the context is one in which he is refuting Herbert Spencer, with particular reference to Spencer's comparison of society to an organism. Durkheim notes that such "centers" had existed in traditional society in the forms of workers' guilds, but we have not lived long enough without them, he suggests, to be sure "if this state is normal and definitive or simply accidental and morbid."

The fact is, Durkheim had little, if any, awareness of the need for such associations when he wrote the *Division of Labor,* for they were manifestly examples of the kind of "mechanical solidarity" that he felt progress into "organic solidarity," based upon division of labor and restitutive law, would in time make unnecessary. As I have indicated above, Durkheim knew in the process of formulating this view of development that it was inadequate and that in truth no society could exist save on the basis of types of authority and solidarity which are, by his original definition, mechanical: that is, assuming the right of direct control of individual behavior. This realization, as we have seen, became a steadily clearer one in Durkheim's life and, in strictly methodological terms, became the basis of *The Rules* as, in moral terms, it became the basis of his next work, *Suicide.* Where Durkheim is indecisive and even confused in the final chapters of the *Division of Labor* on the subject of contemporary disorder, he is utterly forthright on the subject in the final pages of *Suicide.* The crowning need of contemporary society, he there tells us, is for centers of authority and solidarity in which the present anomie and egoism leading to suicide and other forms of deviant behavior will be checked. And this same declaration of need is the theme of the preface to the second edition of the *Division of Labor.*

The second point I want to make about the preface is its historical character. Plainly Durkheim had been stung by some of the criticisms of *Suicide* during the several years leading up to the second edition of the *Division of Labor*—criticisms which referred to the proposals for intermediate association as reactionary, as an effort to re-establish the guilds that had been destroyed by the French Revolution at the end of the 18th century. Here we have an opportunity to see Durkheim the comparative historian at work, and what he says on the matter is still well worth reading.

The argument of retrogression or reaction would carry more weight, he writes, "if we proposed artificially to resuscitate the old corporation as it existed in the Middle Ages." But no such proposal has been made, Durkheim insists, and in any event the question is not one of trying to find out whether medieval institutions can fit contemporary society but is instead "whether the needs which (the occupational association) answered are not always present, although it must, in order to satisfy them, change according to the times."[13]

He goes on to point out that such groups are not, in any event, limited in origin and context to the Middle Ages. Such a point was, for Durkheim's age, a necessary one if its author was to stay clear of suspicion of being in sympathy with the arch-conservative proposals of the integral nationalism of a Maurras, proposals which, in hatred of liberal individualism and democracy, also aimed at reconstitution of society along corporative lines with the Middle Ages the prime inspiration. The *Action Française* that Maurras led brilliantly if banefully had many proposals which, considered abstractly, were of interest to social reformers and revolutionaries who found individualistic capitalism repugnant. But there was little if anything else about the *Action Française,* including its monarchism, total Catholicism, and heavy authoritarianism, that could appeal to the liberal minds of that day, and for good reasons Durkheim wished to take away the possibility of the sting of association.

He thus makes clear in the preface that such occupational associations as he has described are in no way rooted in the medieval ideal. "If they dated only from the Middle Ages, one could believe that, having been born with a political system, they must of necessity disappear with it." In fact, however, these groups are to be found in most ancient societies, in Greece and Rome in early times and then later among the Germanic peoples. He could have added that the same types of grouping, including guilds and cooperatives in agriculture and commerce alike, have been found among the Chinese, the people of India, and many other places in the world. They had existed, as Durkheim notes, in France prior to the Revolution, but the guilds and corporations had become increasingly representative of an unhealthy corporate egoism. But what has followed the termination of this corporate egoism is the equally injurious individual egoism of unregulated industrialism, the alienated and anomic behavior to be found in the modern mass state resting solely upon aggregates of socially unconnected individuals.

The question, Durkheim suggests to his critics, is not whether we try to re-establish the past; that can never be done in any event. It is whether we seek to provide necessary means of a union of economic, social, and political life, drawing from the experiences where necessary of other peoples, past or present, in this endeavor. That intermediate economic associations, guilds and cooperatives, and the like, existed in the Middle Ages and also among other peoples, is in itself neither a reason for favoring nor opposing such associations. But if, as Durkheim's sociological insight suggests, these associations are necessary in modern society as a means of lessening the destructive force of egoism and anomie, then we should, as comparative students of society, draw what we can from other experiences.

There was indeed a great deal of material of this kind available in Durkheim's day, not only in French but in German scholarship. The French Revolution, by its stringent legislation during the years 1791–93 abolishing the historic guilds, prohibiting any new associations, whether of guild or trade union character, and seeking through every means possible to inaugurate a society that would be free of any associative intermediation between the individual and the General Will of the unified nation, had inevitably stirred up a great deal of historical interest among European scholars in such intermediate associations. Durkheim refers to a few of these works, which he apparently had read just prior to the writing of the new preface to the *Division of Labor,* though we should not discount the effect of the scholarship in medieval institutions of his early teacher Fustel de Coulanges which Durkheim was bound to have absorbed during his student days. He does not refer to what is undoubtedly the greatest of all these works, that by the German Otto von Gierke whose monumental researches into the history of intermediate association remain even yet the finest of their kind.

We should also take note of the fact that the place of associations in public law had been a powerful issue in French politics
during the decades preceding Durkheim's work. There were, it
should be emphasized, strong voices from the Right as well as the
Left and the center arguing the importance of restoring to French
life the relative freedom of voluntary, organized association that
France had known prior to the Revolution but had not known,
clearly and unambiguously, since. What had impressed Tocqueville almost above anything else about American democracy on
his visit in 1831 was the profusion of free, voluntary, associations
through which, Tocqueville felt, the Americans were spared the
worst effects of economic individualism and also the extension of
the public power into the innermost recesses of individual life.
In sum, there was a great deal of attention being given to the use
of intermediate associations in both conservative and radical politics in Durkheim's time, and again it is useful to observe that if
such association was a pillar of conservative social Catholicism, it
was not less one in the proposals of many anarchists, syndicalists,
and guild socialists, as well as liberals such as Durkheim.

Durkheim sees the occupational association as one which
would include both owners and workers, management and labor. It would be the central area of direct economic decisions af-
fecting the nation, of matters pertaining to wages, working conditions, profits, and so forth. But the true value, Durkheim argues,
of these associations lies in the fact that, like the guilds of ancient
Rome and of the Middle Ages, they would incorporate social,
moral, and psychological functions as well as economic. They
would do even better indeed than those of the past.

> The corporations of the future will have a complexity of attri-
> butes still greater, by reason of their increased growth. Around
> their proper occupational functions others which come from the
> communes and private societies will be grouping themselves. . . .
> A great many educational institutions (technical schools, adult edu-
> cation, etc.) equally seem to have to find their natural environment
> in the corporation. It is the same for esthetic life, for it appears in
> the nature of things that this noble form of sport and recreation

develops side by side with the serious life which it serves to balance and relieve. In fact, there are even now syndicates which are at the same time societies of mutual aid; others found common houses where there are organized courses, concerts, and dramatic presentations. The corporative activity can thus assume the most varied forms.[14]

Thus, Durkheim concludes, "the great gap in the structure of European societies" would be filled. Instead of the territorial unities or kinship groupings of most ancient times, the occupational association, replete with numerous activities going well beyond the economic sphere, would fill the open spaces which now exist in the mass societies of the present, would supply a sense of membership and at the same time arrest the unhealthy intrusions of the political state into personal life. "To be sure, each of us belongs to a commune, or a department, but the bonds attaching us there daily become more fragile and more slack. These geographical divisions are, for the most part, artificial and no longer awaken in us profound sentiments."[15] Durkheim is possibly exaggerating the decline of the territorial sentiment at least for those still securely placed in their towns, counties, and regions, but his remarks penetrate to the core of the modern problem of mobility. He sees very clearly indeed that for an industrial society, one in which a relatively high degree of worker mobility is virtually built in, there is no substitute for the functional kind of association he is proposing. Once again, we gain appreciation of Durkheim's very skeptical view of the role of the State in communicating the sense of membership. He writes:

A society composed of an infinite number of unorganized individuals, that a hypertrophied State is forced to oppress and contain, constitutes a veritable sociological monstrosity. For collective activity is always too complex to be able to be expressed through the single and unique organ of the State. Moreover, the State is too remote from individuals; its relations with them too external and intermittent to penetrate deeply into individual consciences and socialize them within. Where the State is the only environment in which men can live communal lives, they inevitably lose contact, become detached, and thus society disintegrates.

Now, in that splendid passage we have rich opportunity to see the pluralist roots of Durkheim's political philosophy. Not for him the omnicompetent state of the masses resting on a presumed general will and governed by a centralized, atomizing, administration. It is clearly the pluralist-decentralist tradition of Lamennais and Tocqueville that Durkheim belongs to. Tocqueville, whose study of the French Revolution had been published a half-century before those lines of Durkheim we have just quoted, would have understood Durkheim's message just as clearly as he would have understood the central thesis of *Suicide,* a thesis indeed that Tocqueville, in a very limited and general way, had actually set forth in his *Democracy in America*.[16]

We should not, however, conclude that Durkheim envisaged the functional, intermediate, occupational association as a panacea. "The crisis through which we are passing is not rooted in a single and unique cause. To put an end to it, it is not sufficient to regulate it where necessary. Justice must prevail."[17] Of course it must! No one who had fought for the right to justice of Captain Alfred Dreyfus as passionately as Durkheim had can easily be accused of lacking respect for the liberal and democratic means whereby a corporative society such as Durkheim envisages is to be brought into being. Better an alienated and anomic existence, Durkheim would surely say, if it coexists with legal justice than a fully communalized existence resting on injustice. All that Durkheim is arguing in his political sociology is the necessity of groups in the social order which will protect the individual from the sensations of aloneness to which he is all too often heir in modern mass society and, at one and the same time, protect him from a state that, even in Durkheim's day, was becoming steadily more powerful, more "hypertrophied," and, in Weber's momentous word, rationalized.

One further point should be stressed here. Durkheim never deluded himself that he was either a reformer or statesman. "The work of the sociologist is not that of the statesman." Those words might well hang over every academic door today in America. What Durkheim, in the entirety of his theory of intermediate association, proposes is a structure that, to his mind, has unexceptionable social relevance, one that springs from the sociological scientific imagination. He leaves it at that, however. He does not seek to be philosopher-king!

THE STATE AND INDIVIDUALITY

Still another aspect of Durkheim's political sociology, suggested perhaps, though only obliquely, in the foregoing paragraphs deserves mention here. I refer to the special relation Durkheim saw historically between the rise of the political state and the emergence of the individual from what Durkheim calls the social mass. By way of preface, it should be noted that from the writings of Rousseau on, more and more intellectuals in the West had been made aware of the intimate relation between the distinctive kind of power found in the political sphere and the release of the individual from the constraining ties of kinship, religion, and locality. Rousseau, in some of the most electrifying revolutionary writing of the 18th century, had suggested indeed that only in the absolute community of the General Will—the collective will created by individuals liberated from all corrupting or distracting social ties and dedicated to the political community alone—could true individuality ever be achieved, and, with this, true freedom. Rousseau was not alone in the Enlightenment in his almost ritual dedication to political power conceived in this light. There were others, the Physiocrats, apostles of the natural order in economics, among them who also saw unique significance in the state as the means alone of being able to effect the release of individuals from the net of ties and bonds that, in their judgment, was the traditional society around them.

In the next century, after the French Revolution had demonstrated the affinity that could lie in practice between centralizing political power and the pulverization of society into discrete individual units, the latter the consequence of the Revolutionary government's destruction or weakening of traditional religious, economic, and social groups, there were a good many of opposite ideological persuasion who also stressed the relation I am describing between the state and individualism. The political conservatives such as Burke, Bonald, and Southey all saw, and attacked, the kind of state that, in democratic or revolutionary zeal, bore down heavily on social groups, weakening them where possible, and attracting masses of individuals to itself alone. And the liberal Alexis de Tocqueville, writing in the 1830s, in his *Democracy in America,* also paid heed repeatedly in that work—and then later in his notable study of the French Revolution—to the affinity between political power and the individual. It was, thought Tocqueville, the levelling effect of political power on the social structure of medieval and postmedieval Western Europe that, more than anything else, brought democracy and equalitarianism into being in the first place. The great threat to individual freedom, to cultural liberty, Tocqueville thought, in the modern age lay exactly in democracy's generally levelling effects upon other spheres of association. Hence Tocqueville's celebrated emphasis on the necessity of preserving complete freedom of association, as the means of reinforcing all impulses toward intermediate association in democracy, as well as on such important devices as division of power, decentralization of administration, and an independent judiciary.

There is, however, an interesting ambiguity in Tocqueville's thinking—worth stressing here since it is precisely Durkheim's ambiguity on the subject. Granted that Tocqueville could see the long-run relation between state and society as one inducing the kind of atomization we have already discussed briefly in this chapter, he could also see the power of the central state as a vital bulwark—at least when properly checked by other institutions—as the means of guaranteeing individuals a degree of personal freedom they could not know where the bonds of the small local community, or of the church, or other type of association are close and unchallenged. For all his apprehension about the full impact of equality upon Western culture, Tocqueville makes clear that apart from an appropriate degree of individual equality in the political order there can be no freedom.

Durkheim, in his *Division of Labor,* in one of the most important paragraphs in that book, and in the full spirit of *both* Rousseau's and Tocqueville's views of the matter, wrote:

> Rather than dating the effacement of the individual from the institution of a despotic authority, we must, on the contrary, see in this institution the first step made towards individualism. Chiefs are, in fact, the first personalities who emerge from the social mass. . . . A source of initiative is thus opened which had not existed before then. There is, hereafter, someone who can produce new things and even in certain measure, deny collective usages. Equilibrium has been broken.[18]

In his *Professional Ethics* Durkheim carries the argument a good deal farther. The very idea of individual, positive rights comes from the state, Durkheim argues. He uses ancient Greek and Roman history to illustrate his thesis that the idea of rights belonging to the individual proceeded side by side with the development of political consciousness. And in this argument Durkheim is, of course, right. We need only think of the immense impact in the ancient world of the Cleisthenean reforms at the end of the 6th century B.C., with their reduction of the power of traditional society resting on kinship and their specific granting to the individual of positive rights they had not previously known in a social order in which membership and duty were the cardinal qualities.

"History seems indeed to prove that the State was not created to prevent the individual from being disturbed in the exercise of his natural rights: no, this was not its role alone—rather, it is the State that creates and organizes and makes a reality of these rights."[19]

In such a passage, plainly, the influence of Rousseau is strong. Durkheim, as we know, was keenly interested in Rousseau's whole approach to the social contract and to the relation of the individual to the political community. It is indeed nothing less than the thrust of Rousseau that carries Durkheim into a declaration that following man's incorporation into the political

order "a psychic life of a new kind breaks away which is richer
by far and more varied than one played out in the single individual alone." Rousseau had put the matter more strongly, writing
that the individual, by entering into the political association, en-
dows his actions with "a moral character which was wanting to
them before" and "from a stupid and limited animal he now for
the first time becomes a reasoning being and a man" (*Social Contract*, Bk. I, Ch. 8). And like Rousseau, at least in this discussion
of the political state, Durkheim makes no distinction between
the social and the political—a distinction he made fully, as we
have seen in both *Suicide* and the preface to the second edition
of the *Division of Labor*.

So, too, is there a pronounced Rousseauian ring to Durkheim's treatment in this discussion of the relation of the individual to "secondary groups" within the larger political order.
Rousseau, in the interests of his prized General Will, had recommended a complete absence of secondary, intermediate groups in
the political community on the ground that each of these would
tend to become a kind of General Will for the individuals belonging to it and thus constitute a distraction from the unity that
lay legitimately (in Rousseau's terms) in the General Will alone
of the political state. Durkheim tells us that in the political state,
properly constructed, "there must be no forming of any secondary groups that enjoy enough autonomy to allow of each becoming in a way a small society within the greater. For then, each of
these would behave towards its members as it stood alone and
everything would go on as if the full-scale society did not exist."[20]

How do we account for the seeming discrepancy, even out-
right contradiction, between the Durkheim of the proposed secondary associations, specifically recommended, as we have seen,
for the alleviation of egoism and anomie in society, and the
Durkheim just quoted? The answer lies in the realm of pragmatic
common sense, in the notion of a society in which central authority prevents any local or functional association from assuming
authority so great as to suffocate the liberties of its members but
in which, at one and the same time, the very presence of the local

and functional associations—that is, the secondary or intermediate structures—keeps the central power from itself becoming despotic.

If the individual is to retain the positive rights that large-scale political society makes available, in part through possibilities of individual mobility, it is important that the individual's freedom to move not be curbed and monopolized by the secondary groups. "There must therefore exist above these local, domestic—in a word, secondary—authorities, some overall authority which makes the law for them all. . . ."[21] But will not, Durkheim asks, the state itself threaten to become a formidable power? For Rousseau this question had never obtruded itself once the all-important concept of the General Will had entered his mind. There could be no tyranny, Rousseau declared, if the true General Will was the basis of government, for each individual was, by definition, a constitutive part of the General Will and was participating in the government of himself, no matter how sweeping the effect of this will might be.

Durkheim, however, is far more the pluralist than Rousseau's philosophy could ever have permitted him to be. He concedes that a state possessed of full power over individuals, power unmediated by competing forms of association, could shortly become tyrannical. "In that case, as the sole existing collective force, it produces the effects that any collective force not neutralized by any counterforce of the same kind would have on individuals. The State itself then becomes a leveller and repressive. And its repressiveness becomes even harder to endure than that of small groups, because it is more artificial."[22] In that statement is to be found the pluralist political sociologist we saw so clearly in the discussions referred to above. And in what follows we have, once again, the unambiguous declaration that the political state "in our large scale societies is so removed from individual interests that it cannot take into account the special or local and other conditions in which they exist." By virtue of its political and social distance from individuals, by virtue, too, of its inherent incapacity to deal with local and special needs as well as groups formed specifically around these needs, the State tends to pro-

duce "all kinds of resistance and distressing conflicts." The infer-
ence to be drawn, Durkheim concludes, "is simply that if the collective force, the State, is to be the liberator of the individual, it
has itself need of some counter-balance; it must be restrained by
other collective forces. . . ."[23] In short, the state's authority over
human beings must, if it is to be prevented from becoming the
source of regimentation and mechanical uniformity, be offset by
the recognized authorities and allegiances of other, non- or semi-
political groups and associations.

In summary, then, it is possible to see in Durkheim's political thought adequate recognition of the historical role of the political state in the West in, first, actually creating the seminal
idea of individual positive rights, rights not to be abrogated by
any internal association within the political order, and, second,
by this very fact, a sphere of freedom unknown in simple societies
where the local or functional association is supreme. In this respect Durkheim's political thought is fully up to the mark in that
long tradition of political thought in the West beginning with
Plato and culminating in Rousseau and Austin that has stressed
the profound role of the political state in providing the context
of rights and liberties. But so is it possible also to see Durkheim
in that other—related but different—tradition which reaches from
Aristotle to Burke and Tocqueville and which, without denying
the value, even necessity, of the state nevertheless recognizes, as
the first tradition does not, the vital importance of institutional
checks upon political power, division of authority, pluralism, localism, and the indispensable role of intermediate associations. I
suggested above that there is an element of ambiguity in Durkheim in his political sociology. But, on further reflection, this
would appear to be the kind of ambiguity that is the inevitable
result of bringing equally correct abstract principles down to the
level of pragmatic and empirical human experience. As the exis-
tentialists have told us, ambiguity is an inherent part of the human condition.

SOCIALISM AND COMMUNISM

I shall be brief in this final section of the chapter, for, despite the fact that Durkheim gave a full series of lectures on the subject of socialism and communism while still teaching at Bordeaux (prior to his move to the University of Paris), it can hardly be said that the subject was one of either great interest to him personally through most of his life or of significant consequence in the totality of his work. In fact, the chief value of his *Socialism*—which was published posthumously on the basis of the written lectures he left behind—is its often acute analyses of the works of Saint-Simon, the mind that Durkheim regarded as the true beginning (rather than Auguste Comte) of the sociological tradition in France. From Saint-Simon's trenchant analyses of the political and economic scene the French Revolution had created issued not only, Durkheim tells us, the authentic socialist philosophy in France but also the seminal reflections which Saint-Simon's sometime follower and secretary, Auguste Comte, was later to convert into his celebrated Positive Philosophy and into the science for which he coined the name "sociology." There is no mistaking Durkheim's admiration of Saint-Simon, and also of Comte, as philosophical minds and as pioneers in the positivist ideal of a creative relation between science and social policy.

There are two ways, Durkheim tells us, of envisaging socialism. It may be seen as a scientific doctrine concerned with analysis of society and history. Or it may be seen instead as an ideal, as a plan for the reconstruction of society. Both conceptions of socialism were, of course, current—especially among Marxists—in Durkheim's own time. But Durkheim makes it evident that he conceives socialism solely in the second light—as an ideal. "It is above all a plan for the reconstruction of societies, a program for collective life which does not yet exist in the way it is dreamed of. . . . It concerns itself much less with what is or was than what ought to be."[24] Granted that in its best forms, socialism does not repudiate social analysis and use of empirical data, even so its use of both clearly removes it from that body of work fully deserving of the name science.

Socialism presumes to predict about the future. But "the bases for rigorous prediction about the future, especially one of such breadth, are not established." Far worse from Durkheim's point of view is the assumption contained in modern socialism that it is at one and the same time a body of theory and a set of practical principles. But socialism is not a body of theory in the true sense of this word, for it reaches conclusions long before its basic questions are answered.

> That is why, to speak precisely, there cannot be a scientific socialism. Because, were such a socialism even possible, sciences would be necessary that are not yet developed and which cannot be improvised. The only attitude that science permits in the face of these problems is reservation and circumspection, and socialism can hardly maintain this without lying to itself. And, in fact, socialism has not maintained this attitude. Not even the strongest work —the most systematic, the richest in ideas—that this school has produced: Marx's *Capital*. What statistical data, what historical comparisons, what studies would be indispensable to solve any one of the innumerable questions that are dealt with there![25]

Plainly, socialism is not for Durkheim—that is as an area of personal commitment, however sympathetic he might be about its overall aims and ideals. For, as does not require elaboration at this point, Durkheim is first, last, and always the *scientist*. The nearest we can place Durkheim in the socialist movement is, as observed above, with respect to his proposals for intermediate, guildlike organizations in modern society. There were, in his time, the guild-socialists whose ideas had, as we observed, limited likeness to Durkheim's in this respect. But such coincidence is not enough. Durkheim presented his idea of intermediate associations for the specific purpose of alleviating the citizen's atomized aloneness in modern society, of providing contexts in which a renewed sense of community might be found, and also of providing buffers between man and the increasingly centralized state. Such purposes, limited as they are, stand in marked contrast to those of the socialists who, in effect, began with the purpose of total reconstitution of the social order.

What Durkheim gives us in his treatment of socialism—that is, apart from .his valuable and interesting analyses of the doctrines of Saint-Simon which fall in the history of thought or the sociology of knowledge—is, at bottom, nothing especially revealing. It is hard for the reader to believe that his heart was in his task. As Marcel Mauss, his nephew, student, and one of the most distinguished of the scholars who had their education under Durkheim, tells us, there was not very much reason in the first place for undertaking the course of lectures except the fact that students were keenly interested in socialism as a movement and Durkheim felt the pressure. We know that he did not complete what he had originally planned for his study of socialism—sections on Proudhon, Lassalle, and Marx. "He intended," Mauss writes, "to confine himself to the works of the masters, to their thought, rather than to their personal lives or to works of the second rank.

"But in 1896 Durkheim, undertaking the *L'Année Sociologique*, returned to pure science, and the History of Socialism remained incomplete. He always regretted his inability to continue or resume it."[26]

It is permissible to doubt that last. In the very next year Durkheim's *Suicide,* was published, and toward the end of that study we find him listing socialism, at least in its revolutionary forms, along with anarchism, mysticism, and estheticism, as being among the symptoms of cultural malaise and social degeneration in France.[27] Despite Mauss's admittedly well-founded words on the subject, it is hard to imagine Durkheim, working strenuously and zestfully at his scientific studies, really regretting time away from historical treatment of a social movement that did not much interest him in the first place.

So what we get, basically, are a few definitions: socialism he deems to be primarily occupied with the economic sphere and with collective ownership of the larger means of production; communism on the other hand seeks to penetrate man's moral and psychological nature, to become a total community in the individual's life. There is, Durkheim tells us, far more contrast than similarity between socialism and communism. "Communism is prompted by moral and timeless reasons; socialism by considerations of an economic sort."[28] Indeed, Durkheim goes so far as to declare that where socialism falls in the "profane" sphere, being simply a proposed form of social engineering, utilitarian in form, communism belongs to the "sacred," with its ends and elements regarded in much the same way that the religious communicant reacts to his gods and values.

Clearly, Durkheim was interested in the ideas of socialism and communism which had become so much a part of the Western scene in his lifetime, but his interest was far from intense, and he seems to have regarded these ideas as being, for the most part, elements in the larger problem of solidarity in society rather than viable proposals for solution of this problem. The conservative vein in Durkheim's own morality and politics was perhaps enough to leave him uneasy at best in the presence of socialist proposals and communist panaceas, and, even beyond this, his profound dedication to science, and to the unending task of science, could not but have alienated him from doctrines which rested upon a combination of (for him) unacceptable philosophy of history and premature rush into the area of grand social policy or reconstruction.

In summary, Durkheim's political sociology contains a very large share of what in both France and England in his day was called pluralism. He saw the inevitable diversity of allegiances in any society that was rooted in the long history of mankind— allegiances to family, parish, local community, region, religion, and occupation—and, seeing this diversity, built his essential political theory around it. Not that he was without awareness of the role of the central power of the state, primitive or modern, in the creation of circumstances within which individuals could, at least temporarily and partially, liberate themselves from the constraints of traditional society. As we have seen, Durkheim dates the emergence of the individual in history—emergence from the primordial social mass—from the time of the first upthrust of political power, the power that in the beginning lay in the hands of the military-political chief alone. And there is nothing to suggest that Durkheim wished to see society take on anarchist character, one totally devoid of political structure and sovereignty, one composed solely of traditional and spontaneous groups. Nevertheless, Durkheim, even above Max Weber—who also distrusted the centralized, bureaucratized state—prescribed in detail the alternative to nationalist collectivism rooted in the atomized masses. And this alternative for Durkheim was a society strong in the intermediate ties which he saw best exemplified by new occupational associations whose own capacity to arouse the loyalties of their members would be the best indicator of their buffer-like protection of the individual from the ever-increasing demands of the state.

5 Religion

To this day Durkheim remains, along with Max Weber, one of the two preeminent sociological interpreters of religion. Different as are the approaches of the two minds to religion—Weber's overwhelmingly historical and comparative, involving in the process whole civilizations, ancient and modern; Durkheim's predominantly analytical and structural, basing his conclusions largely upon a single people, the primitive Australians—they are alike in their fascination with religion and its relations to society and personality. If Durkheim cannot match in any of his writings the smallest part of Weber's comparative-historical sweep, it has to be said that Durkheim supplied an intensiveness and brilliance of analysis of the sacred, the cult, and ritual that neither Weber nor anyone else since in sociology has equalled in originality.

How do we account for the unremitting interest in religion we find in both Weber and Durkheim? Answers usually dwell in biographical fashion upon Durkheim's Jewish roots and their rabbinical overtones, the impact made upon his youthful mind by a devout Roman Catholic teacher, and, in Weber's case by his devotion to a very religious mother. Such answers take us very little of the way. What is much more relevant to the lives of two scholarly sociologists in the latter part of the nineteenth century is the fact that this century, for all its generally vaunted secularism, is one of the two or three most important centuries in Western history so far as religious life and thought are concerned. One has only to look at the sheer number of philosophers, historians, ethnologists, sociologists, and psychologists in the century who made religion the central object of research and thought.

Not only was the nineteenth century one of immense scholarly and scientific exploration of religion, it was also an age of nearly unprecedented spawning of new faiths, sects, and churches in Christianity. That process of permanent schism or fission in Christianity that Bishop Bossuet had warned against in the seventeenth century from his Catholic point of view became major religious reality in the nineteenth century. Side by side with this proliferation of Protestant faiths went also one of the more impressive efflorescences of Roman Catholic activity in the long history of that church. The nineteenth is the century of the emergence of what was called Social Catholicism, a movement intellectual in origin, taking both capitalism and centralized nationalism as its enemies, but that spread shortly to prominent role in the labor union and cooperative histories of the century. In addition are to be noted the large number of utopian communities, most of them deeply religious in inspiration, which occupy a great deal of the social history of the century. And, not least, were the great millennialist-salvationist eruptions among the working classes and the, mostly American, revival meetings.

Against this religio-social background in the 19th-century West is to be found a veritable torrent of books, articles, essays, and tracts on one or another aspect of religion. If the greater number of these were written by the religiously committed, there was still a very substantial body of writing on religion by minds as personally aloof to religion as James, Renan, and Durkheim, by those who may have had no room in their individual lives for religious experience but who nevertheless recognized religion as one of the most powerful of influences in human history and were willing to give religion its due. In many ways this is the single most impressive aspect of 19th-century interest in religion: its roots in the rationalist- or utilitarian-minded who, despite personal indifference or hostility, were able to see religion's profound relation to the structure of human society and to the deepest regions of human consciousness. More than anything else, I think, it is this ethnological, historical, sociological, and psychological envisagement of religion that separates the nineteenth from the eighteenth century.

The Enlightenment, for all its undoubted preoccupation with the single force, the Church, it feared and hated above all other forces, never was able to see religion as much more than a tissue of superstitions, follies, and tyrannies of the mind; as, in short, a largely intellectual rather than emotional and social phenomenon that might be expected in time to vanish, given sufficient education and exposure to the wonders of science. Rousseau was, of course, a partial exception with his proclaimed Civil Religion—a spiritualized patriotism of absolute intensity—but so far as other *philosophes* were concerned, religion and most especially Christianity, was much less something to try to understand in its roots than it was to obliterate as quickly as possible. There was little doubt that the shape of progress in the future of humanity was overwhelmingly secular, with religion increasingly retreated to the lumber room of history. So thought *philosophes* and radicals everywhere.

Very different is the approach of the nineteenth century; even, as I have noted, of that large and important element that did not itself accept religion as a matter of personal commitment. One need only think here of the attitudes of Marx and Engels toward religion. Neither man himself accepted religion, of course, and both undoubtedly thought the sway of religion would be short-lived once the march toward classless society, society devoid of private property and personal exploitation, was completed. But there is a very different attitude toward the role of religion, indeed toward the *value* of religion to the people, in presocialist society, which is to say in human history up to the age in which Marx and Engels lived, in these two thinkers from anything that could be found in the secular eighteenth century. What Marx has in common with Durkheim and Weber is a clear sense of the *functional* relation of religion to human life, and if he did not, as did Durkheim and Weber, think religion in some form at least to be eternal and ineradicable from social organization, he nevertheless saw it as something rooted deeply in the roles, statuses, and tissues of any social system where alienation existed.

In Auguste Comte, founder of systematic sociology, the vein

of religion is a deep one in his works, by no means confined to the final years of his life. Even in his early *Essays,* written while still in young manhood and before the writing of *The Positive Philosophy,* we find Comte appealing for a new "spiritual power" that would serve the modern world as Roman Catholicism had served the Middle Ages. Among other criticisms of the French Revolution in Comte's early works is that of the Revolution's repressive and destructive effect upon religion. Comte tells us that most of the dislocations of Western society stem from the spiritual disorganization that began with the Reformation. It is, however, in *The Positive Polity* that the full force of Comte's religiosity is to be seen. Not Christianity, of course, but Positivism is to be the religion of the future, with society as the Grand Being of worship. What we are given in rich detail in the four volumes of this work is hardly less than "Catholicism minus Christianity," as someone has put it: that is, a structure of religion every bit as hierarchical, liturgical, canonical, and sacramental as anything to be found in medieval Christianity but with Society, not God, as its center.

It is easy to smile at the extravagances of Comte's devotion to his new religion of humanity, but we should not miss the often brilliant analyses of the relation of religion to personality, socialization, and to society as a whole. Granted that Comte's primary purpose was that of advancing the positivism which in his thought had begun as science but had become religion; granted, too, that Comte's own role in this mission seems to have been perceived by him and his closest followers as no less than papal: there yet remain in the voluminous pages of the *Positive Polity* a wealth of insights regarding religion as a social system, as a structure of authority, and as an indispensable source of consensus.[1] Comte detested Protestantism as much as any ardent Catholic, and there is no hint of any individualism or asceticism in his portrayal of legitimate religion. A great deal of Durkheim's emphasis upon the commonal-corporate nature of religion, upon the cult and its rites, and upon the ineradicability of the sense of the sacred, not to mention the profound stress Durkheim lays upon society as the real source of all religion, could have come directly from his reading of Comte.

So too could he have drawn a good deal of his perspective from Tocqueville's *Democracy in America,* a work that has much more in it than what its title might suggest. Given the instant popularity of this book everywhere in the West from the time of its publication (Vol. 1, 1835, Vol. 2, 1840), the boundless respect in which it was held by minds as rigorous as John Stuart Mill's and Ernest Renan's, we may safely assume that it was a staple of reading in moral philosophy by the time Durkheim began his career as student.

For Tocqueville, religion is the ultimate source of man's conceptions of reality.

> There is hardly any human action, however particular it may be, that does not originate in some general idea men have conceived of the Deity, of his relation to mankind, of the nature of their own souls, and of their duties to their fellow creatures. Nor can anything prevent these ideas from being the common spring from which all the rest emanates.[2]

Religion is as natural to human nature and society as any way of thought and membership could possibly be. "Men cannot abandon religious faith without a kind of aberration of intellect and a sort of violent distortion of their true nature. . . ."[3] The main function of religion so far as society is concerned is that it furnishes a framework of belief, one that enables individuals to convert external chaos into order they may live by. If religion manifests itself in ways which are inseparable from society—community, rite, hierarchy, authority, and so on—it yet manages to remain above all of these, or at very least transfuse the social into the spiritual, into a world of meaning that man everywhere regards as utterly different from the utilitarian.

For Tocqueville the word *dogma* best expresses the social and psychological essence of religion. Dogma is the steel spring of both personality and social structure.

> In order that society should exist and, *a fortiori,* that a society
> should prosper, it is necessary that the minds of all the citizens
> should be rallied and held together by certain predominant ideas;
> and this cannot be the case unless each of them sometimes draws
> his opinions from the common source and consents to accept cer-
> tain matters of belief already formed.
>
> If I now consider man in his isolated capacity, I find that dog-
> matic belief is not less indispensable to him in order to live alone
> than it is to enable him to cooperate with his fellows. If man were
> forced to demonstrate for himself all the truths of which he makes
> daily use, his task would never end. He would exhaust his strength
> in preparatory demonstrations without ever advancing beyond
> them. . . . There is no philosopher in the world so great but that
> he believes a million things on the faith of other people and ac-
> cepts a great many more truths than he demonstrates.[4]

Whatever else religion is, it is for Tocqueville a system of
order and authority intimately fused with society with roots deep
in the most primary needs of human personality. However it be
called, religion is a necessary stabilizing, orienting force in human affairs. "When there is no longer any principle of authority
in religion any more than in politics, men are speedily frightened
at the aspect of this unbounded independence. The constant agi-
tation of all surrounding things alarms and exhausts them."
From spiritual insecurity, men tend to run to political refuge,
despotism: "As everything is at sea in the sphere of the mind,
they determine at least that the mechanism of society shall be
firm and fixed; and as they cannot resume their ancient belief,
they assume a master."[5] Religion is, then, a structure of belief,
one extending to all aspects of experience, and—far from being
an impediment to reason, as the *philosophes* argued—it is the
very sinew of reason.

If it is religion's integrative role in thought that Tocqueville
stresses, it is religion's capacity for investing society and culture
with a sacred nature that Fustel de Coulanges so memorably emphasizes. His *The Ancient City* (1861), an account of the rise and
fall of the ancient city-states of Athens and Rome, was written
from a rationalist position nearly as rigorous as Durkheim's.

What made this book unique in that age of monumental classical scholarship was its single-minded emphasis on religion—and specifically on the sacred—as the prime cause of all that was foremost in the social, political, and intellectual structure and the vicissitudes of these two ancient communities.

It was religion, Fustel de Coulanges concluded in his study, that formed the foundation of the kinship system: it "established marriage and paternal authority, fixed the order of relationship, and consecrated the right of property, and the right of inheritance." And from religion came also

> . . . all the institutions, as well as all the private law, of the ancients. It was from this that the city received all its principles, its rules, its usages, and its magistracies. But in the course of time, this ancient religion became modified or effaced, and private law and political institutions were modified with it. Then came a series of revolutions, and social changes regularly followed the development of knowledge.[6]

The heart of religion, Fustel emphasized, is not belief or faith or external authority, but the idea of the sacred; in its first form, the sacred fire. The sacred fire in each family hearth was, in the beginning, the very identity of the family:

> The fire ceased to glow upon the altar only when the entire family had perished; an extinguished hearth, an extinguished family, were synonomous expressions among the ancients. Not everything could be fed into the fire; some woods could be, some not. Some stones could be used for preparation of the hearth, some not. It was a religious precept that this fire must always remain pure; which meant, literally, that no filthy object ought to be cast upon it, and, figuratively, that no blameworthy deed ought to be committed in its presence.[7]

The essential point of Fustel's treatment of the early Athenian and Roman communities is that everything in the social bond proceeded from the sacredness of the flame on the hearth, epitomizing as it did the unbroken chain of familial succession from the past through the present to the limitless future. It is impossible to believe other than that Durkheim got his own sense of the fundamental importance of the sacred in society and of the profound distinction between the sacred and the merely utilitarian—or, as Durkheim would word it, the *profane*—from Fustel de Coulanges. Fustel's thesis, in his *Ancient City*, is that early Greek and Roman social organization acquired its sinews from the profound sense of the sacred, that ancient thought did likewise, and that the eventual disintegration of these ancient communities came only when that sense of the sacred had become sapped by skepticism set in alien contexts of power.

Finally, the religious works of Ernest Renan should be mentioned here. In the Introduction I referred to Renan as a much neglected mind at the present time and almost certainly a profound influence upon Durkheim in a number of ways. Far from least of these ways were Renan's remarkable studies of the origins of Christianity and, separately, of the nature of the religion and culture of the ancient Jews. Renan had begun in training for the priesthood, lost his faith completely in religion as a personal experience or belief, and became a devoted exponent of the scientific approach to both nature and man. At no point, however, did Renan ever abandon interest in the study of religion and its relationship to society. The first volume of his *Origins of Christianity* is his by-now historic *Life of Jesus,* one of the very first, if not the first, of such works to deal in strictest objectivity and regard for verifiable historical propositions with the life of the founder of Christianity. Both the volume on Jesus and the work as a whole were bitterly attacked by clerics and others in the late nineteenth century for what they regarded as Renan's impiety and his flouting of sacred text. But the *Origins of Christianity* remains, despite inevitable flaws which only later scholarship could have corrected, one of the truly great works in religious history and sociology of the age.

In some ways, even more remarkable was Renan's multivolume study of the ancient peoples of Israel. Here, as in the study of Christianity, we are treated to an almost astonishing learning—Renan had acquired facility in almost all the ancient languages of the Mediterranean world while still in training for the priesthood and of these Hebrew seems to have been one of his favorites—coupled, however, with brilliance of insight and perspective. As a picture of the circumstances involved in the rise of a nation, of the relation between religious belief and social organization, of the social sources of the most abstract points of doctrine, and of the social structures in ancient Israel within which religion arose, *The History of the Peoples of Israel* would be difficult even today—again omitting only the specific matters which later scholarship has been required to correct—to improve upon. To a degree that not even Durkheim ever exceeded, and that certainly impressed itself upon the young Durkheim in his own beginnings of interest in religion and society, Renan dealt with religion and its beliefs and symbols in the concrete terms of *society:* of household, clan and kindred, tribe and nation; of rite and ceremony, of social ways of behavior, in short, which only over a long period of time became transmuted into letter and doctrine.

Both the study of Christianity and that of ancient Israel are, finally, superb insights into the more general histories of their times and settings—military, economic, social, and political.

I have mentioned briefly four of the many minds which may be found throughout the nineteenth century concerned with religion in its relation to man and society; concerned in ways native to scholars and scientists. The background to Durkheim's own interest in religion is, in short, a large one. As we look at this background of scholarly interest in religion in the century, to be found in sociology, history, anthropology, and psychology, as well as in older disciplines such as philosophy, four perspectives become apparent. I will summarize these succinctly; each of them, as we shall see, is to be found luminously in Durkheim's own treatment of religion.

First, religion is necessary to society, not merely in an abstract or general sense, but as a vital mechanism of integration of human beings and as a realm of unifying symbols. No matter how personally indifferent to religion any of the investigators here referred to may have been, how hostile indeed, there is yet conviction that throughout the human race the deepest roots of social membership are to be found in the nonrational sphere of religion.

Second, religion is a key element and a basic context of social change. The interest both Weber and Durkheim had in Protestantism as a seedbed for modern individualism and secularism was a wide one in the nineteenth century, and it in turn was but a part of a still wider interest in the relation of religion to social movements and other forces in history involved in historical change.

Third, religion is much more than creed and faith; its most fundamental and enduring elements are social; that is, rite, ceremony, hierarchy, and community. The greatest power of religion lies not in what it teaches man about the after-life or about cosmology, but in what its symbols and rituals, its cults and churches and sects, do to stimulate in man the sense of membership in society, the feeling of belonging to what Edmund Burke had called the partnership of the dead, the living, and the unborn. The sacraments and the varied other rites concerned with birth, marriage, and death bespeak the inalienable union of religion with the crises of social existence.

Fourth, there is an unbreakable relation between religion and the origins of human language and thought. From the time that the conservative-Catholic writer Bonald, at the very beginning of the nineteenth century, writing in fierce opposition to both Enlightenment and Revolution, set this proposition forth in his remarkable work, *The Theory of Authority,* we find unremitting interest in this problem. Not all, to be sure, were willing to go as far as Bonald had in his declaration that religion and society precede man and his reason, but more and more minds in the century commenced exploration of the relation between religion and the rise of reason, and, as we have already seen, Durkheim himself derived the very categories of the mind from the prior authority of society and religion.

All of these perspectives are to be found, though set forth with rare insight and power, in Durkheim's sociology of religion.

THE METHOD OF STUDY OF RELIGION

The Elementary Forms of Religious Life, in which is to be found the most detailed, fully articulated, and mature of all Durkheim's analyses of religion, is basically an investigation of a single people, the aboriginal inhabitants of Australia, then widely regarded as the most "primitive" of all known peoples on earth so far as their social organization, culture, and beliefs were concerned. Durkheim did not himself ever visit Australia, or, for that matter, any primitive people or setting, and his study is based exclusively upon the ethnological accounts of the Australians, of which there were many. This total lack of field work in Durkheim's investigation of primitive religion has not seldom been the basis of criticism of Durkheim's conclusions, but it is worth emphasizing that, this lack notwithstanding, *The Elementary Forms* has drawn far more praise than censure from ethnologists, is the immediate foundation on which a great deal of English social anthropology under Malinowski and Radcliffe-Brown was built, and is widely acclaimed by anthropologists as well as sociologists and specialized students of religion as an authentic milestone in the scientific understanding of religious culture.

At the base of Durkheim's method, then, is intensive analysis of a single people. That mode of work, of approach to religion, has no novelty today, but it had a great deal of novelty in Durkheim's day, when sociology and ethnology alike were so widely constructed in terms of the so-called Comparative Method which involved the extracting of thousands of traits from cultures all over the world, their taxonomic arrangement, and their conversion into an imagined linear series declared to be mankind's evolutionary ascent in society. There is no need to repeat here what I wrote about, and quoted from, Durkheim's repudiation of this in the opening chapter of this book.[8] Suffice it to say that behind Durkheim's concentration upon the religion of one people lay, in largest part, revulsion for the ruthless tearing of traits—beliefs, rites, and cults—from literally hundreds of cultures and societies and their presentation in a proclaimed but in fact imaginary universal evolution.

His interest in, and, of course, choice of the Australians for his study of religion stem from his belief, as I have said, that by any reasonable standard they and their religious practices were the "simplest" to be found in the world. In this belief Durkheim was, of course, not alone. At that time there was wide assent that the Australians and the inhabitants of Tierra del Fuego were the two "simplest" or most "primitive" of all peoples on earth. Durkheim's study of the Australian practices was based in some degree upon the desire to demonstrate, so far as was possible, what the origins of mankind's religions are. He makes this plain, though indicating at the same time that by "origins" he has something in mind more nearly logical than anything that might be thought to be *the* beginnings of religion for all mankind. In a footnote he writes: "It is to be seen that we give a wholly relative sense to this word "origins" just as to the word "primitive." By it we mean not an absolute beginning, but the most simple social condition that is actually known or that beyond which we cannot go at present."[9]

Let us not make too much of Durkheim's explanation. There is no ignoring the fact that whatever else his treatment of religion is—and it is a very great deal else—it is a product of a mind oriented in substantial degree toward the social evolutionism that had flourished in the nineteenth century and been the immediate context of his first published work, the *Division of Labor*. I shall have more to say about this aspect of Durkheim in the chapter below on social change. For the moment, in order to give emphasis to Durkheim's very definitely evolutionary intent, the following quotation will suffice:

> Every time that we undertake to explain something human, taken at a given moment in history—be it religious belief, a moral precept, a legal principle, an esthetic style or an economic system— it is necessary to commence by going back to its most primitive and simple form, to try to account for the characteristics by which it

was marked at that time, and then to show how it developed and became complicated little by little, and how it became that which it is at the moment in question.[10]

Those words could have been used by Comte, Spencer, McLennan, Morgan, Tylor, and the other great social evolutionists of the nineteenth century—and with slight variation were so used. But what gives lasting distinction to Durkheim's study of religion is not the flavor of evolutionism, unmistakable though it is, but the purely analytic and structural framework that is overwhelmingly the essence of the book. Here it is, of course, the concentration upon one people, the Australians, that is crucial. Though comparative references are not wanting altogether when Durkheim is discussing some aspect of the Australian religion, these are held not only to a minimum but to purely explanatory significance; they are not intended to suggest universal stages of religious development for mankind.

The intent of the book is, basically, analysis of the constituent elements of religion, the really fundamental and essential elements, and it is to this end that Durkheim settles upon what was generally regarded in his day as the simplest of all religions to be found in the world. He would, he thought, through intensive analysis of the simplest of religions known, thus be able to define religion as a discrete human experience and also decompose it into its basic elements. He would do this not through the Cartesian method of logical deduction but through empirical observation.

> It was one of Descartes's principles that the first ring has a predominating place in the chain of scientific truths. But there is no question of placing at the foundation of the science of religions an idea elaborated after the Cartesian manner, that is to say, a logical concept, a pure possibility, constructed simply by force of thought. What we must find is a concrete reality, and historical and ethnological observation alone can reveal that to us.[11]

It is in this light, then, that we are able to gain an overview of the specific contents of Durkheim's study of religion. His distinction between sacred and profane, his stress upon totemism, upon the cult, and upon positive and negative rites—all to be found in the Australian religion, all, equally, to be found, Durkheim argues, in other religions, including the most complex and historically recent—have to be understood as efforts to deal with the constituent elements of religion, no matter where religion, properly so-called, may be found.

> *A religion is a unified system of beliefs and practices relative to sacred things, that is to say, things set apart and forbidden—beliefs and practices which united into one single moral community called a Church, all those who adhere to them.* The second element which thus finds a place in our definition is no less essential than the first; for by showing that the idea of religion is inseparable from that of the Church, it makes it clear that religion would be an eminently collective thing.[12]

RELIGION AND SOCIETY

Religion, like almost everything else, is made a reflection of society, more specifically of collective representations, by Durkheim. Well before he had written his *Division of Labor* in final draft, Durkheim had, in book reviews and lectures, insisted upon the fact that religion is a derivation of man's earliest *social* experience, that is, of man's absolute dependence upon society and upon its symbolic representations. In the *Division of Labor* Durkheim made this point emphatic. We cannot, he there writes, make religion a function of belief in gods, for there are religions without apparent gods and in all religions there are vital elements pertaining to the mundane sphere, to food and drink, to body, to immediate associations, and to physical environment, which do not in any way link themselves with a deity.

". . . The sole characteristic that all ideas such as religious sentiments equally present seems to be that they are common to a certain number of people living together, and that, besides, they have an average intensity that is quite elevated. It is, indeed, a constant fact that, when a strong belief is held by the same community of men, it inevitably takes on a religious character. It inspires in consciences the same reverential respect as beliefs properly religious."[13]

What history demonstrates, Durkheim goes on, is that religion tends to encompass an ever-smaller portion of human life. Whereas in the beginning it permeates everything—polity, economy, war, technology, and so forth—, with the passing of time, each of these important areas liberates itself, so to speak, from the tentacles of religion and becomes a part of the ever-widening nonreligious or profane world. "God who was at first present in all human relations, progressively withdraws from them; he abandons the world to men and their disputes." This process, Durkheim writes in a passage that is highly suggestive of Simmel's treatment of "autonomization" of cognitive life in man, has the effect of making individuals more active in personal terms, more aware of themselves as heterogeneous rather than homogeneous elements of the social body, but without actually diminishing the role of religion. Religion, from being inseparable from all institutionalized activities, now increasingly has its seat in the individual mind or faith. "The individual really feels himself less *acted upon;* he becomes more a source of spontaneous activity. In short, not only does the domain of religion grow at the same time and in the same measure as temporal life, but it contracts more and more."[14]

Durkheim's argument with respect to religion here is all of a piece with his larger argument in the *Division of Labor* which is, as we noted above, the progressive differentiation of society, emergence of individuality, and utilization of contractual rather than mechanical-repressive relationships as the principal tissues of the social order. It is impossible not to conclude from Durkheim's discussion of religion in the *Division of Labor* that he regards the trajectory of history as overwhelmingly toward the individualization of religion as well as society generally.

What we find in Durkheim's ensuing work, however, to the very end of his scholarly career, is an emphasis upon, certainly a clear direction of his interest toward, the communal and corporate aspects of religion, the *collective representations* rather than the individual representations of religion. We are obliged to conclude that religion, along with law, became for Durkheim so preeminently reflective of the constraining and coercive qualities he deemed essential in social facts and so overwhelmingly illustrative of the depth and reach of the social bond that he took the model of religion pretty much as he had described it under the rubric of "mechanical solidarity" in the *Division of Labor* as his ideal-type for all analytical purposes.

Certainly, in just about everything pertaining to religion thereafter Durkheim demonstrated the degree to which the social basis of religion and, with this, the religious basis of society dominated his mind and investigations. There were the studies of the origins of contract and property, discussed in Chapter 2 above, in which Durkheim showed the roots of both these institutions in the sacred covenant and the sacred ground. There was his effort to show, in *Suicide,* that the greater immunity of the religious to suicide was the result, not of religious commandment or doctrine, but of the stronger element of sociality religion afforded its members in contrast to those who knew little or no sociality relatively in their lives. And there were his lectures on morality, much later to appear as *Moral Education,* in which he affirmed once again, first, the profound affinity between the moral and the religious experience and, second, the ineradicable foundation of each in the disciplines and also the images supplied by society. Moral conscience and religious faith alike have their origins, Durkheim argues, in the supremacy of society and in the social formation of the self.

In *The Elementary Forms of Religious Life* we see stated as firmly as in the *Division of Labor,* but with immeasurably greater refinement of argument, the point that religion is at bottom nothing more than man's respect for society carried to a superlative degree of symbolic intensity. Religion is emphatically *not* what the rationalists and utilitarians have declared it to be, writes Durkheim: that is, a state of mind with the physical world the direct object. Religion is, on the contrary, a consecration of community. Religion is not a hallucination or tissue of superstitions, as the secularists of the eighteenth century had argued. There is nothing hallucinatory about religion so far as the role of the communicant is concerned. "Religion ceases to be an inexplicable hallucination," Durkheim writes, following earlier reference to the efforts of rationalists to account for it, "and takes a foothold in reality. In fact, we can say that the believer is not deceived when he believes in the existence of a moral power upon which he depends and from which he receives all that is best in himself: this power exists; it is society." Before all else, religion is, and will always be as it always has been, a reflection of man's relation with society.

> Before all, it is a system of ideas with which the individuals represent to themselves the society of which they are members, and the obscure but intimate relations which they have with it. That is its primary function; and though metaphorical and symbolic, this representation is not unfaithful. Quite on the contrary, it translates everything essential in the relations which are to be explained: for it is an eternal truth that outside us there exists something greater than us, with which we enter into communion.[15]

SACRED AND PROFANE

How does society specifically become religion? What are the processes or structures which make religion so unique a manifestation of that force, society, which for Durkheim lies at the base of all institutions? We begin with the momentous distinction Durkheim makes between the sacred and the profane. This, not the existence of believed-in gods, not animism, not pantheism, not anything of belief-character at all, lies at the foundation of religion everywhere. That the distinction is generated by man's social experience does not in any way lessen the uniqueness of the particular form of social experience that is symbolized by the awareness man has of the profound difference between the sacred and the profane. Here one notes the influence of Fustel's classic work. Durkheim carries the sacred much further, however. In-

stead of limiting the distinction between the sacred and the profane to primitive or ancient consciousness, as Fustel tended to do,
Durkheim makes it crucial and determining for all time. The object, the specific identity, of the sacred may vary from age to age
and from people to people, but the category itself is immutable
and eternal. Religion, reduced to its essentials, is a society's classification of some things as sacred (beyond the rule of interest and
reason) and of other things as profane.

It is important to keep in mind that Durkheim, in distinguishing between the sacred and the profane, is not distinguishing between good and evil. Far from it. There are "sacred" objects limitlessly evil in their conceived relation to man and society,
and there are "profane" objects wholly acceptable—even advan-
tageous—to both.

> The division of the world into two domains, the one containing
> all that is sacred, the other all that is profane, is the distinctive
> trait of religious thought; the beliefs, myths, dogmas, and legends
> are either representations or systems of representations which ex-
> press the nature of sacred things, the virtues and powers which are
> attributed to them, or their relations with each other and with pro-
> fane things. But, by sacred things, one must not understand simply
> those personal beings which are called gods or spirits; a rock, a
> tree, a spring, a pebble, a piece of wood, a house—in a word, any-
> thing—can be sacred. A rite can have this character, in fact, the rite
> does not exist which does not have it to a certain degree.[16]

Sacred things are, by nature, superior—in dignity and power
—to profane things, and particularly is this true in their relation
to man himself. Man looks up to them, immolating himself in
one degree or other. Man's relation to the sacred is sometimes
one of awe, of love, or even of measureless dread; sometimes one
of ease and pleasure. Man is not always in a state of expressed in-
feriority before his gods, for he may joke with and about them,
and he may beat the fetish which has caused him mishap. But
the superiority of sacred things is assumed nevertheless.

The distinction between the sacred and the profane is absolute:

> In all the history of human thought there exists no other ex-
> ample of two categories of things so profoundly differentiated or so
> radically opposed to one another. The traditional opposition of
> good and bad is nothing beside this; for the good and the bad are
> only two opposed species of the same class, namely morals, just as
> sickness and health are two different aspects of the same order of
> facts, life, while the sacred and the profane have always and every-
> where been conceived by the human mind as two distinct classes,
> two worlds between which there is nothing in common.[17]

The absolute and universal nature of the contrast between
the sacred and the profane does not mean that things and beings
cannot or do not pass from one sphere to the other. The passage
quoted, however, highlights the division between the two. Purifi-
cation rites, as in initiation or eucharistic ceremonies, are the
means through which a person or thing passes from the profane
state to the sacred. By contrast, the passage from the sacred state
to the profane is more often the consequence of an erosion of
values or the dislocation of deities and entities by the entrance of
new manifestations of the sacred (new religions) or from the
spread of skepticism.

The erosion and disappearance of one set of sacred observances is invariably followed by the appearance of new entities or
states to which sacred status is granted. There is, Durkheim
emphasizes:

> . . . something eternal in religion which is destined to survive all
> the particular symbols in which religious thought has successively
> enveloped itself. There can be no society which does not feel the
> need of upholding and reaffirming at regular intervals the collective
> sentiments and the collective ideas which make its unity and its
> personality.[18]

This is also the fate of intellectual and social systems that begin
in the most utilitarian or rationalistic circumstances—even those
dedicated, in the name of critical reason, to the overthrow of
some existing system of sacred values. Durkheim cites the eventu-
ation of political rationalism during the French Revolution in

worship of the Goddess of Reason, in the establishment of new commemorative festivals.

Durkheim applies the perspective of the sacred and the profane to specific institutions in society in order to show the historical and psychological source of their authority. An example already noted is his use of the sacred with respect to contract. Contract presupposes society, but society gains the authority communicated to the idea of contract only by making contract sacred; hence, the origins of contract lie in ritual. The same applies to property. Whence comes the notion of the right of property?— not, Durkheim argues, from any instinct or sense of self-interest, for these would result only in a desire for aggrandizement, not in a respect for the property of others. And it is this respect which is crucial to the conception of right. Rather, Durkheim concludes, the notion of right of property comes from the sacredness originally diffused in things—some things—and fixed by ritual. His words here are among the finest he wrote anywhere:

> The sacredness diffused in things, which withheld them from any profane appropriation, was conducted by means of a certain definite ritual either to the threshold or to the periphery of the field. It there established something like a girdle of sanctity or sacred encircling mound, protecting the domain from any trespass by outsiders. To cross this zone and enter the little island insulated from the rest of the land by ritual, was reserved to those alone who had carried out the rites, that is, those who had contracted especial bonds with the sacred beings, the original owners of the soil. By degrees, this sacredness residing in the things themselves passed into the persons: they no longer possessed this quality, except indirectly, because they were subject to persons who themselves were sacred. Property, from being collective, became individual.[19]

The idea of the sacred—and, with it, the communal—becomes the basis of Durkheim's interpretation of the character of religion. He rejects the view that religion is defined by belief in gods or transcendent spirits. Nor does he believe its origins can be made synonymous with those of magic. And it is his development of the distinction between religion and magic that forms the heart of Durkheim's theory. Characteristically he makes the distinction between religion and magic in terms of the group and its relative value to each.

Religious beliefs, Durkheim maintains,

> . . . are always common to a determined group, which makes profession of adhering to them and of practicing the rites connected with them. They are not merely received individually by all the members of the group; they are something belonging to the group, and they make its unit. The individuals which compose it feel themselves united to each other by the simple fact that they have a common faith. A society whose members are united by the fact that they think in the same way in regard to the sacred world and its relations with the profane world, and by the fact that they translate these common ideas into common practice is what is called a church. In all history we do not find a single religion without a church.

Very different is the case with magic. Magic can be—and often is—diffused throughout considerable sections of the populations, and among some peoples it has as many adherents as religion.

> But it does not result in binding together those who adhere to it, nor in uniting them into a group leading a common life. *There is no church of magic.* Between the magician and the individuals who consult him, as between those individuals themselves, there are no lasting bonds which make them members of the moral community, comparable to that formed by the believers in the same god or the observers of the same cult. The magician has a clientele and not a church, and it is very possible that his clients have no other relations between each other, or even do not know each other; even the relations which they have with him are generally accidental and transient; they are just like those of a sick man with his physician.[20]

THE CULT

If the origin of the sacred is to be found in the immeasurable value man has always tended to place upon the social order, upon the collectivity that alone stands between him and the social void with all its nameless fears, we are yet obliged to ask, what is the most elemental form of collective representation of the sacred? For Durkheim the answer is the *cult,* the smallest possible collective unity of a religious character. The cult is in every sense the social molecule of religion—or, more accurately, of the church which is for Durkheim inseparable from religion properly so-called.

Specifically, it is the *totemic* cult that Durkheim finds at the basis of religion in its most primitive form. Not for Durkheim any origin of religion put in psychological or emotional terms—such as Tylor's animism or Müller's and Lang's "awe." The origin of religion lies in society, in man's dependence upon society, and in man's consecration of the social bond. The very earliest and most primitive manifestation of this dependence and consecration is the totem: the plant, insect, bird, or animal that the kinship group may make its visible symbol. But, for Durkheim, there is not the slightest trace of worship of the totemic entity as such; that is, of the animal or bird, as the case might be. The totem, in Durkheim's view, has no intrinsic importance at all; it becomes an aspect of the sacred only insofar as it has been taken over as a symbol of the unity and indestructibility of the group—the clan, which is in its strictly religious role the cult. The essence of totemism is, then, not plant- or animal-worship but use of something external as the visible symbol of the social fabric, the ties of belonging.

> Thus the totem is before all a symbol, a material expression of something else. . . . In the first place it is the outward and visible form of what we have called the totemic principle or god. But it is also the symbol of the determined society called the clan. It is its flag; it is the sign by which each clan distinguishes itself from the others, the visible mark of its personality, a mark borne by everything which is a part of the clan under any title whatsoever, men, beasts, or things. So if it is at once the symbol of the god and of the society, is that not because the god and the society are only one. . . . The god of the clan, the totemic principle, can therefore be nothing else than the clan itself, personified and represented to the imagination under the visible form of the animal or vegetable which serves as the totem.[21]

What Durkheim is presenting us with is a highly sophisticated theory of symbolism, one that explores the roots of symbolism in man's relation to nature and, above all, society. All religions, he indicates at the outset of the book, are "true in their fashion; all answer, though in different ways, to the given conditions of human existence . . . There are no religions which are false."[22] We can be assured in advance, he tells us, that whatever the movements of the cult in its dedication to totem, however bizarre and even seemingly delirious they may be, they are profoundly functional. "By the mere fact that their apparent function is to strengthen the bonds attaching the believer to his god, they at the same time really strengthen the bonds attaching the individual to the society of which he is a member, since the god is only a figurative expression of the society."[23] Society is a reality, Durkheim tells us, sui generis. Collective representations are at bottom an "immense cooperation" which reaches out in space and backward and forward in time. A special intellectual activity is concentrated in these communal, social phenomena that is richer and more complex than anything to be found in the individual, no matter how learned or talented he may be.[24]

The totem—whether this be bird or animal, a flag, a cross, whatever—is the visible symbol of the organic unity of society. To suggest that the martyr is dying for the cross as such, or the soldier for the piece of bunting called a flag, is absurd. It is, at bottom, one's community, his cult, nation, as the case may be, that one gives his life for.

The essence of religion, then, is not to be found ever in the individual, but only in the community of believers. Admittedly, religion becomes a matter of purpose and devotion in the individual mind. Everything social, as Durkheim repeatedly reminds us, is carried in the consciousnesses of individuals; nowhere else. But behind the faith of the individual lies the cult. "In a word, it is the church of which he is a member which teaches the individual that these personal gods are, what their function is, how he should enter into relations with them, and how he should honor them."[25] Durkheim is very critical—as critical as any Roman Catholic might be—of the Protestant stress upon the residual individuality of religion, of the Lutheran or Calvinist declaration that religion commences in the individual breast and is directed solely to God. Such a view, Durkheim argues, misconstrues the communal nature of all religion and is possible at all only in a society or age such as that of Reformation Europe when religious minds and characters have already been well established by a historical and corporate church.

Durkheim is as critical of rationalist explanations of religion as any religious conservative might be:

> The theorists who have undertaken to explain religion in rational terms have generally seen it before all else a system of ideas, corresponding to some predetermined object. This object has been conceived in a multitude of ways: nature, the infinite, the unknowable, the ideal, and so on; these differences matter little.[26]

In such theories, conceptions and beliefs are considered as the essential elements. Religious rites, from this point of view, appear to be "only an external translation, contingent and material, of these internal states which alone pass as having any intrinsic value."[27]

But, Durkheim notes shrewdly, this appraisal of religion, made by outsiders, is very different from that made by individuals who are within the compass of religion and committed to it. For such individuals, the essence of religion is not what it says about things—external or internal—but what it does toward making action possible, life endurable:

> The believer who has communicated with his god is not merely a man who sees new truths of which the unbeliever is ignorant; he is a man who is *stronger*. He feels within him more force, either to endure the trials of existence, or to conquer them.[28]

The first article of belief, where belief is explicit, may well be belief in salvation; but this idea could never have acquired its transforming meaning or profound human sustenance apart from its place in a community of acts, of observances, of rites.

It is, therefore, the cult that is fundamental. According to Durkheim anyone who has ever "really practiced" a religion knows

> . . . it is the cult which gives rise to those impressions of joy, of interior peace, of serenity, of enthusiasm, which are, for the believer, an experimental proof of his beliefs. The cult is not simply a system of signs by which the faith is outwardly translated; it is a collection of the means by which this is created and recreated periodically.[29]

Durkheim concludes the long passage (part of which is quoted above) by declaring: "Our entire study rests on the postulate that the unanimous sentiment of the believers of all times cannot be purely illusory." In short, the sociology of religion must begin with religion as it is practiced, as it is experienced, as it *is*—as far as objective observation can convey it. From Durkheim's point of view, the critical rationalists who have sought to dismiss religion as a tissue of superstitions, "expendable" once men are correctly informed, are as much in error as those theologians—especially of the Protestant faith—who have endeavored to express its nature in terms of creed and dogma. Religion is community—cult—or it is nothing but a precarious assemblage of impressions and words with no power to integrate and transfigure.

Every cult presents a double aspect: one, negative; the other, positive. Although the two aspects are inseparable, they can be distinguished. Both aspects flow from the all-important separation of the sacred and the profane:

> A whole group of rites has the object of realizing this state of separation which is essential. Since their function is to prevent undue mixings and to keep one of these two domains from encroaching upon the other, they are only able to impose abstentions or negative acts. Therefore, we propose to give the name negative cult to the system formed by these special rites. They do not prescribe certain acts to the faithful, but confine themselves to forbidding certain ways of acting; so they all take the form of interdictions, or as is commonly said by ethnographers, of *taboos*.[30]

The function of the negative cult is to free man from contamination—or possible contamination—by the profane in order that he may be put in position to achieve the sacred; hence, the value placed upon acts (often extreme) of self-abasement, self-denial, or rigorous asceticism.

> [But] . . . whatever the importance of the negative cult may be . . . it does not contain its reason for existence in itself; it introduces one to the religious life, but it supposes this more than it constitutes it. If it orders the worshipper to flee from the profane world, it is to bring him near to the sacred world. Men have never thought that their duties toward religious forces might be reduced to a simple abstinence from all commerce; they have always believed that they upheld positive and bilateral relations with them, whose regulation and organization is the function of a group of ritual practices. To this special system of rites we give the name of *positive cult.*[31]

In the positive cult is effected the relationship of god and man that is, Durkheim emphasizes, a reciprocal one. Unlike such observers as Robertson Smith, who defined the chief function of the cult as that of uniting men, Durkheim points out that the cult is as important to the gods as to men themselves—for (and here again is the essence of Durkheim's entire system of sociology) the gods are but manifestations or personifications of society:

> We now see the real reason why the gods cannot do without their worshippers any more than these can do without their gods; it is because society, of which the gods are only a symbolic expression, cannot do without individuals any more than these can do without society. Here we touch the solid rock upon which all the cults are built and which has caused their persistence ever since human societies have existed.[32]

The cult is cellular to religion and constitutive to society as a whole. Without the cult, Durkheim declares, society would weaken. The first effect of religious ceremonies is to put the group's members into action: "to multiply the relations between them and to make them more intimate with one another. By this very fact, the content of their consciousness is changed." Ordinarily, in utilitarian or "profane" activities, there is a strong tendency for individualism—or even divisiveness—to operate among men, thus weakening the web of society. But when the cult exists and rituals are celebrated, men's thoughts are centered upon

> . . . their common beliefs, their common traditions, the memory of their ancestors, the collective idea of which they are the incarnation; in a word, upon social things. . . . The spark of social being which each bears within him necessarily participates in this collective renovation. The individual soul is regenerated, too, by being dipped again in the sources from which its life came; consequently, it feels itself stronger, more fully master of itself, less dependent upon physical necessities.[33]

RITES

Here, then, is the context within which religious rites become crucial to the sociologist: they are the visible manifestation of a communion of spirits, of a coalescence of ideas and faiths. Two essential rites are *sacrifice* and *imitation*. The first, through some mode of transubstantiation, symbolically bridges the gap between the profane and the sacred. The second, by focusing upon an ideal conception, be it totem or god, supplies the means whereby men may emulate the ideal and thus be spiritually and morally elevated. The idea or category of cause originates in the human mind through the performance and use of imitative rites.

Beyond these are two other types of rite, which Durkheim calls, respectively, *representative* and *piacular*. The primary function of representative rites is to commemorate the group's continuity with past and future, emphasizing—through sacred observances—the links each living member has both with history and with posterity. It is thus that totemic identification with animals or plants is born. Out of these representative rites also come, in time, esthetic and recreational activities—dramatic pageants and games—which give the rites added purpose. The gradual disengagement of these activities from the original religious matrix constitutes one important phase of the secularization of culture. Of them, Durkheim writes:

> Not only do they employ the same processes as the real drama, but they also pursue an end of the same sort: being foreign to all utilitarian ends, they make men forget the real world and transport them into another where their imagination is more at ease; they distract. They sometimes even go so far as to have the outward appearance of a recreation: the assistants may be seen laughing and amusing themselves openly.[34]

Piacular rites introduce another element: the notion of sadness, of fear, of tragedy. All the other rites—sacrificial, imitative, and representative—have one thing in common: "they are all performed in a state of confidence, joy, and even enthusiasm." But there are also rites which are performed in a spirit of unease, of latent pessimism, of apprehension. These Durkheim summarizes under the heading of *piaculum*—that is, "expiation"—the ritual cleansing of man from his sins or his affronts to the sacred powers:

> Every misfortune, everything of evil omen, everything that inspires sentiments of sorrow or fear necessitates a *piaculum,* and is therefore called *piacular*. So this word seems very well adapted for designating the rites which are celebrated by those in a state of uneasiness or sadness.[35]

Between the joyful rites and the piacular, there is, of course, deep affinity. The two poles of religious life correspond to the two states between which any society must oscillate.

> Between the propitiously sacred and the unpropitiously sacred there is the same contrast as between the states of collective well-being and ill-being. But since both are equally collective, there is, between the mythological constructions symbolizing them, an intimate kinship of nature. The sentiments held in common vary from extreme dejection to extreme joy, from painful irritation to ecstatic enthusiasm, but in any case there is a communion of minds and a mutual comfort resulting from this communion.[36]

The functional value that Durkheim gives to sorrow in individual life is noteworthy. Only in his oscillation between sorrow and joy is man made human. So it is with the oscillation between ritual states of spiritual deliverance and spiritual abasement: each is necessary to the other; both are necessary to religion and to society. The sense of sin (enforced by piacular rites) is as important to social integration as the commission of crimes (in due proportion), which is the only force that can cause the mobilization of moral values—the warp of society and of human conscience.

Precisely as he makes religion into a manifestation of society and its crucial phases, Durkheim makes society, in turn, depend upon a nonrational, supraindividual state of mind that can only be called *religious*. Between religion and society there is a functional interplay. It is only because society atttains, through sacred-making processes, a limitless majesty over man that the development of his own distinctive qualities of personality and mind becomes possible. These include man's most profoundly rational, as well as his deepest emotional, qualities. Even logic and its laws are premised upon society:

> It is under the form of collective thought that impersonal thought is, for the first time, revealed to humanity; we cannot see by what other way this revelation could have been made. From the mere fact that society exists there is also, outside of the individual sensations and images, a whole system of representations which enjoy marvelous properties. By means of them, men understand each other and intelligences grasp each other. They have within them a sort of force or moral ascendancy, in virtue of which they impose themselves upon individual minds. . . . Hence, the individual at least obscurely takes account of the fact that above his private ideas there is a world of absolute ideas according to which he must shape his own; he catches a glimpse of a whole intellectual kingdom in which he participates, but which is greater than he. This is the first intuition of the realm of truth. . . . Thus the faculty of conception has individualized itself. But to understand its origins and function, it must be attached to the social conditions upon which it depends.[37]

RELIGION AND SCIENCE

The cult and its rites form the essential and distinctive elements of religion. But also present in religion are speculative and interpretative ideas—ideas that touch upon cosmology, morality, and the nature of society and of man. Here, and here alone, Durkheim says, may conflict between religion and science occur, for science is—by its nature—both a successor and rival of religion in these specific matters. The gradual recession of religion as an explanatory idea may be observed historically in area after area of man's speculative interest. First, it is the physical world—the stars, the mountains, water, subhuman organisms—that is given over to the secular mind of the scientist. His findings, at first inevitably antireligious, are gradually granted exemption from the dominion of religion. Then it is the nature of man—his behavior and his mind—that is relinquished. But this is attended historically by more conflict, for here scientists are dealing with souls and "it is, before all else, over souls that the god of the Christians aspires to reign." That is why the idea of submitting the psychic life to science led for a long time to a feeling of profanation, and is even today repugnant to many minds: "[T]he world of religious and moral life is still forbidden. The great majority of men continue to believe that here there is an order of things which the mind cannot penetrate except by very special ways."[38]

It is the functional similarity of religion and science, so far as man's understanding of—and belonging to—the world is concerned, that insures a certain amount of conflict between religion and science. Religion can never escape a certain speculative function in physical and social matters of cause and substance, even though cult and rite are its true forms. Conversely, science—though the speculative or interpretative function is its primary one—cannot escape a certain degree of ritualization that follows from its institutional character and from its ever-rising position in society's hierarchy of values:

> We have said that there is something eternal in religion: it is the cult and the faith. Men cannot celebrate ceremonies for which they see no reason, nor can they accept a faith which they in no

way understand. . . . Science is fragmentary and incomplete; it advances but slowly and is never finished; but life cannot wait. The theories which are destined to make men live and act are, therefore, obliged to pass science and complete it prematurely.[39]

But the authority of science was established, and it has had to be reckoned with:

From now on, faith no longer exercises the same hegemony as formerly over the system of ideas that we may continue to call religion. A rival power rises up before it which, being born of it, ever after submits to its criticism and control. And everything makes us foresee that this control will constantly become more extended and efficient, while no limit can be assigned to its future influence.[40]

6 Morality

No other major sociologist has given the moral dimension of human behavior the sustained and penetrating attention we find in Durkheim's writings. In part, to be sure, the recurrence of the word "moral" in his works proceeds from the virtual interchangeability of the social and the moral, as concepts, in a great deal of 18th- and 19th-century French thought. To a degree not approached in either England or Germany the "moral sciences" and the "social sciences" are equivalent terms in French writing from at least the time of Montesquieu down through Durkheim's works. But even allowing for this, no one can come away from the reading of Durkheim without realizing the unusual extent to which morality—using that word in the stricter and more specialized sense in which it is to be found in contemporary writing—suffuses his conception of society. Along with religion it is fair to say that morality bulks largest among the subjects to which Durkheim applied his sociological method. A scholar of passionate commitment to the moral values which underlay science, reason, and also, in the crisis of war, love of country, Durkheim was yet able to declare morality as proper and successful a subject for scientific analysis as any other within the range of the sociologist.

We shall begin here with his observations on moral facts in his first major work, the *Division of Labor,* although if there were space it would be possible to glean a great deal of his starting assumptions from some of the early articles and reviews written from 1883 on. Particularly in two articles published in 1887 is it possible to see the formation of Durkheim's interest in the moral sphere: one on philosophy as he found it in the German universities during his year there, the other on the subject of positivistic science in Germany and the role of moral facts in that science. We shall nevertheless commence with the *Division of Labor,* for here, and especially in the early sections of that work, we can see the maturation of earlier thinking and, at the same time, the clear beginning of interests which would be unbroken during the next two decades.

He describes the purpose of the *Division of Labor* as "an attempt to treat the facts of the moral life according to the method of the positive sciences." This does not mean, Durkheim immediately explains, any effort to extract a morality from the positive sciences rather than from, as is so common, the a priori. Quite the contrary. "We do not wish to extract ethics from science, but to establish the science of ethics, which is quite different." Moral facts, he continues, are phenomena like others; "they consist of rules of action recognizable by certain distinctive characteristics. It must, then, be possible to observe them, describe them, classify them, and look for the laws explaining them."[1] By the time Durkheim developed the methodological ideas which would form his *Rules of Sociological Method,* published but a very short time later, "moral facts" would become "social facts." Indeed the attributes which we have already seen Durkheim endow in social facts—exteriority, coerciveness, and so forth—are precisely the attributes we find him giving to moral facts in his preliminary discussion in the *Division of Labor.* Whatever else moral phenomena are, they are not to be dredged up from individual consciousness through introspection or other self-discovery; they are external to the individual observer and possessed of an autonomy, scientifically speaking, that permits dispassionate study. Such study demands a posture, Durkheim readily concedes, very different from that of the revolutionary. There is in fact a built-in conservatism whenever a genuine science of morality is found.

> While the science of ethics does not make us indifferent or resigned spectators of reality, at the same time it does teach us to

treat it with extreme prudence, imparting to us a conservative attitude. There has been good reason to upbraid certain theories which are thought to be scientific for being destructive and revolutionary; they are scientific in name only. They construct but do not observe. They see in ethics, not a collection of facts to study, but a sort of revocable law-making which each thinker establishes himself.[2]

What we must take as our point of departure, Durkheim declares, is the view of morality or ethics as consisting of nothing more than habits and prejudices. If we take the opposite view, that there is an absolute, prescriptive morality, with all else but a spurious or proximate manifestation of morality, we cannot possibly treat moral facts scientifically. Granted, Durkheim writes, that each of us may follow to the end a given moral principle, believing it eternal in truth. This is our privilege as men and citizens. But the scientist must adopt for his purposes "a complete freedom of mind. We must rid ourselves of that habit of seeing and judging which long custom has fixed in us; we must submit ourselves rigorously to the discipline of the methodological doubt."[3]

These are the written reflections with which Durkheim commences his first signal effort to deal with the problem of society. From these reflections he proceeds directly into discussion of the nature of division of labor, of the two types of solidarity, and of the several patterns of disorganization of solidarity which contemporary society reveals. These are matters already discussed in part in earlier chapters and to which in other part we shall return later. It is important for the moment to stay closely to the conception of morality that emerges from the *Division of Labor*.

We find this well stated in the Conclusion of the *Division of Labor*. Here he picks up the reflections once again with which he had begun the book, reflections on the nature of morality and its susceptibility to scientific treatment. The two great types of solidarity, mechanical and organic, reduce themselves, he tells us here, to moral rules. Indeed the very function of these rules "is that they enunciate fundamental conditions of social solidarity.

Law and morality are the totality of ties which bind each of us to
society, which make a unitary, coherent aggregate of the mass of
individuals. Everything which is a source of solidarity is
moral. . . ."4 And, in a passage that could well serve as the
epitome of Durkheim's sociology of morality, he writes:

> Society is not, then, as has often been thought, a stranger to
> the moral world, or something which has only secondary repercus-
> sions on it. It is, on the contrary, the necessary condition of its
> existence. It is not a simple juxtaposition of individuals who bring
> an intrinsic morality with them, but rather man is a moral being
> only because he lives in society, since morality consists in being
> solidary with a group and varying with this solidarity. Let social life
> disappear, and moral life will disappear with it, since it would no
> longer have any objective.5

How preoccupied Durkheim was from the very beginning of
his career with a science of ethics and with the nature of morality
can be inferred from some twenty-five pages of rather fine print
which form the Appendix of the English translation but which
had been a major part of the Introduction Durkheim wrote for the
first edition of the *Division of Labor*.6 I shall treat briefly the contents of this Appendix, for the really central ideas are to be found
in more developed form in a later piece Durkheim wrote on the
subject of the determination of moral facts.

The first point to note in the Appendix is Durkheim's sharp
criticism of Immanuel Kant's celebrated idea of the categorical
imperative. Kant, in one of the most influential moral treatises
ever written, had declared morality—and with it the human conscience—to arise from what Kant called a "categorical imperative"
ingrained in man's very nature and antecedent to actual experience. Kant had put the essence of moral imperative in its universality, suggesting that irrespective of social and cultural differences there is to be found a deeply embedded sense of "oughtness"
in human nature that transcends immediate culture or locality,
that in fact lies anterior to man's cultural experience. Durkheim
is critical in high degree of Kant, it goes without emphasis at this

point, and he would resume his criticism of Kant two decades later in his *Elementary Forms of Religious Life* where, as we have already seen, Durkheim seeks to refute the Kantian idea of innate categories of the mind. But whereas in that later work Durkheim made the direct power of society over individual consciousness the basis of his criticism of Kant—deriving the categories from religio-social rituals, tribal organizations, and so forth—what we find in this earlier critique, concerned solely with morality, is something more in the nature of evolutionary development of morality than with the dynamics of interaction of individual and group.

In his refutation of Kant's moral theory, he does indeed declare for a relativism of morals that is related to his sense of the diversity of social organizations in the world, but his primary goal is to set this relativism in the evolutionary scale that was, in a real sense, the very structure of the *Division of Labor*. As I have indicated, the typology of mechanical and organic solidarity he presents in that book is developmental to the core, with firm insistence upon the fact that although elements of the organic can indeed be descried embryonically in the mechanical, the path of civilization has nevertheless been from the mechanical to the organic. So with the path of human morality.

"One considers as a normal moral fact for a given social type, at a determinate phase of its development, every rule of conduct to which a repressive diffuse sanction is attached in the average society of this type, considered at the same period of evolution. . . ."[7]

Observe in that definition the strong emphasis given to the idea of the normal in relation to phase of development and, with this, emphasis also on the notion of the average society of relevant type. This brings me to the second point I want to make about Durkheim's analysis of morality in the *Division of Labor*. We find in this same discussion the clear beginnings of his interest in deviance, an interest that would be heightened considerably in his *Rules* two years later. There are, Durkheim tells us, cases in which it is not enough to refer to the "normal type" when one wishes to distinguish between the healthy and the sick in social behavior. At certain times crises overtake peoples when "the moral conscience of nations is not yet adapted to the changes which have been produced in the milieu, changes which, partaking of the past which holds it from behind and the necessities of the present, keep it from becoming fixed."[8]

Durkheim would never really abandon the idea that the Western society he knew was undergoing a major crisis and that that crisis consisted at bottom in a pathological loosening of moral authority upon the lives of individuals. As we first encounter this idea it is set, as I have just said, in an evolutionary context. That context continues strongly into his *Rules* where we are given, at much greater length, an analogous discussion of the normal, the average type, as this may be inferred from degree of development, although toward the end of the *Rules* we are also given some of the sharpest criticism of the whole theory of social development to be found anywhere in the nineteenth century. We shall come to that later, as we shall come also to Durkheim's ideas of deviance. For the moment it is important only to observe that, as is true of so much else in his thinking, his fundamental interest in morality goes back clearly and deeply to the *Division of Labor*. For Durkheim the analysis in that work of solidarity in social organization carries with it the assumption that all such solidarity is basically moral, a phase of mankind's *moral* development.

THE NATURE OF MORAL FACTS

In his *Sociology and Philosophy* is to be found a short essay, "The Determination of Moral Facts" that is of much value to us. One gathers that originally Durkheim had been invited to set forth some propositions regarding morality for reading and discussion with the members of the *Société Française de Philosophie*. This he did, and the comments made by Durkheim at the meeting of the Society in reply to questions or observations have been preserved and, together with the original propositions, made into the text of the essay. I think it is without question the most succinct account to be found anywhere in Durkheim's writings of the substantive character of morality. Here we shall find that he has gone much beyond the point of his thinking on morality that was in effect the underlying structure of the *Division of Labor*. We may take this essay as not only a splendid evidence of the maturation of his moral theory during the fifteen years that had followed the writing of the *Division of Labor* but also an admirable point of departure here for consideration of his major work, *Moral Education,* which we shall come to next.

Moral reality, Durkheim begins, can be studied from either of two different points of view (in this respect being indeed like all other aspects of reality): that of exploration and analysis, on the one hand and, on the other, that of practical evaluation of given rules of conduct. Characteristically, it is the first that is of principal appeal to Durkheim, though he does not evade the second.

All morality reduces itself to a system of rules of conduct, but if we are to understand why such rules have greater influence in human lives than those rules of technical character which are the stuff of any activity, craft, or ordinary relationship, we are obliged to turn to the concept of *duty.* The preeminent attribute of morality is its capacity for inspiring in the individual the sense of obligation, of oughtness. In this Durkheim is, of course, concurring with Kant who had, as I have noted, made the sense of duty into what he called the categorical imperative. But Durkheim seeks to go beyond Kant. Duty, while a vital element, is by no means all there is to morality. There must be, Durkheim tells us, an element also of the *desirable* in the moral injunction or precept.

> Something of the nature of duty is found in the desirability of morality. If it is true that the content of the act appeals to us, nevertheless its nature is such that it cannot be accomplished without effort and self-constraint. The *élan,* even the enthusiasm, with which we perform a moral act takes us outside ourselves and above our nature, and this is not achieved without difficulty and inner conflict. It is this *sui generis* desirability which is commonly called *good.*[9]

In order to convey something of the flavor of the combination of the obligatory and the desirable that makes up morality,
Durkheim compares the two qualities to the *sacred*, which we
have already found to be his concept for what is essential in religion. The sacred being has a commanding authority that may not
be violated, nor reduced to the merely utilitarian. But at the
same time, the sacred being is sought after, is adored, is declared
good and the source of man's happiness. So also with respect to
the moral principle or law. One may deem it an imperative, the
source of one's sense of binding duty, but this does not mean it is
not at the same time desirable, capable indeed of generating happiness and of pleasure in the very act of being moral in a given
circumstance. The ethic of honesty or loyalty or chastity may be a
commanding ethic, but it does not follow from this fact that individuals do not find such values ends which they very much wish
to pursue, ends which they regard as desirable.

This does not mean that Durkheim is falling into the trap of
hedonism. His critical strictures in the *Division of Labor* on
utilitarianism and its underlying psychology have not been—nor
would they ever be—forgotten in Durkheim's thinking on morality or on any other aspect of society. If morality were no more
than an assemblage of acts which participant individuals each
found gratifying to the pleasure-sense, there would be no morality
at all. Such a conception of human behavior is in any event sim-
plistic, reductionist, and false from Durkheim's social psychological point of view. No, while the element of the desirable
must be seen in morality—in contradistinction to Kant's approach
—so too must the idea of duty, of obedience to an authority
greater than, outside, the individual. Characteristically, Durkheim finds the reconciliation of the components of morality—duty
and the desirable—in society.

> Morality begins with membership of a group, whatever that
> group may be. When this premise is accepted the characteristics of
> the moral fact become explicable. First, we shall show how society
> is good and desirable for the individual who cannot exist without it
> or deny it without denying himself, and how, at the same time, be-

cause society surpasses the individual, he cannot desire it without to a certain extent violating his nature as an individual. Secondly, we shall show that society, while being good, constitutes a moral authority which, by manifesting itself in certain precepts particularly important to it, confers upon them an obligatory character.[10]

Now, we shall not follow Durkheim in the detailed explanation that follows this statement, for we have already had ample opportunity in this book to observe the desirability, the authority, and the psychological indispensability of society in everything that may truly be called social behavior in the individual's life. I have been concerned thus far only with showing how, in morality as in religion or mind, Durkheim carries the analysis to the social, to the functionally antecedent social bond. Suffice it to say that for Durkheim the authority *and* the desirability of society in human life transpose themselves into the constitutive tissues of morality.

Durkheim is not insensitive to the fact that circumstances of crisis may arise in any individual's life with respect to moral principles or facts. The source of morality is society, and between man and society there is an indissoluble bond. But this does not mean that convulsions in the social order or conflicts in the moral sphere outside the individual do not register themselves in individual thought and behavior. In periods of sharp change, of the succession of one phase of society for another, the consequences are to be seen, not in conformity but in what may be widely regarded as revolt against the social and moral orders. In fact, as Durkheim tirelessly explains, the individual is rebelling not against the social order as a whole but against one or more aspects of it, and it is his very conformity to some other aspect or aspects —perhaps new, still only dimly perceived aspects to most persons— that supplies the rebel indeed with the motive force of his opposition that seemingly is directed to the whole of society. We shall have much more to say about this in the next chapter, on deviance.

Nor is Durkheim unaware of the fact that, while both duty and desirability are involved in the moral act, there may be tension between the two elements; there may be at times in the history of a society a greater emphasis upon the desirable than upon the obligatory. Such a period Durkheim thought to be upon the West in his own day.

> For the feeling of obligation to appear in all its strength there must exist a closely wrought moral system prevailing without opposition. Today traditional morality is shaken and no other has been brought forward to replace it. The old duties have lost their power without our being able to see clearly and with assurance where our new duties lie. Different minds hold opposed ideas and we are passing through a period of crisis. It is not surprising that we do not feel the pressure of moral rules as they were felt in the past.[11]

But none of this is tantamount to finding the individual separated from society; only from a traditional, perhaps passing phase of society or from a specialized aspect of society to be found in an economic or ethnic grouping that is "official" but yet by no means inclusive of all individuals in the society at large. At no point does Durkheim ever lose sight of the multiple and diverse character of what we are prone to call "the morality" of a given modern nation. In the very simplest and most homogeneous societies alone does a monistic morality exist. That morality may have been defined by a very large number of Americans—to use one example here—in essentially middle-class WASP terms earlier in the century, with little if any regard paid to other codes, did not mean that such other codes did not exist in fact in the diversely ethnic and socially variegated "melting pot" that was the American nation. More to the point here, what the "official" culture in America often pronounced immoral was no more than conformity to "nonofficial" but not the less morally binding ways of behavior to be found in America.

If there is one other trait Durkheim finds in morality beyond those mentioned, the obligatory and the desirable, it is the one previously referred to for purposes of comparison, the one that is fundamental to religion: the *sacred*. Between morality and moral values on the one hand and, on the other, religion and the sense of the sacred there is, Durkheim argues, a vital relation.

Certainly I will maintain the sacred character of morality. I base my opinion, not upon any feeling that I personally may have, but upon the facts. It is impossible to imagine, on the evidence, that morality should entirely sever its unbroken historic association with religion without ceasing to be itself. . . . Morality would no longer be morality if it had no element of religion. . . . The respect which we have for the human being is distinguishable only very slightly from that which the faithful of all religions have for the objects they deem sacred.[12]

THE SOCIAL CONTEXTS OF MORALITY

There is a passage toward the end of the essay from which I have just been quoting that admirably puts into focus Durkheim's position with respect to the social character of morality. He writes:

Society has consecrated the individual and made him preeminently worthy of respect. His progressive emancipation does not imply a weakening but a transformation of the social bonds. The individual does not tear himself from society but is joined to it in a new manner, and this is because society sees him in a new manner, and wishes this change to take place.[13]

From this sounding of the major theme we may move immediately to the work in which Durkheim has set forth in greatest detail his ideas on not merely the nature of normality but the processes of socialization through which codes of morality become internalized in the individual, *Moral Education*. It is this work, perhaps above any other, that establishes in a very concrete way affinity between Durkheim and Mead. The subtitle of the book is "A Study in the Theory and Application of the Sociology of Education." While Durkheim does indeed address himself to education in the ordinary sense of the word, the book is in larger part what its title implies, an analysis of the processes operative in the individual's interaction with the codes and norms of morality in society. That these are without exception social may be assumed in advance on the basis of what has already been quoted from Durkheim in this chapter.

There are, Durkheim argues, three basic sociological processes involved in the individual's internalization of moral values.
First, what he calls "the spirit of discipline"; second, "attachment
to social groups"; and third, "autonomy" or self-determination.

DISCIPLINE   There is a substantial difference between Durkheim's
view of the function of discipline in the formation of the moral
personality and that which can be extracted from the writings of
most utilitarians and critical rationalists in his day. For them, as
Durkheim observes, discipline is a necessary evil at best, a means
of socialization that is artificial and invasive of the real being of
man.

> For Bentham, morality, like law, involved a kind of pathology.
> Most of the classical economists were of the same view. And doubt-
> less the viewpoint has led the major socialist theoreticians to deem
> a society without systematic regulation both possible and desirable.
> The notion of an authority dominating life and administering law
> seemed to them an archaic idea, a prejudice that could not persist.[14]

This, Durkheim declares flatly, is a false view of the function
of authority in the molding of human personality and of the relation between authority and morality. Authority not only but-
tresses morality; in a real sense authority *is* morality. Authority
"performs an important function in forming character and personality in general. In fact, the most essential element of character is this capacity for restraint or—as they say—of inhibition,
which allows us to contain our passions, our desires, our habits,
and subject them to law."[15] In his *Professional Ethics,* along the
same line, Durkheim writes: "There is no form of social activity
which can do without the appropriate moral discipline. . . . The
interests of the individual are not those of the group he belongs
to and, indeed, there is often a real antagonism between the one
and the other." There must, therefore, be some (external) system
which brings into some degree of reconciliation the interests of
the group and those of the individual, some system "which obliges
him to respect them, and this system can be not other than a

moral discipline. For all discipline of this kind is a code of rules that lays down for the individual what he should do so as not to damage collective interests and so as not to disorganize that society of which he is a part."[16]

Morality is at bottom discipline; such discipline has the double objective of promoting regularity in human behavior and of providing individuals with "determinate goals" which are the necessary anchors of human existence. To argue as the utilitarians and other progressive-rationalists of the time argued, that the ideal of socialization is an atmosphere devoid of discipline or authority, is to miss utterly the role of discipline in the development of personality. It is as vital to psychological growth as oxygen is to physiological growth.

> By means of discipline we learn the control of desire without which man could not achieve happiness. Hence, it even contributes in large measure to the development of that which is of fundamental importance for each of us: our personality. The capacity for containing our inclinations, for restraining ourselves—the ability that we acquire in the school of moral discipline—is the indispensable condition for the emergence of reflective, individual will.[17]

None of this means, of course, that discipline is a constant thing from group to group or from age to age. There is, Durkheim insists, a history or evolution of discipline as surely as of any other aspect of society or of personality. "Not only does the content of discipline change, but also the way it is and should be inculcated."[18] In simple societies where social life tends to be very direct, without necessity of complex techniques of mediation, morality and discipline are also direct, assimilated almost unconsciously. In our own society, however, with its far greater complexity, "the rules of morality require intelligence in their application." There must be much greater effort expended in clarifying, in making intelligible, and also in allowing for certain deviations on the part of the individual. It does not follow from a belief in the need for discipline that discipline involves "blind and slavish submission." "Moral rules must be invested with that authority without which they would be ineffective. However, since a certain point in history, it has not been necessary to remove authority from the realm of discussion, converting it into icons to which man dare not, so to speak, lift his eyes."[19] We shall say more on this point when we come in a moment to Durkheim's treatment of individual autonomy.

Nevertheless, with whatever allowance made for modernity and for individual reason, some form of discipline is absolutely crucial to morality in any proper sense of the word. Discipline is, we can conclude from Durkheim's statement of the matter, the steel spring not only of development of personality but of the social bond.

> In sum, the theories that celebrate the beneficence of unrestricted liberties are apologies for a diseased state. . . . Through the practice of moral rules we develop the capacity to govern and regulate ourselves, which is the whole reality of liberty. Again, it is these same rules that, thanks to the authority and force vested in them, protect us from those immoral and amoral forces besetting us on every hand. "Rules" and "liberty" are far from being exclusive or antithetical terms. The latter is possible only by virtue of the former.[20]

ATTACHMENT TO GROUPS The second main aspect or context of individual morality is to be found in the social group, or rather in the individual's attachment to the group. Apart from such attachment the all-important qualities of duty and desirability which we have seen to be the chief identifying elements of morality could never germinate at all; nor could the psychological force of discipline ever come into being and shape the personality and its moral content. We saw that even in his first book, the *Division of Labor,* Durkheim had given profound emphasis to the social basis of morality. "Let social life disappear," he there wrote, "and moral life will disappear with it, since it would no longer have any objective."[21]

Society is the most natural thing in the world. "Between it and us there is the strongest and most intimate connection, since it is a part of our own being, since it in a sense constitutes what is best in us. Under these conditions, one can understand how uncertain the life of the self-centered persons, the egoist is. For he goes contrary to nature."[22]

But man does not interact with society at large; only with its concrete manifestations, its groups, communities, and associations. It is the essence of social life, especially modern, that man lives in the midst of many groups. There is the family, the local community, the political association, church, and many others. Only in the individual's highly specific interaction with, socialization by, one or more of such groups in each of the successive phases of the individual's life, is it possible for the social context of morality to reveal itself. "Family, nation, and humanity represent different phases of our social and moral evolution, stages that prepare for, and build upon, one another. Consequently, these groups may be superimposed without excluding one another. Just as each has its part to play in historical development, they mutually complement each other in the present."[23]

We must not forget at this juncture the significance Durkheim gave to the intermediate associations we considered in the chapter on political sociology. That significance was, as we noted, basically moral, though not the less psychological. Because the sense of atomism increases in modern life, because there is an acceleration of tendencies toward anomie and estrangement, results of large-scale capitalism and of the centralized, remote, national state, associations must be created which will be adequate contexts for the development and reinforcement of moral bonds among individuals. Durkheim has little to say of these in *Moral Education* for in this work he is primarily concerned with the processes of socialization to be found in the individual. But what he had already said on the subject of intermediate associations in *Suicide* and the second edition of the *Division of Labor* can be seen, so to speak, between the lines of *Moral Education*.

Durkheim does not deny for a moment that there are great moral figures in the history of mankind, the kind of figures to which Weber applied the concept of charisma. Without such in-

dividuals—Buddha, Socrates, Christ, Mohammed, and others—
there would never have been any breaks in the routine, any
deviations from existing codes. In this Durkheim is one with
Weber. But Durkheim sees the real effect and power of such individuals in terms of the "great human groupings that they personified." Granted that in a Socrates or Confucius purely individual genius is to be found at a higher level than we see in ourselves
and with this the sense of commanding influence upon other lives.
We still cannot isolate such individuals from either their personal
attachments to human groupings—call them followers, disciples,
or believers—around them or from the much larger human groupings which they and their initial groupings have created over time
and within which the essence of these exhalted individuals' appeal continues to be found. Writing of Moses, Socrates, Buddha,
Confucius, Christ, Mohammed, and Luther, Durkheim says of
their greatness:

> We consider them so not only because they are great men—
> that is to say persons like ourselves although endowed with more
> talent; but because in our minds they identify themselves with the
> impersonal ideal that they embodied and the great human group-
> ings that they personified, we see them as raised beyond the condi-
> tion of human beings and transfigured. That is why popular imagi-
> nation, if it has not deified them, has nevertheless felt a need to
> set them apart and to identify them as closely as possible with
> divinity.[24]

AUTONOMY   The third of the contexts of morality is more nearly
what most of us would deem to be individual and at the same
time rational, though Durkheim does not yield a bit in his declaration that even this context is basically derived from society.
What Durkheim has in mind here is strikingly analogous to what
Simmel called "autonomization" as a process in the formation of
abstract thought. Genuine thought begins in the human mind,
Simmel tells us, when it becomes possible for thought to become
disengaged in rising degree from the struggle for existence. Originally cognition was no more than a means by which man engages

environment for survival purposes. But with the advance of culture, with the differentiation of functions in society, cognition increasingly becomes its own reason for being: a condition resulting in the appearance of philosophical systems in due time. There are, of course, other examples of autonomization Simmel gives us, including law, which is in the beginning inseparable from religion and family but in the course of time becomes distinct and autonomous from these realms.

Durkheim has this Simmelian sense of autonomy in mind, and he also is suggesting to us that one of the principal results of social development is the individual's ever greater sense of being "liberated from direct dependence on things." He uses the example of our knowledge of the outside world. Given this knowledge, "the world, properly speaking, is no longer outside us; it has become a part of ourselves, since we have within us a system of symbolic representations that adequately express it. Everything in the physical world is represented in our consciousnesses by an idea. . . ."[25] Consequently in order to know—that is, given very large knowledge of the physical world—what the physical world is like, in most instances, simply look within ourselves to our ideas of that physical reality.

In the moral sphere, Durkheim goes on, there is precisely the same autonomy to be found. Just as the mind's awareness of and internalization of the external physical world is in fact the individual's liberation from that world to a degree the unknowledgeable, insentient individual can never know, so also is the mind's comprehension of the moral world the basis of liberation—or autonomization.

> This is the only kind of autonomy to which we have any claim; and the only kind having value for us. It is not an autonomy that we get prefabricated from nature, that we find at birth among our constituent attributes. Rather, we fashion it ourselves to the extent that we achieve a more complete knowledge of things. It does not imply that the human being, in any of his aspects, escapes the world and its laws. We are an integral part of the world; it acts on us, it penetrates every part of us, and it must be so; without this

pervasive influence our consciousness would be empty of all content. . . . But if in some measure we are the product of things, we
can, through science, use our understanding to control both the
things that exert an influence upon us and this influence itself. In
this way, we again become our master.[26]

Morality is inseparable from the social world, and, Durkheim
writes, "it is a dangerous illusion to imagine that morality is a
personal artifact; and that consequently we have it completely
under our control." That, he tells us, is as much an illusion as is
primitive man's belief that by incantation or other assertion of
personal will he can stop the course of the sun or change the atmosphere around him. But while this is unalterably true and
while the individual by himself can never be the author of moral
existence, properly so-called, he can nonetheless be aware, be conscious, and reflective. What Durkheim is saying at some length
and in sociological detail is not substantively different, it seems to
me, from what Pascal—a French philosopher whom Durkheim is
bound to have read—wrote in one of his most memorable *pensées*,
that while man is a reed, a frail reed the universe can crush, he is a
thinking reed, and in this fact of consciousness lies man's superiority over the universe. Durkheim would surely have agreed with
that, both in its reference to the physical world and to the moral.
Such consciousness is the essence of the element of personal autonomy in morality.

TWO TYPES OF MORALITY: A NOTE

Buried away in Durkheim's *Moral Education* is a brief discussion
of personality types that deserves special consideration here, although it flows clearly enough from the preceding discussion of
autonomy in morality. One can distinguish, Durkheim writes,
"two extreme and opposed types in men's moral character," both
to be found in the pages of history as well as around us in ordinary society.

In the first type, it is "sensitivity to the rule," a predisposition to discipline and its regular processes, that one finds domi-

nant. These, Durkheim suggests, are the persons who do their duty and, more important, are really happy only when they are doing their duty as they see it. Such individuals can contain major intellects among them, and Durkheim puts the great Kant in this category indeed. The emotional faculties appear to be less developed among them than among individuals of the opposite type.

> As soon as reason speaks, they obey; but they hold their feelings at a distance. Thus, their bearing suggests firmness and resolution and at the same time conveys a sense of coldness, severity, rigidity. The power of self-control is characteristic of them. This is why they do not go beyond their rights, do not trample on those of others. But they also have little capacity for those spontaneous impulses in which the individual gives or joyfully sacrifices himself.

The second type of personality is characterized not by the overriding sense of limits and proportions but by that of "spending themselves, by an outward expansiveness." Such individuals enjoy the company of others and, with this, the sense of participating in the moral lives of others—their ends and norms.

> They love to attach, and devote themselves to others. These are the loving hearts, the ardent and generous souls. . . . If they are capable of great deeds they find it hard to tie themselves down to the performance of mundane obligations. Their moral conduct lacks, then, that consistent logic, that beautiful moral bearing of the former. One is less sure of these passionate men. For passions, even the most noble, blow successively hot and cold under the influence of chance circumstances and in the most erratic ways.[27]

What we have here, it would seem, is something rather like that contrast David Riesman has made famous, between the "inner-directed" and "other-directed" types of personality. There are differences, of course, and I would not wish to push the comparison very far. And yet as one reads Durkheim's contrast between those with "self-mastery, the power of inhibition, and of authority over themselves" and those at opposite corners who are "characterized by active and creative energy that is developed through the most continuous and intimate communication" it is impossible not to see resemblance between Durkheim's and Riesman's typologies.

Durkheim extends the contrast to whole societies or to periods in the history of a given society. When a people has achieved a condition of "equilibrium and maturity," Durkheim writes, when the major social functions are articulated, however temporarily, and "when the collective sentiments are incontestable for the great majority of people," then there is a strong, not easily yielded, preference for discipline, for law, and for the rule of order. Such preference may even extend to the arts and letters of that people, resulting in the kinds of "classical" norms we find in an age of Louis XIV, the 18th century in England, or, long before, the age of Augustus in ancient Rome. Such periods are relatively quiet, and there is even a distaste for the energies many would think in our own day to be vital to creativity. But there is the opposite type of society or age in which such energies—"romantic," as they are so often called in the histories of literature—abound in the arts with consequent valuing of innovation, of the breaking of the bounds of convention. In such times "the spirit of discipline cannot preserve its moral vigor since the prevailing system of rules is shaken, at least in some of its parts." Durkheim makes plain that he believes his own age is of the second kind. History, he tells us, records no crisis "as serious as that in which European societies have been involved for more than a century. Collective discipline in its traditional form has lost its authority, as the divergent tendencies troubling the public conscience and the resulting general anxiety demonstrate. Consequently the spirit of discipline has lost its ascendancy."[28]

Such observation is not, it should go without saying, excuse in Durkheim's mind for repressiveness either in family, school, or the social order at large. He does not doubt that society must somehow rescue itself from present ongoing currents of disorder and near-anarchy in some of its sectors, for without the social framework of general stability it becomes impossible for reason to maintain itself as an ideal, even for the genuinely creative minds to assert themselves. But precisely as Durkheim has shown elsewhere how weak and ineffectual the power of the political order, he makes vividly clear in this context how self-defeating the state is where it seeks to become a substitute for social and moral disciplines as the proffered antidote to moral breakdown.

It is innate in the character of society, Durkheim argues, that where moral anarchy is to be found there are also to be found, however dim to ordinary perception, emerging elements of a new morality. Human beings cannot endure a moral vacuum, and, as Durkheim has tirelessly stressed, it is the very nature of the social bond to reveal itself in terms of moral, even religious values over the long run. Durkheim does not doubt that ideas and perspectives of a new, different morality are existent in his own time. The difficulty is, such ideas and perspectives are still in large degree germinal, not yet sufficiently evident to public consciousness to become rallying points of a public morality.

This is the role, the appointed function, Durkheim argues, of the school, of the entire educational apparatus: to nurture these new ideas and perspectives, and above all to seek to communicate their reality and pertinence to generations of pupils. Only thus can a new moral order come into being, for the ideals of any society are rooted in the predispositions to these ideals which are somehow communicated to the young. Once, in a simpler and more homogeneous society, family and religion were sufficient to this task. Today, in our far-flung, variegated, and rationalized society, it is the school, Durkheim thinks, that has become the heir of the function of socialization, and, thus, the institution best qualified to give leadership in the search for proper alternative to the present moral disintegration that everywhere pervades the social order. In the school, Durkheim declares with almost religious faith, is to be found the best means of combining morality and reason, of giving practical representation to those basic elements of morality, duty, and desirability, and of providing the necessary social contexts of discipline, attachment to groups, and autonomy.

To many a reader of our own day, accustomed to the "blackboard jungle" for his image of the school in America, Durkheim's faith in the school will seem perhaps naïve, certainly one that has been betrayed by the history of education during the past three-quarters of a century. Not a community responsible for moral education but, rather, a bleak, grim setting of incarceration, one of repressiveness of spirit, one characterized by bureaucratization that has lost any semblance of devotion to original function, and, at opposite extremes in this same setting, the spirit of revolt, of contempt for authority in any of its manifestations, even of sabotage of the mind and its works. It is unlikely that Durkheim, were he alive today, would believe the moral crisis in the West which so haunted him in his time was anywhere near resolution even yet.

7 Deviance

There is little question that Durkheim has been for three-quarters of a century, and remains today, the preeminent theorist in socio-logical treatments of deviant behavior. Remove the uniquely Durk-heimian content of contemporary analyses of social disorganization, of delinquency, of problems such as narcotics addiction, alcoholism, family breakdown, mental illness, sexual deviance, suicide, and others which fill the pages of textbooks on social problems, and there would be very little left above the level of simple description and enumeration. So pervasive in sociology has become the Durkheimian theory of social structure in all these matters, of the social functions of deviant behavior, of processes and motivations arising in the social milieu, and of the mirroring in individual behavior of structure conflicts and constraints in the social order that it is today seldom thought necessary even to identify Durkheim's concrete historical role in this vital area of modern sociological theory.

From the treatment of crime and punishment Durkheim gives us in his *Division of Labor* down through his classic account of social pathology in the *Rules of Sociological Method,* and, perhaps above all, his remarkable account of the social basis of the incidence of suicide—an account that proved flexible enough for others to extend it to the incidence of other types of deviant behavior—in his *Suicide,* Durkheim's interest in the nature of crime, delinquency, and pathological behavior generally proved a powerful one in his life's work. There is every reason to regard his specific analyses of deviant behavior as but special instances

of his general theory of social structure, a point we noted earlier
in this book. Nevertheless, given the sheer importance of the
study of deviance in our own day and also the central and stra-
tegic role of deviance in Durkheim's theoretical and empirical sociology, there is excellent reason for giving the subject distinctive
attention here.

Predictably, Durkheim's theory of deviance rests solidly upon
social, not individual or psychological foundations. Not for Durkheim the kinds of explanation of crime and immorality which
were only too rife in his day: those which purported to find the
roots of the criminal act in personality types, even physiological
types, in instinctual or racial predispositions, or in any claimed
disharmony between individual ego and society. The antinomy
between individual and the social order which orthodox religion-
aries might explain in terms of original sin and psychologists in
terms of a persisting id or substructure of the ego was, for Durkheim, not a timeless or universal thing but, rather, one closely related to currents of history and constraints of society. It was Durkheim's genius to see that so-called nonconformity is in fact as
socially rooted and structured as the kind of behavior conventionally labelled conformist. There is a clarifying passage in the
essay on "The Determination of Moral Facts" on this important
point:

> The individual can free himself partially from the rules of so-
> ciety if he feels the disparity between them and society as it is, and
> not as it appears to be—that is, if he desires a morality which corre-
> sponds to the actual state of the society and not to an outmoded
> condition. *The principle of rebellion is the same as that of con-
> formity.* (Italics added—R. N.). It is the *true* nature of society that
> is conformed to when the traditional morality is obeyed, and yet it
> is also the *true* nature of society which is being conformed to when
> the same morality is flouted.[1]

That passage is a very instructive one and, carefully read,
suggests that the difference between Durkheim and, say, Mead or
W. I. Thomas in such matters as revolt and conformity is small
indeed. For what Durkheim is telling us in his reference to "true

nature of society" is basically what Thomas was to tell us years later in his *Polish Peasant* and what Mead pointed out in his notable passages on *perceived* social reality. Rarely if ever does the rebel act from internal drives or from any sense of being utterly cut off from society and thrown back upon his own resources. He acts in terms of motivations and constraints arising from society—but that part of society, or that representation of society, which is for him the *true* or *meaningful* society. Thomas's phrase "definition of the situation," through which he emphasized that, not society in the large or abstract, but society as it is defined to be real in the individual's life sphere is what is crucially involved in social causation would have been perfectly acceptable to Durkheim, as the passage just quoted makes clear enough.

In *Moral Education* there are abundant references to the relation between the social order and the springs of what we commonly call immorality or deviance. In his flouting of society's conventional norms the deviant, whether at the level of a Christ or Buddha, of a Caesar or Napoleon, or at the level of the criminal or suicide, is in fact drawing upon social currents which loom large in his life even if they are thought nonexistent or unimportant in the lives of those forming society at large. That great moral or political figures in history fall in some degree in the annals of deviance Durkheim did not doubt.

> We have contended that the erratic, the undisciplined, are morally incomplete. Do they not, nevertheless, play a morally useful part in society? Was not Christ such a deviant, as well as Socrates? And is it not thus with all historical figures whose names we associate with the great moral revolutions through which humanity has passed? Had their feeling of respect for the moral rules characteristic of the day been too lively, they would not have undertaken to alter them. To dare to shake off the yoke of traditional discipline, one should not feel authority too strongly. Nothing could be clearer.[2]

But, as Durkheim was fully aware, neither Jesus nor Socrates nor any other major figure of moral revolt in history ever imagined that he was operating from purely internal drives or from strictly nonconformist motivations. Jesus, as he repeatedly says in the Gospels, came not to destroy but to fulfill the law, meaning, of course, the law—the norms and codes in society which were for him real and true—that alone mattered, the law that stood for Jesus in utter contrast to what the misled and misguided were accepting. And Socrates too appealed to a justice that he could never have given his life for had that justice not possessed for him an objective, external reality in the social sphere, however different it was from the kind of justice that to his executioners alone seemed real.

What holds for the great prophet or revolutionary in history holds also, Durkheim argued, for the ordinary deviant or delinquent. Such a being may not conceive himself as, nor in fact be, in the same realm with the moral rebels that history comes in time to honor, but his acts are not the less motivated by conformity to some social constraint that for him outweighs in importance the constraints which the nondeviant obey. The suicide who, at first glance, seems to have broken by his act from society in any manifestation has in reality, Durkheim tells us, simply become obedient to those social currents which have put high, even extreme, value upon individualism, upon the "cult of the personality."

THE ROOTS OF DEVIANCE

Durkheim's initial interest in deviant or criminal behavior is to be found in the *Division of Labor*—still another instance of the extraordinary fertility of that book so far as his life interests and pursuits are concerned. We find it in his description of mechanical solidarity.

> This solidarity does not consist only in a general and indeterminate attachment of the individual to the group, but also makes the detail of his movements harmonious. In short, as these collective movements are always the same, they always produce the same

effects. Consequently, each time that they are in play, wills move spontaneously and together in the same sense.[3]

Repressive law—which, as we have seen, is the mechanism of the maintenance of mechanical solidarity in tribes, clans, villages, and other manifestations of this type of solidarity—is the agency both of definition of deviance (and in degree at least of creation of it) and of punishment. The function of punishment is protection of all the vital links of the social bond. The acts that repressive law identifies and punishes as criminal are of two kinds:

> Either they directly manifest very violent dissemblance between the agent who accomplishes them and the collective type, or else they offend the organ of the common conscience. In one case as in the other, the force that is offended by the crime and which suppresses it is thus the same. It is a product of the most essential likenesses, and it has for its effect the maintenance of the social cohesion which results from these likenesses. It is this force which penal law protects against all enfeeblement, both in demanding from each of us a minimum of resemblances without which the individual would be a menace to the unity of the social body, and in imposing upon us the respect for the symbol which it expresses and summarizes these resemblances at the same time that it guarantees them.[4]

In his next work, *The Rules of Sociological Method*, we can see the extent to which Durkheim had remained fascinated by the problem of social solidarity and of crime. The book is, of course, methodological in aim, and the immediate context of Durkheim's development of his theory of deviance is a chapter on how the investigator should distinguish between the normal and the pathological in his analysis of social facts. He disposes quickly of the then-conventional views of the pathological as being a reflection of either the "socially morbid (in the medical sense)" or the immoral. The diversity of human behavior and the relativity of morals throughout the world make impossible any declaration that some offense is a violation of "social health" or that it is universally immoral with respect to a set of standards. All one needs do, Durkheim suggests, is survey in the literature the practices, religious or lay, that one group or other deems iniquitous. For the modern Christian plural marriage is evil; for the ancient patriarch of the Old Testament such marriage was both necessary and good. The socialist regards capitalism as evil; the capitalist sees socialism in the same moral light. "The common flaw in these definitions is their premature attempt to grasp the essence of phenomena."[5]

And yet it would be myopic to ignore the social reality everywhere of distinctions between good and evil, between normal and pathological. Such distinctions are as much social data as any other forms of behavior or thought. There is, however, no alternative in social science to what is basically a statistical differentiation between the two modes of behavior. "We shall call 'normal' these social conditions that are the most generally distributed, and the others 'morbid' or 'pathological.' "[6]

We may consider average that hypothetical being capable of being constructed in thought, composed of the most commonly found traits of behavior in a given people at a given phase of its history. The so-called normal individual "merges with the average type," and, by the same token, the deviant individual is identified by his departure in one degree or another from that normal individual. Just as the physiologist deals perforce with "the average physiological type" in his treatises, identifying as pathological those types and organs which diverge from the norm or average, so, Durkheim concludes, does the social scientist. Observe, though, that Durkheim is not blind to the phenomena of history and development. Practices once sanctioned in a given people often become regarded as morally wrong at a later time. And, obviously, the reverse is true, with many a custom accepted at a later time that would have been considered evil earlier.

Durkheim offers the following three rules in summarization of his methodological preface to the understanding of deviance:

1. A social fact is normal, in relation to a given social type at a given phase of its development, when it is present in the

average society of that species at the corresponding phase of its evolution.

2. One can verify the results of the preceding method by showing that the generality of the phenomenon is bound up with the general conditions of collective life of the social type considered.

3. This verification is necessary when the fact in question occurs in a social species which has not yet reached the full course of its evolution.[7]

With these rather stark methodological considerations in mind we can turn now to what is very probably still the most famous single treatment of crime and punishment to be found in sociological literature.

If there is a single proposition on which all reasonable men are agreed, Durkheim writes, it is that crime is pathological, an example of social morbidity. This view is held despite the fact that no society has ever been discovered, in history or in travel, without crime. Crime, it is said, is abnormal by its very definition, for, leaving to one side religious or ethical systems, what identifies the criminal act everywhere is its departure from the norm that is represented and upheld by the social organization in which the act takes place. Hence the widespread tendency to be found among scholars to deal with crime, in its many manifestations, in the literature of pathology.

But, Durkheim argues, we must, in the light of all the evidence place the study of crime among the "phenomena of normal sociology." If there were evidence that with the development of human society rates of criminal behavior were declining, there might be some warrant for removing such behavior from the analysis of normal phenomena. But there is no such evidence; in truth, Durkheim suggests, there is excellent reason to believe that crime is increasing with the advance of modern society. Hence, on developmental as on other grounds, deviant behavior must be seen in terms of the same processes which are operative in behavior that is not declared deviant.

In the first place crime is normal because a society exempt from it is utterly impossible. Crime, we have shown elsewhere, consists of an act that offends very strong collective sentiments. In a society in which criminal acts are no longer committed, the sentiments they offend would have to be found without exception in all individual consciousnesses, and they must be found to exist with the same degree as sentiments contrary to them. Assuming that this condition could actually be realized, crime would not thereby disappear; it would only change its form, for the very cause which would thus dry up the sources of criminality would immediately open up new ones.[8]

Thus does Durkheim state his thesis of the inevitability of crime in one form or other. To be sure there is an ancient and profuse literature, chiefly sacred, making much the same point. But this literature reaches the point through a view of human nature that finds it basically evil and incorrigible. That is anything but Durkheim's view of the matter. He has no view of the intrinsic character of human nature, beyond declaring, as we have seen, human nature in whatever manifestation to be shaped by its surrounding culture. And if he is impervious to ancient theological conceptions of original sin, Durkheim is equally impervious to declarations by socialists and other progress-oriented minds that a form of society is at least theoretically imaginable in which there will be no crime at all. There were more than a few in his day to argue that inasmuch as some linkage is to be found between crimes and a social order like that of capitalism, all that would be necessary for the abolition of crime is the prior abolition of such structures as social class, profit-based industry, and private property.

Crime is, however, absolutely necessary—though Durkheim does not deny that its incidence can be increased through bad legislation and decreased by good laws and policies. It is inevitable simply because man is a normative creature; he judges as he perceives, and both judgment and perception are to be seen as shaped everywhere by the web of morality that is inseparable from any social system known or imaginable. None of this is to argue that any *specific type* of crime is inevitable; that would be absurd; it would lead one to a conclusion of lack of relation at all between crime and social order. But it is to argue that, normative behavior being what it is, there will always be types of behavior pronounced deviant—on a scale ranging from simple attribution of bad taste at one end to pronouncement of felony or worse at the other.

> Imagine a society of saints, a perfect cloister of exemplary individuals. Crimes, properly so-called, will there be unknown; but faults which appear venial to the layman will create there the same scandal that the ordinary offense does in ordinary consciousness. If, then, this society has the power to judge and punish, it will define these acts as criminal and will treat them as such. For the same reason, the perfect and upright man judges his smallest failings with a severity that the majority reserve for acts more truly in the nature of an offense.[9]

Durkheim is applying here a shrewd mode of reasoning he might well have acquired in the first instance from Montaigne's famous essay on cannibals or from Tocqueville's treatment of equality in his *Democracy in America*.[10] In both, with their different referents, the point is made that so long as a gross offense or inequality exists, one's perceptions will be dulled to the multitude of small offenses and inequalities. But, remove the gross manifestation of anything and human faculties will be instantly fixed upon occurrences which will suddenly take on new significance. To be sure, Durkheim would be among the first to declare that there is good in this; that even if human beings will forever find themselves declaring one type of behavior criminal, given the nature of the social bond and the broad statistical variation of human behavior, there is the ever-present possibility that the *level* of crime and punishment will rise. Those in the toils of the law and police system may forever find instances of police brutality, but something has been gained if this "brutality" rises from the hideous tortures applied a few hundred years ago in the West to verbal assault or calculated negligence today in the police courts and jails.

The inevitability of deviant behavior arises, then, not from abnormal or evil circumstances but from those which we are obliged to regard as both normal and vital for any society. It is good that there is a wide statistical differentiation in the behavior of individuals; without such differentiation there would be no geniuses, no towering moral prophets. But the same statistical range that has a Newton or Einstein, or Buddha or Jesus, at one end is bound to have, at the other end, the inept or delinquent. "Thus, since there cannot be a society in which the individuals do not differ more or less from the collective type, it is also inevitable that, among these divergences, there are some with a criminal character." Then follows Durkheim's most celebrated single paragraph:

> Crime, then, is necessary; it is bound up with the fundamental conditions of all social life, and by that very fact it is useful, because these conditions of which it is a part are themselves indispensable to the normal evolution of morality and law.[11]

Now, that paragraph must be understood for what it says, not for what it doesn't say. Durkheim, as we have seen, has a very high sense of the necessity of moral authority in any human community or organization. He was himself, both in personal life and in assessment of others, of almost stern cast of mind. Without reigning moral values, without a system of authority, and without a generalized consensus underlying that authority, there cannot be, in Durkheim's view, any society worth the name. Furthermore, while declaring the inevitability of deviant behavior in any organization, he assuredly is not declaring the inevitability of all rates of deviance, much less of any particular kind. For Durkheim in this, as in any other context of sociological analysis, the purpose indeed of analysis is the gaining of scientific knowledge that will serve as the proper foundation of social policy. And we have seen in several connections that Durkheim regarded the society around him as one in crisis, as one requiring, through the uses of reason, the achievement of a much higher degree of stability, of relief from the historically formed intensities of deviant and anomic behavior current in his age.

Nevertheless, if all of this is to be accepted and understood, what Durkheim is arguing is that in some degree deviance is both inevitable and necessary, social behavior being what it is. The scale of differentiation of behavior among individuals, the inevitable variations of correspondence between act and norm, and, above all, the normative character of the socially formed human mind, a normative character in which pronouncement of right and wrong is constitutive, all combine to make deviance necessary in some proportion. Furthermore, deviant behavior arises from precisely the same basic processes which contain nondeviant behavior.

Nor is this all. There is, Durkheim continues, a vital relation between deviance and progress; not all types of deviance, to be sure, but deviance nonetheless. "To make progress, individual originality must be able to express itself. In order that the originality of the idealist whose dreams transcend his century may find expression, it is necessary that the originality of the criminal, who is below the level of his time, shall also be possible. *One does not occur without the other.*"[12] Crime implies that, moral consensus notwithstanding, the way is open for variations which may bespeak social and moral change. According to the reigning mores of late 5th-century B.C. Athens Socrates was a criminal, and he was put to death for the crime of corrupting the morals of youth through his teachings on the rational basis of true morality and justice.

> Nor is the case of Socrates unique; it is reproduced periodically in history. It would never have been possible to establish the freedom of thought we now enjoy if the regulations prohibiting it had not been violated before being solemnly abrogated. At that time, however, the violation was a crime, since it was an offense against sentiments still very keen in the average conscience. And yet this crime was useful as a prelude to reforms which daily became more necessary.[13]

Again let it be stressed that from such a declaration Durkheim does not draw the conclusion that there is therefore no difference to be found among types of deviance. Theories that "celebrate the beneficence of unrestricted freedom" Durkheim has already told us in his theory of morality, are but "apologies for a diseased state." How do we distinguish between the creative deviant—the Socrates or Christ—and those for whom deviance is no more than a form of assault on a social order? The answer for Durkheim lies in a distinction between those for whom deviance is but the necessary step toward advocacy of a new moral code, one believed to be higher, more just, indeed the only true moral code, and those for whom "abhorrence of all discipline" is the key, those who make destruction or violation its own justification and who manifest no interest in any new or higher principle of moral conduct.

> Doubtless, with some of the great moral innovators, a legitimate need for change has degenerated into something like anarchy. Because the rules prevailing in their time offended them deeply, their sense of evil led them to blame, not this or that particular and transient form of moral discipline, but the principle itself of discipline. But it is precisely this that has always vitiated their efforts; it is this that rendered so many revolutions fruitless, not yielding results corresponding to the effort expended. At that point when one is rising against the rules, their necessity must be felt more keenly than ever. It is just at the moment when one challenges them that he should always bear in mind that he cannot dispense with the rules.[14]

It would be difficult to fault Durkheim on that statement of the matter. One need but think of the successful revolutionaries— or if we like deviants—in history: Buddha, Moses, Jesus, Mohammed, Luther, those who led the American Revolution, Gandhi, Lenin, among others. Revolt there was indeed, major revolt. But without exception there is among these a deeply rooted sense of discipline and of law. What we so often find indeed is the revolutionist calling revolt as such to a halt at a certain point, declaring the immediate necessity of stabilization, even when this means, as it so often does, dividing followers between a "Left" that wishes to continue the work of destruction and a "Right" that wishes to build a new order with discipline its cornerstone. The same Luther who declared war on Rome, successfully taking a large number of Germans out of the Roman Catholic Church, did not hesitate, when a certain point was reached, to call for order even at the price of widespread killing of those who would not be brought to order. We do not find a prescription for killing in the teachings of a Buddha, Jesus, or Gandhi, but we find ample prescription for obedience to law—the new law!

To return now to deviance and crime in their normal connotations, we can no longer, Durkheim tells us, consider the criminal as a "totally unsociable being, a sort of parasitic element, a strange unassimilable body, introduced into the midst of society."[15] Quite the contrary. There are indeed types of crime, Durkheim writes, the very existence of which is sound indication of general well being in the social order. "Thus the number of assault cases never falls so low as in times of want." To which Durkheim might well have added the truth that a great many types of crime are at their lowest ebb during time of warfare—the more intense and demanding the war in terms of human lives and fortunes, the lower the rates of crimes of assault, trespass, rape, murder, and others.

Moreover, the existence of crime in rising volume can often result in the attention of society being called to conditions which are deserving in themselves of reform but which would undoubtedly continue to be ignored apart from the association with them of rising rates of criminal behavior. Or, putting the matter in reverse, the *drop* in rates of certain types of crime can lead to a revision of a society's system of punishment.

> With a drop in the crime rate, and as a reaction to it, comes a revision, or the need of revision, in the theory of punishment. If, indeed, crime is a disease, its punishment is its remedy and cannot be otherwise conceived; thus all the discussions it arouses bear on the point of determining what the punishment must be in order to fulfill this role of remedy. If crime is not pathological, at all, the object of punishment cannot be to cure it, and its true function must be sought elsewhere.[16]

THE FUNCTION OF PUNISHMENT

It is impossible, from Durkheim's point of view to deal with crime and deviance except in the terms of punishment or announced penalty.

In *Moral Education* Durkheim asks

> What is there in common between punishment and offense? They seem to be two heterogeneous things coupled artificially. But this is because we do not see the middle term that links them, that makes a bridge from one to the other: the sentiment evoked by the offense and from which the penalty results, the feeling that is the result of the act and the essence of the punishment.[17]

The whole effect of Durkheim's continuing interest in the problem of deviance and punishment in society is to underscore this statement, that of continuity of the sentiment resulting in the collective mind from the offense and the sentiment that underlies the penalty set. In the *Division of Labor,* in the chapter on mechanical solidarity, Durkheim had stressed the fact that punishment's function lies in nothing so rational or utilitarian as simple deterrence or quid pro quo, much less anything resembling rehabilitation. The origins of punishment lie in what Durkheim calls "passionate reaction,"[18] the direct and powerful reaction of a community to violation of its customs or laws. Among primitive peoples there appears at first sight to be no relation at all between either the character or stringency of the punishment and the offense committed. But, Durkheim points out, the roots of punishment lie less in a community's desire to do something about the offender than in the desire to do something for itself; something that manifests itself in vengeance but that is, at bottom, a mechanism of protection of itself from both the offense and any and all associations with the offense. Precisely as the individual in the presence of evil or cowardice or treason may, and often does, seek with every means at his disposal to demonstrate to all around his own perfection, his goodness, courage, and loyalty, so, Durkheim notes, does the primitive community. Hence the passionate and even undiscriminating character of punishment. The object is not the offender as such but the violation that has been done to the honor or collective conscience of the community.

Nor, at bottom, Durkheim continues, has the essence of punishment changed in modern society. We may rationalize in terms of rehabilitation or protection of society from the criminal, but, at bottom, "punishment has remained, at least in part, a work of vengeance." The basic structure of punishment remains the same, "the essential elements of punishment are the same as of old."[19] Punishment remains for us what it was for our ancestors, a means of regaining the sense of collective good through passionate reaction, through vengeance, and through vicarious expiation for the sin of having contained in the community the individual maldoer. The continuity of crime and punishment lies in the fact that it is through crime and punishment, in their spasmodic eruptions, that a community is able to reaffirm, give emotional intensity to support of the community's most fundamental values.

> Thus the nature of punishment has not been changed in essentials. All that we can say is that the need of vengeance is better directed today than heretofore. The spirit of foresight which has been aroused no longer leaves the field so free for the blind action of passion. It contains it within certain limits; it is opposed to absurd violence, to unreasonable ravaging. More clarified, it depends less on chance. One no longer sees it turn against the innocent to satisfy itself. But it nevertheless remains the soul of penalty. . . .[20]

Always Durkheim considers the roots of punishment, of reaction to deviance and crime, in the assembled moral values which for him is the collective conscience. Just as deviance is itself based in the social order, in, first, the inevitable differentiation of behavior that must exist wherever human beings congregate and, second, in the identification with values, social in origin but possessed by but small minorities or individuals, so is punishment itself a manifestation of the social bond.

Every strong state of conscience is a source of life; it is an essential
factor of our general vitality. Consequently, everything that tends to
enfeeble it wastes and corrupts us. There results a troubled sense
of illness analogous to that which we feel when an important function is suspended or lapses. It is then inevitable that we should
react energetically against the cause that threatens us with such
diminution, that we strain to do away with it in order to maintain
the integrity of conscience.[21]

Durkheim continued this line of analysis in all of his subsequent writings: in *The Rules of Sociological Method*, in *Suicide*,
in *The Elementary Forms of Religious Life*, as well as in the lectures and notes later brought together in *Moral Education* and in
Professional Ethics and Civic Morals. His notable treatment of
interdictions in the *Elementary Forms* is clearly rooted in the theory of punishment he had elaborated twenty years earlier in the
Division of Labor.[22] Interdictions in primitive (and modern) religions have their origins in the systematic efforts by individuals
and cults to purge themselves of any sign of profanation. The
willingness to endure abstinences and mortifications, often nearly
lethal in character, arise in religion from the communicant's desire to insulate himself from any possibility of contact with the
evil or the profane. Punishment in society at large serves vicari-
ously much the same objective; it is a means of action through
which, by infliction of suffering and pain upon the offender, the
community purges itself of the guilt generated by the criminal
act. Again we see how profoundly held by Durkheim is the essentially moral perspective he takes toward association of any kind.
Society and morality are but two sides of the same coin.

The essence of punishment, then, is vengeance or blame.
This holds as true for the school, profession, or athletic contest
as it does for the modern state with its apparatus of law. In *Moral
Education* there is an interesting and valuable discussion of the
kind of punishment that is in our day appropriate to the pupil
who breaks the rules.

Since punishing is reproaching, the best punishment is that which
puts the blame—which is the essence of punishment—in the most

expressive but least expensive way possible. . . . It is not a matter
of making him suffer, as if suffering involved some sort of mystical
virtue, or as if the essential things were to intimidate and terrorize.
Rather it is a matter of reaffirming the obligation at the moment
when it is violated, in order to strengthen the sense of duty, both
for the guilty party and for those witnessing the offense—those
whom the offense tends to demoralize. Every element of the penalty
that does not promote this end, all severity that does not contribute
to this end, is bad and should be prohibited.[23]

One of the more arresting discussions in *Moral Education* is
concerned with the history of punishment in schools in Western
Europe. Durkheim begins with the observation that, despite popular opinion, the treatment of apprentices and pupils in primitive and folk societies is much gentler than what may be found to
have existed in Renaissance and Reformation Europe. What one
finds in the so-called lower societies is almost excessive indulgence
of childrens' delinquencies. Among more than a hundred of such
societies compared, Durkheim tells us, only thirteen were found
with severe systems of penalty for children and pupils. In ancient
Rome, before the age of Augustus, punishment of children seems
to have been mild, despite the *patria potestas* which in theory allowed the household father the punishment of death for any er-
rant member of the family, young or old. So long as the household remained the context of education, physical punishment or
extreme penalty of any kind was rare, almost unknown. But all
of this changed drastically, Durkheim writes, when, after Augustus commenced his massive transformation of Roman society in
the wake of the Civil Wars, the institution of the public school
arose—where instruction was carried on by professional teachers,
mostly Greek in the beginning—and where, accompanying the inevitably greater impersonality of atmosphere, the system of discipline became harsher and ever more corporal. The use of the rod
on the bare body of the erring pupil became, before the end of
the 1st century, very common, and in more extreme offenses, the
same lash was used on the pupil that had long been used on the
recalcitrant slave.

Far more severe, however, was the school punishment of the Middle Ages and also the Renaissance. "Here again the severity was less at the beginning than at the end. It was toward the thirteenth century that such harshness attained its maximum, that is to say, at the time when universities and colleges were established and peopled, when the scholarly life of the Middle Ages itself achieved its highest point of development and organization."[24] So harsh were the corporal punishments in the later Middle Ages and the Renaissance in Europe that in a great many places expressions of opposition to such harshness, declarations of need for regulation of punishment, may be found. The chief correctional means were the lash, the rod, kicking, slapping, striking with the fist, incarceration, prolonged kneeling, and the *vellicatio* or punitive tickling. Effective opposition to this harshness came chiefly from the Jesuits, Durkheim notes, although Rabelais, Montaigne, and Erasmus have their due passages of opposition to it. To explain this harshness by declaring it but the transfer from the family to school of household discipline is false, Durkheim argues. Everything we know about the disciplining of children in societies where kinship is the exclusive or dominant means of socialization indicates the relatively mild nature of that disciplining. "There is something in the nature of the school that strongly inclines it to this type of punishment (harsh, corporal punishment); once established, it persists for centuries despite all protests against it and even despite the most frequently repeated legal prohibitions."[25]

Why is this the case? How do we account for the fact that in more advanced civilization the school, "the very seedbed of humane culture," should reveal a degree of cruelty to children unknown in the simpler societies? Durkheim's answer suggests that in the process of transfer of familial function to the school a certain dislocation has occurred, a dislocation of context. What tends repeatedly to happen is that the residual authority of the father over the child gets transferred to the schoolmaster, who makes it actual and operative, but what does *not* get transferred is the spirit of the kinship community, a spirit in which discipline is seen as but the stepping stone to personal autonomy, to self-discipline. Add the fact that the content of the school curriculum is alien to the life the child has known in the home. There is not the same continuity of function and discipline, with the latter serving simply as the format of the former. Hence the abstractness of the school curriculum, its seeming irrelevance to the child's perceived realities around him.

The solution to this does not lie for Durkheim in any relaxation of authority as such, for, as we have seen, the spirit of discipline is absolutely necessary in Durkheim's view for the inculcation of morality. All the more important is discipline when the content of education is the content of civilization itself—language, literature, mathematics, science, and so forth, fields which by no stretch of the imagination can be expected to come easily to the child, to become as easily and quickly a part of his nature as the more primitive life and norms of simpler cultures does through the mediation of family alone. What must be done, Durkheim suggests, is to convey the idea to the child that the authority seemingly wielded by the teacher is not in fact the teacher's authority, his personal rule over the child, but is rather "a moral power superior to him," the teacher, as well as to the child. The teacher "must make the students understand that it imposes itself on him as it does on them; that he cannot remove or modify it; that he is constrained to apply it; and that it dominates him and obliges him as it obliges them."[26]

The firmest authority, in short, is that which epitomizes the social conscience itself, which gives fullest expression to *all* of the attributes of morality, especially attachment to group and personal autonomy, as well as the spirit of discipline alone. The most effective and humane punishment is that which is made to seem a reflection of the impersonal but nonetheless communal authority of the social order; not the mere possession of an individual to wield in seeming isolation from that social order. Whether it is the school, the profession, the church, or society as a whole, both the deviant act and the responding punishment must be perceived in terms of the collective conscience.

SUICIDE AS DEVIANCE

No treatment of Durkheim's theory of deviant behavior could be complete without reference to his most famous single empirical work, *Suicide*. That it is fundamentally a study in deviance Durkheim makes clear both at the beginning and the end of the work. By every reasonable sociological standard, suicide must be regarded as an immoral act, one in contravention of the social bond. It is an error, Durkheim tells us, to assume that the suicide, in killing himself, injures himself alone and not society.

> Society is injured because the sentiment is offended on which its most respected moral maxims today rest, a sentiment almost the only bond between its members, and which would be weakened if this offense could be committed with impunity. . . . From the moment that the human person is and must be considered something sacred, over which neither the individual nor the group has free disposal, any attack upon it must be forbidden. . . . If violent destruction of a human life revolts us as a sacrilege, in itself and generally, we cannot tolerate it under any circumstances. A collective sentiment which yielded so far would soon lose all force.[27]

Suicide is at once a work in applied and theoretical sociology. Durkheim's announced intent in making his study is to seek causes of and therefore remedies for what he regards as the alarming increase in rates of suicide in the Western countries during the modern age. But while this is assuredly Durkheim's intent, so also is it his intent to demonstrate that suicide, properly regarded as perhaps the most individual, the most intimately personal of all human acts, can be best understood through structural analysis; that is, by commencing with society, not the individual. What we have in *Suicide* is, then, a work of profoundest theoretical and methodological importance but also one that does not shrink from consideration of vital matters of social policy.

How do we account for variable rates of suicide in human society? In precisely the same way we account for variable rates of deviance in general and, for that matter, for all types of human behavior: through inquiry into the variable social structures we find in history and in any complex society and into the variable relationships of such structures to individual human beings. It is not necessary to repeat here what was dealt with generally in the chapters on social structure and social psychology. Suffice it to say that it is on the basis of his general theory of structure and social psychology that Durkheim builds his analysis of the incidence of suicide in society. There are, Durkheim argues, three major types of suicide, or, if we prefer, of suicidal currents: *egoistic, anomic,* and *altruistic.*

EGOISTIC Suicide, Durkheim discovered, varies with the degree of integration, of cohesion, of the groups individuals live in; varies, that is, inversely. His initial investigation had shown that there is less suicide among the religious, particularly among those who belong to the traditional and corporate religions which exercise a great deal of discipline over individual lives, among the rural-agricultural, and among those living in strongly articulated kinship systems. Conversely, there are higher rates of suicide among the nonreligious, or among those belonging to the more individualistic and rationalistic religions, among urban-industrial workers, and among the unmarried. The reason for this variability is not to be found in any distinctive or unique attribute possessed by religious, kinship, or local society, but, rather, in an attribute that is common to them all. And this is degree of integration of the individual to the group.

> . . . The more weakened the groups to which he belongs, the less he depends on them, the more he consequently depends only on himself and recognizes no other rules of conduct than what are founded on his private interests. If we agree to call this stage egoism, in which the individual ego aserts itself to excess in the face of the social ego and at its expense, we may call egoistic the special type of suicide springing from excessive individualism.[28]

As we observed in the chapter on social psychology, Durkheim sees in man a duality of nature, the first side physical, inherited through germ plasm, the second and the more important the social, acquired through acculturation and socialization.

Social man necessarily presupposes a society which he expresses and serves. If this dissolves, if we no longer feel it in existence and action about and above us, whatever is social in us is deprived of all objective foundation. All that remains is an artificial combination of illusory images, a phantasmagoria vanishing at the least reflection; that is, nothing which can be a goal for our action. Yet this social man is the essence of civilized man; he is the masterpiece of existence.[29]

It must not be thought, however, that hyperindividualization is the result of forces lodged in the individual which seek release from social constraint. There is no flavor of Freudianism in Durkheim's analysis of egoistic suicide and of the nature of the processes involved in the individual's release from group cohesion. Even the individualism that is the context, that is, indeed, but another name for social disintegration, is itself a social current, one formed by historico-social forces, not psychological or physiological ones. History shows us that waves of depression and disillusionment can come over entire societies, their consequences to be seen in diminishing relation between the individual and social groups to which he belongs. There are, in sum, *social* currents to which we may give the labels "individualism," "secularism," and the like but which are at bottom currents of social disintegration, of weakened relation between men and their accustomed communities.

. . . As these currents are collective, they have, by virtue of their origin, an authority which they impose upon the individual and they drive him more vigorously on the way to which he is already inclined by the state of moral distress directly aroused in him by the disintegration of society. Thus, at the very moment that, with excessive zeal, he frees himself from the social environment, he still submits to its influence.[30]

Egoism, the excessive falling-back upon one's self, conceived by the subject as a self ever-more disconnected from the selves of others, is thus not simply a descriptive term to cover the type of

suicide here referred to; it is explanatory in that it goes right to
generating cause. Ages of history, or societies, overwhelmingly
characterized by cultural emphasis upon the self, the ego, and the
states of mind, philosophy, literature, and art which are recur-
rently associated with such emphasis, are invariably ages, Durkheim concludes, of sharp rise in rates of suicide—and also of other
types of equally deviant behavior.[31]

ANOMIC This type of suicide is, as Durkheim describes and ana-
lyzes it, closely enough linked to egoistic suicide to lead a good
many students to the conclusion that anomie could be made a
special manifestation of egoism rather than a distinguishable
state. I am myself inclined to agree with Durkheim, however,
that anomic suicide, like the state of anomie from which it proceeds, is worthy of separate analysis.

"No living being can be happy or even exist unless his needs
are sufficiently proportioned to his means. In other words, if his
needs require more than can be granted, or even merely something of a different sort, they will be under continual friction and
can only function painfully."[32]

In this statement Durkheim draws our attention to the role
of norms once again in human behavior. Needs, as Durkheim
uses the word here, go well beyond the physiological needs of
man; while these are basic and inextinguishable, they coexist
with and often manifest themselves entirely through acquired social needs. And when we refer to means we have the phenomenon
of differential or marginal behavior in mind. One's needs, even
his obsessing, gnawing needs, may be at a level of human affluence or social morality that to the outsider might seem meretri-
cious and artificial. But what matters, as Durkheim was one of the
very first to realize, is differential or relative deprivation. The
man with a million dollars may acquire so agonized a need for
increasing his wealth that failure can plunge him into depths of
depression and destructive torment unimaginable to the individual with only meager needs. It is the phenomenon of relative
abundance and deprivation that alone can throw light upon the

well-attested fact that contentment may coexist with poverty while discontent of extreme degree may go with wealth that by all ordinary standards is ample.

It is not within the resources of man's physiologically born character to set limits to desires. Such desires are essentially unlimited insofar as they depend upon the individual alone. "Irrespective of any external regulatory force, our capacity for feeling is in itself an insatiable and bottomless abyss."[33] If there is nothing outside man in the way of social and normative limits upon his desires, these can become imperious and a "source of torment." As Durkheim puts it, "in extinguishable thirst is constantly renewed torture." To pursue a goal that is in substance unattainable—that is, happiness, absolute power, success, or prestige—is to condemn oneself to a state of perpetual torment.

Thus "a regulative force must play the same role for moral needs which the organism plays for physical needs. This means that the force can only be moral. The awakening of conscience interrupted the state of equilibrium of the animal's dormant existence; only conscience, therefore, can furnish the means to reestablish it."[34] Again we are brought back by Durkheim, thus, to the all-important attributes of morality: discipline, attachment to the group, and autonomy.

Crises in history often manifest themselves in terms of dislocation of the equilibrium between social needs and social means that we find ordinarily in individual lives. It does not matter, Durkheim argues, whether the overriding character of the crisis is in elevation of depression of one's existence. A sudden increase in means of wealth, power, or status may prove to have as destructive an effect upon this equilibrium as does a sudden decrease.

> With increased prosperity desires increase. At the very moment when traditional rules have lost their authority, the richer prize offered these appetites stimulates them and makes them more exigent and impatient of control. The state of de-regulation or anomie is thus further heightened by passions being less disciplined, precisely when they need more disciplining.[35]

So too, however, with a sharp diminution of prosperity, with a plunge into relative poverty. It is not poverty as such that induces toward anomie and anomic suicide. Poverty, as Durkheim points out, is associated with very low rates of suicide. Poverty is an evil in itself, if we like, but it cannot be used as explanation for either anomie or suicide.

> Poverty protects against suicide because it is a restraint in itself. . . . Wealth on the other hand, by the power it bestows, deceives us into believing that we depend on ourselves alone. Reducing the resistance we encounter from objects, it suggests the possibility of unlimited success against them. The less limited one feels, the more intolerable all limitation appears. Not without reason, therefore, have so many religions dwelt upon the advantages and moral value of poverty.[36]

Hence the relation Durkheim finds between rise in incidence of suicides during periods of sudden onset of prosperity as well as of depression. Hence too the greater proneness to suicide of individuals who have lost suddenly religious or moral or political conviction—assuming such conviction was deep and permeative of all spheres of an individual's life. What is crucial in these instances is the sudden dislocation of human needs from means, the former in large part socially formed, the latter inseparable from external social structures. To suffer anomie is in the moral sphere precisely like the onset of extreme egoism in the social sphere. In each instance the individual has been thrown back upon himself to a degree that is unbearable for some persons, leading to self-destruction through one means or other.

ALTRUISTIC   The third type of suicide, also social in its roots, Durkheim finds to be relatively rare, especially rare in the modern West, and the result of, not hyperindividualism or release from social ties, but of unusually great identification of the individual with his social organization. Examples of altruistic suicide are to be found among the very elderly or infirm in certain types of society where suicide proceeds from the individual's sense of duty to his society and his consequent desire to spare that society further burden rising from his infirmity. Still another example is to be found where the custom exists of a woman destroying herself at her husband's death, as in the *suttee* of traditional upper-caste India. Similarly with the suicides of loyal followers upon the death of their chief. In all such instances, plainly, it is not egoism or anomie that is involved but rather a heightened sense of obligation and duty to the organization or relationship of which one is a part. So too with the practice of suicide among the military of traditional Japan when such suicide seemed to redound to the interest of the class or the nation. And in the West Durkheim found suicides among soldiers to exist at a higher rate than among civilians, nearly all of which reflected an individual soldier's conviction that his only way of making amends for some disgrace he had brought upon the corps was through self-destruction.

In all such instances, altruism is the essence; the desire of the suicide to serve through his death a larger community of purpose.

> We actually see the individual in all these cases seek to strip himself of his personal being in order to be engulfed in something which he regards as his true essence. The name he gives it is unimportant; he feels that he exists in it alone, and strives violently to blend himself with it in order to have being. He must therefore consider that he has no life of his own. . . . While the egoist is unhappy because he sees nothing in the world but the individual, the intemperate altruist's sadness, on the contrary, springs from the individual's seeming wholly unreal to him."[37]

THE CONTROL OF SUICIDE

As I noted above, Durkheim's purposes in writing his book on suicide included the practical purpose of seeking some means whereby the rate of suicide among sectors of the population could be reduced. He leaves us in no doubt of his belief that, while suicide in some degree is as normal to a society as any other form of deviant behavior in proper degree, the West is experiencing a rate of suicide that can only mean, or at least suggest, crisis. We have seen that Durkheim's view of authority and of morality in his age contained a diagnosis of severe breakdown of the kinds of social groups alone capable of instilling in the individual the elements of legitimate authority and morality. He had made that diagnosis central in his *Division of Labor* and there are occasional hints in *The Rules of Sociological Method* of the same point of view. It is, however, in *Suicide,* the third in time of his major works, that we get the first full statement of what Durkheim regarded as a feasible and effective antidote to social crisis.

Inasmuch as the two major types of suicide in the West, each increasing in rate for relevant sectors of Western society, both spring from social disintegration, from diminished sense of relation between the individual and the social group, response to suicide must be made in social terms also. What is necessary, Durkheim tells us in the final section of *Suicide,* is the restoration of the sense of social integration in those elements of the population where this sense is now attenuated.

How shall this be achieved? Durkheim considers a number of possibilities, all of them consonant in theory at least with diagnosis. The family might, through wise legislation and benign policy, be made once again the effective force of socialization it was once in the West and still is in many non-Western parts of the world. But, Durkheim argues, the family in the West has, by force of economy and polity, become too small a group, both in numbers and functions, for it to serve the ends here of necessary policy. The extended family is a barrier to the suicidal sense of egoism and anomie, but the conjugal family is inadequate. And, given the structure of modern industry and democracy, each based in large degree upon the kind of mobility that the small, conjugal family alone can supply, it is highly debatable whether the West should seek to enlarge and strengthen the kinship sphere even if it could.

There is the possibility of religion, and Durkheim is well aware of the record of the more corporate and authoritative types of religion in the reduction of suicidal impulses. The difficulty, he suggests, lies in the fact that the religions which on the evidence are the most effective in controlling suicide—primitive religions, those of highly ritualized and liturgical character, those which declare their absolute sovereignty over the individual communicant—are precisely those which appear to be waning in the modern, secular West. The kind of religion that modern man tends most to be at home with, the liberal, rationalistic, service type of religion, shows no greater capacity on the record for reducing suicide than purely secular types of belief and association. There is no doubt in Durkheim's mind that science and rationalism are firmly based in the West, are destined to increase, not diminish their sway, and the consequence, he thinks, for religion will be an ever-continuing decline of those authoritarian, disciplinary elements which alone appear to be able to prevent the rise of suicidal impulses.

Equally futile would be any effort toward reinstituting harsh penalties for suicide—the kind which in earlier centuries led to public display of the suicide's body after it had been flayed or mutilated by the civil authorities as a means of discouraging others from suicide or announced severe reprisals against the suicide's family. The modern conscience would not permit such penalties to be restored. To suggest a heightening of moral penalty is to be confronted by the social structure that would be needed for the meting out of such penalty. What would it be? There is education, but, as Durkheim has repeatedly emphasized for us, he sees the educational system as at best little more than a mirror for the society around it; society's ills are inevitably to be found in the educational structure. And, finally, there is the possibility of the State—not through legal punishment but through State-initiated humanitarian means. But in our day, Durkheim tells us, the great States are too far removed from individuals, too impersonal by their very nature to be effective. Some external or internal crisis of immense importance is required for the State to assume even briefly the kind of authority that can affect individual conduct or motivation.

Nowhere among existing institutions, in short, is there to be found the possibility of the kind of social structure, and with it the kind of moral authority, within which modern man might achieve the degree of social integration his forefathers knew.

It is at this juncture that Durkheim proposes those occupational, intermediate, guild-like organizations we have already dealt with in the chapter on political sociology. It suffices to state once again that in such structures Durkheim saw a possible antidote to not just suicide alone, not just deviant behavior alone, but to other moral and intellectual elements of what Durkheim thought of as the modern social crisis in the West.

8 Social Change

Earlier treatments of Durkheim, especially in this country, did not give much attention to Durkheim's envisagement of the problem of change or to his theory of development apart perhaps from what was unmistakable and inescapable in his consideration of social solidarity in the *Division of Labor*. There, as will be recalled, Durkheim had argued, or attempted to argue, the evolutionary supersession of ancient mechanical solidarity by the modern structure of organic solidarity. He also tried to set forth a theory of the conditions—chiefly those of increasing population density, leading in turn to social density—responsible for the emergence from traditional society of an ever more differentiated social organization, an ever greater division of labor, and, with these, an ever greater role of the restitutive sanctions which form the legal structure of Durkheim's organic solidarity. Few students of Durkheim have found themselves satisfied with either the larger theory of development of solidarity or the correlative theory of density as the efficient cause of the development. And, as I have noted, there is every reason to believe that Durkheim himself was dissatisfied with what he had done in the *Division of Labor,* for he never again in his work picked up, even for typological purposes, his categories of the mechanical and the organic.

Nor can any systematic theory of change be easily drawn from Durkheim, though as I shall show in this chapter there are certainly to be found a good many elements of such a theory even if they are sometimes in discordant relation to one another. There is certainly not to be found in Durkheim the kind of attention to either social change or to the materials of history which lie so richly in Weber's work. Durkheim was without question a historically learned mind. The teaching he had from Fustel de Coulanges established a sensitivity to history and to historical perspective that was never to leave Durkheim. And the record makes clear that among the many students in Durkheim's own classes to be lastingly affected by the master's insights were budding historians of the first water. Even so, it would be absurd to claim for Durkheim any of the passion for history, comparative or other, that we find in, say, Weber. What we have in Durkheim is a mind largely dominated by concern with the nature and effects of social structure, with the relation of the individual consciousness to the norms, roles, and other elements of the social bond, and with the whole problem of social order. For Durkheim history is for the most part an occasional means of illustrating or reinforcing propositions on these matters. Nevertheless, this much said and emphasized, there is still a great deal of importance to observe in Durkheim's works with respect to our own contemporary interests in social development, social change, and the nature of the historical process.

THEORY OF DEVELOPMENT

Those who have argued that Durkheim's "functional" sociology is incompatible with a developmental or evolutionary perspective have simply not given enough attention either to Durkheim or to the real character of functionalism in contemporary social science. Functionalism, as one finds it in the works of its chief contemporary spokesmen, is in every pertinent respect compatible with the canons of the kind of social evolutionary theory that flourished in the 19th century. I have dealt with this in some detail in my *Social Change and History*, and will not repeat either the argument or the illustrations there used to support my contention. It will do here to note merely that contemporary functionalism, despite widespread misunderstanding, *does* include a theory of change and development, one predicated upon the role-

and status-conflicts and upon the dysfunctions to be found in all social structures, and is indeed an offshoot of classic evolutionary interest. The principal difference between classic evolutionism and contemporary functionalism lies in the latter's concentration upon the micro-elements of development rather than upon the grand, encompassing stages of evolution in institutions and societies which so engaged minds like Comte, Marx, and Spencer in the nineteenth century. Durkheim's relation is a very close one, on the evidence of his writings, to both large-scale and small-scale developmentalism.

Development, like any major idea, is a perspective. It is a conceptual framework, one in which certain characteristic questions lie ready for the asking, depending upon the special interests of the investigator. Thus, if one assumes that society or any of its institutions is in the process of development, any one or all of the following questions can be asked: (1) What is the *origin,* or the early conditions or states, from which all succeeding conditions and states have emerged? (2) What are the *stages,* or phases of development, that intervene between original conditions and the present? (3) What are the *causes* of the process of development? Are they external—to be found in wars, invasions, climate, and so on? Or are they internal—to be discovered in the structure of the thing itself? (4) What is the significance, the meaning, the *direction* of development?

All these questions are integral elements of the perspective of developmentalism. It is short-sighted and incomplete to assume that this perspective is limited to works (such as those of a Spencer or a Marx) that set out to identify unilinear stages in the process. If sociologists today pay little attention to the long, unilinear vistas of the past that marked so many nineteenth century works, they nevertheless have a continuing interest in "stages" of development in such matters as economic growth and in the "causes" and "mechanisms" of change considered internal to social systems. With few exceptions, sociologists deal with the problem of change largely in terms of a search for the self-resident, self-generative forces that the developmental perspective has always emphasized.

How does Durkheim's thought fit the pattern just described? The author of *Suicide* and *The Elementary Forms of Religious Life* could not, certainly, be considered an evolutionist in the ordinary sense of the term, but this does not mean that the assumptions and interests of evolutionism passed him by entirely. Certainly Durkheim himself did not think they had. There is scarcely an institution or group that he does not place within the framework of developmentalism.[1] The *Division of Labor* is only the most obvious example; it is, like dozens of other works written in that period, an effort to explain the present in terms of the development of society: in this instance, the development of moral solidarity. That this work proved to be the point of departure for much more than developmentalism in Durkheim's thought, and in the thought of his students, in no way belies the truth of this statement. Not only social solidarity, but also kinship, property, contract, the categories of the human mind, religion—all are couched in a framework that is as clearly premised on the reality of social evolution as anything to be found in Marx, Spencer, or Ward. In this respect, Durkheim is much closer to the evolutionary tradition in nineteenth century sociology than either Weber or Simmel, each of whom combined social analysis, not with developmentalism (in the strict sense of the term), but with history —comparative history.

Durkheim's achievement is that, although accepting the framework of developmentalism (including its search for origins, comparative stages, and endemic causes), he was yet able to deal with problems of social cohesion, personality, authority, and religion in ways that have left his work as relevant to the interests of our own age as though he had approached these problems directly.

Four points are raised by Durkheim within the perspective of development: (1) the search for origins; (2) the recapitulation of stages; (3) the causes of development; and (4) the trend or direction of the assumed development.

THE PROBLEM OF ORIGIN   The first point to emphasize is that Durkheim seems to have accepted, as completely as any social evolutionist in his century, the validity of what had come to be known as *the comparative method*. This, in nineteenth century ethnography, meant much more than simple comparison: it meant that the institutions and norms of coexisting preliterate peoples could be generally regarded as clues to the primitive origins of advanced societies; and it also meant that the logical order of simple-to-complex in which existing peoples could be placed was, in all probability, the actual order of development undergone by advanced societies. The comparative method was not born in the nineteenth century, but it was most widely used and accepted during that period. Almost every social scientist in the age regarded preliterate peoples as, in one degree or another, "living ancestors."

Nowhere in Durkheim's work can one find the kind of exploitation of the comparative method exhibited in the writings of Spencer, Ward, and nearly all the ethnologists. Few were as ingenuous, even childlike, in the telling as Spencer was (in his autobiography he relates how slips of paper, each with an abstracted primitive custom or belief written on it, were arranged in piles on his living-room floor—the arrangement reflecting, in logical order, the assumed development of the institution over an immense period of time). But all of them took for granted the reality of the conclusions drawn from the comparative method. Durkheim was much more sophisticated than most in this respect, but his work too reflects an interest in social origins that remained constant throughout his life.

The interest begins, as has already been seen, in the *Division of Labor*. No purpose would be served here by again reconstructing the argument of this work. It suffices to recall that he viewed mechanical solidarity as the earliest and most primitive form of social organization, and that his illustrations of this phenomenon are drawn from accounts of existing primitive peoples or from studies of the evolution of law based upon "traces" found in earliest legal records. But what is germane here (and too often neglected in the literature on Durkheim) is the fact that he found in primitive life more than simple mechanical solidarity; he found also the beginnings of organic solidarity. Thus, beneath the dominant patterns of early society lie the seeds of modernity. Even in the primitive family, Durkheim notes, there is some degree of division of labor and dim manifestations of restitutive law, of cooperation:

> The history of the family, from its very origins, is only an uninterrupted movement of dissociation in the course of which diverse functions, at first undivided and confounded one with another, have been little by little separated, constituted apart, apportioned among the relatives according to sex, age, relations of dependence, in a way to make each of them a special functionary of domestic society. Far from being only an accessory and secondary phenomenon, this division of familial labor, on the contrary, dominates the entire development of the family.[2]

In the same work, Durkheim attacks the problem of origins even more fundamentally, and in a way that leads directly to his later systematic treatment of this problem in *The Rules of Sociological Method:*

> There are in each of us . . . two consciences: one which is common to our group in its entirety which, consequently, is not ourself, but society living and acting within us; the other, on the contrary, represents that in us which is personal and distinct, that which makes us an individual. . . . There are, here, two contrary forces, one centripetal, the other centrifugal, which cannot flourish at the same time. We cannot, at one and the same time, develop ourselves in two opposite senses. If we have a lively desire to think and act for ourselves, we cannot be strongly inclined to think and act as others do. If our ideal is to present a singular and personal appearance, we do not want to resemble everybody else.[3]

Conflict between these "two consciences," both of which are aboriginal, is to a very large extent what motivates the whole process of social development.

In *The Elementary Forms of Religious Life* Durkheim gives a detailed account of the need for study of origins and, for that matter, of the evolutionary perspective. In the following passage, he justifies utilization of the materials of primitive religion (specifically, Australian totemism):

> In the first place, we cannot arrive at an understanding of the most recent religions except by following the manner in which they have been progressively composed in history. In fact, historical analysis is the only means of explanation which it is possible to apply to them. It alone enables us to resolve an institution into its constituent elements, for it shows them to us as they are born in time, one after another. On the other hand, by placing every one of them in the condition where it was born, it puts into our hands the only means we have of determining the causes which gave rise to it. Every time that we undertake to explain something human, taken at a given moment in history—be it a religious belief, a moral precept, a legal principle, an esthetic style, or an economic system—it is necessary to go back to its most primitive and simple form, to try to account for the characterization by which it was marked at that time, and then to show how it developed and became complicated little by little, and how it became that which it is at the moment in question.[4]

It would be hard to find, even in the nineteenth century, a more forthright defense of the evolutionary study of origins. Yet it remains true that the long-run significance of Durkheim's study of religion—and that which seems to have impressed itself on his own consciousness—is not so much developmental, in the ordinary sense of the term, as it is what can best be thought of as microsociological. In Durkheim's mind, the totemism of the aborigines in Australia was important, not so much for its assumed exemplification of religion in its earliest form, as for its exemplification of religion in its *simplest* form. It was not so much the primitive origins of religion that interested him, but the discovery of its constitutive elements. Yet it remains true that the idea of development, of unfolding, was a vivid one in his mind.

STAGES OF DEVELOPMENT   There is little in Durkheim's work to compare with the imposing sequences of stages that are to be found in the writings of such men as Westermarck, Hobhouse,

Frazer, and others who dealt with religion and morality in Durkheim's time. The middle chapters of the *Division of Labor* give some indication of the phases involved in the developemnt of social solidarity. And, after all, this book was conceived as a kind of evolutionary treatise—one in which the relation between mechanical and organic types of solidarity in human history is shown to be genetic as well as sequential. Durkheim provides brief glimpses into the transitional or intermediate types of solidarity that may well have intervened between these two major stages. Durkheim's interest in stages is to be seen in other works, as in the sections of *Professional Ethics and Civil Morals* concerned with the development of contract and property. Contract, for example, is explained in terms of stages: ritual contract, real contract, consensual contract, and finally just contract. The usual illustrations, drawn from preliterate and ancient peoples, are provided. The same approach characterizes his treatment of property. Durkheim was, in short, no stranger to the nineteenth century's fascination with stages of social evolution.

THE CAUSES OF DEVELOPMENT AND CHANGE   The nineteenth century search for causes took two main forms: external and internal. Not often—indeed, if ever—are these completely separated in the works of a single writer, but they have to be distinguished from one another. In the main line of sociology we are struck for the most part by the effort to uncover immanent, more or less autonomous and continuous, forces leading to social change. Thus Comte found the dominant motivation toward mankind's development to lie in the human capacity for awareness of the discrepancy between the actual and the desirable, a kind of built-in itch toward improvement and perfectibility. Throughout man's long history, Comte declared, the consequences of this motivational force are to be seen in the constantly ascending curve of progressive development. Marx, on the other hand, found the mainspring of social evolution to lie in certain dialectical processes rooted in class conflict; the latter being a constant in human affairs down through the final great stage of capitalism, the dissolu-

tion of which would usher in man's first real opportunity for
participation in history, that is, socialism. Tocqueville saw the
source of development to lie in the twin forces of maximization
and centralization of power, on the one hand and, on the other,
the incessant levelling of social strata. For Spencer the key to
evolutionary change lay in the evolutionary obligation of the best
possible degree of adaptation to immediate environment. All evil
is rooted, Spencer thought, in maladaptation, all progress in increasing adaptation, with the human race increasingly composed
of those who had secured an effective adjustment to environment.
Almost wherever we look, in short, in the 19th-century line of
sociology, we find an effort to descry internal and uniform causes
of change.

Here Darwin's *Origin of the Species* took greatest effect—not,
certainly, in establishing the idea of evolution (for this had been
deeply embedded in social thought long before 1859), but in increasing the scientific prestige of a single principle of explanation
of long-run change. Change was expressed in terms of processes
("variations," in Darwin's case) that are to be found in the present as well as in the past and may also be confidently assumed for
the future. Attention is directed—not toward external events and
impacts never to be repeated—but toward internal processes that
are inalienable aspects of the structure itself—be it the biological
species, the family, or the society as a whole.

Durkheim's reference to the two consciences in man—the collective and the individual—and the conflict between them has already been noted. It is this type of cause, rather than that em-
bodied in his not-very-successful effort to deal with demographic
and social density in the *Division of Labor,* that became of increasing interest to him and that was to register greatest effect on
subsequent sociological and ethnological thought. The conflict
between the two consciences is not, to be sure, a mode of psychological explanation. In his important chapter on the explanation
of social facts in *The Rules of Sociological Method,* Durkheim is
emphatic on this point. Social evolution, he insists, does not have
its origin in the psychological constitution of man, for "we would

then have to admit that its motivating force is some inner spring of human nature." He dismisses both Comte and Spencer on this matter, finding in each man an appeal to what is no more, no less, than instinct. Hence, the famous principle: *"The determining cause of a social fact should be sought among the social facts preceding it and not among the states of the individual consciousness."*

And, further, "the function of a social fact ought always to be sought in its relation to some social end." The emphasis here, in context, is on the word *social*. Any misplaced psychological effort to reduce social function to psychogenic has no support from Durkheim:

> Psychological training, more than biological training, constitutes . . . a valuable lesson for the sociologist; but it will not be useful to him except on the condition that he emancipate himself from it. . . . He must abandon psychology as the center of his operations, as the point of departure for his excursions into the sociological world to which they must always return.

This leads directly to the crux of the problem of origins in the study of social change: "The first origins of all social processes of any importance should be sought in the internal constitution of the social group." It is clear, Durkheim argues, that "the impulsion which determines social transformations can come from neither the material nor the immaterial, for neither possesses a motivating power." What is important to the sociologist is what Durkheim calls *the social or human milieu*. The principal task of the investigator ought to be that of discovering "the different aspects of this milieu which can exert some influence on the course of social phenomena." *Milieu* must be understood as comprising human beings and cultural patterns, as well as strictly social processes of interaction.

Because a number of sociologists have interpreted this—both in their commentaries and in their empirical work—as sanction for confining attention to what lies solely within the group, one point should be emphasized: Durkheim makes plain that the milieu goes beyond the simple structure of the group. The group has, to be sure, a milieu of its own (Durkheim calls it a *special milieu),* and study of this milieu—whether in a family or a pro-fession—is vital:

> Nevertheless, the action of these particular milieux could not have the importance of the general milieu, for they are themselves subject to the influence of the latter. We must always return to the general milieu. The pressure it exerts on these partial groups modifies their organization.[5]

In sum, there is every reason to think of Durkheim's sociol-ogy as falling within the outlines of 19th-century social evolution-ary philosophy. Different as his larger system of thought is from that of Comte, Marx, or Spencer, or any other major evolutionist of the century, it remains true that Durkheim, in a great deal of his work, starting with the *Division of Labor,* casts his ideas in developmental form. The *Division of Labor* is as evolutionary a treatise in its essentials as anything Spencer wrote. *The Elemen-tary Forms of Religious Life* takes its greatness today in our minds largely from its superb interpretation of the extant mate-rials on a single people, the Australians, and their religion. Mod-ern ideas of function, structure, ritual, and of the detailed rela-tion of individual to the social bond flow in great measure from this classic. It is as far as a book could be from the studies of ori-gins of institutions we find in so much 19th-century anthropol-ogy, with traits and ideas wrenched from separate cultures and fused by the anthropologist into some kind of initial stage in an evolutionary ascent. It is *one people* alone that Durkheim studies in unexcelled rigor of analysis. And yet, having noted all of this plainly, Durkheim himself, as we have seen, regarded his work as more than just a study of social and religious structure among the primitive Australians. He saw it as an investigation into *the* origin of religion in mankind, as an account of the first and most elemental of the stages which link primitive society with modern. In short, Durkheim was, despite all the commentaries which have sought to remove his "functionalism" and his "structuralism" from evolutionary contexts, very much a part of the 19th-century developmentalist tradition.

CRITIQUE OF DEVELOPMENTALISM

So much is true, but what is equally true, even if far more limited in scope, is that in Durkheim we can find some of the most brilliant criticism to be found in his age of the presuppositions of developmentalism. I refer to remarks on the subject of change contained in the final part of *The Rules of Sociological Method* where Durkheim indicates the fallacy of all asserted growth- or genealogical-linkages among events and changes in society and of the imagined capacity of "stages" of social development to engender other stages. I shall come to the details of his criticism in a moment.

How far was Durkheim himself aware of the fact that he was, on the evidence of his writing, both developmentalist and antidevelopmentalist? It is impossible to say. His first full-blown developmentalism is, of course, his first major book, the *Division of Labor.* The criticism I refer to here of developmentalism is to be found in the final pages of his second work, *The Rules.* It should be noted, though, that in this same work, in the chapter on "the classification of social types," all of the preceding work's evolutionary thrust is to be seen once again. And, although Durkheim's next published book, *Suicide,* is clearly enough devoid of social evolutionary intent or format, his final book, *The Elementary Forms of Religious Life,* falls, as I have stressed, very clearly indeed within this intent and format.

Perhaps Durkheim saw the evolutionary pattern as descriptively useful when we are concerning ourselves with society in the abstract or in the whole, or with institutions in the same light. Who can doubt, as we survey, or imagine we are surveying, the whole of mankind through the past several hundred thousand years that certain "stages" may be discerned and, with these, certain seeming patterns of change—continuous, immanent, directional, and so on? To take a single institution such as property

or contract—as Durkheim does in his *Professional Ethics*—and set
for one's self the problem of arranging probable stages of development of each of these, or of any other institution conceived abstractly, is to move instantly into the familiar evolutionist practice of seizing upon aspects of the institution from all over the
world and then, through classificatory procedures united with
imagination, present them as "the" stages of development.

It is a very different matter, however, when one is concerned
with the concrete processes of change encountered in the study of
some actual, historically concrete institution or social organization. Here the kind of massive continuities of type, the uniformities and directionalities, and the immanence of change are assuredly not to be descried—not if one stays with the historical
record.[6]

Perhaps these considerations were in Durkheim's mind; perhaps not. There is always the possibility, by no means a unique
one in Durkheim's writing, of simple contradiction. It is a rare
book of major philosophic importance that does not have an in-
consistency or two in it. We will leave it at this. What is important, having noted the strongly developmentalist thrust of much
of Durkheim's work, is to describe now in appropriate detail his
very searching criticism of this thrust.

We can begin with his penetrating criticisms of psychological
interpretations—already dealt with in other connections in this
book—for in these are to be seen valuable criticisms also of the
conventional evolutionary view of society in the nineteenth century. Thus he takes note in *The Rules of Sociological Method* of
the large number in his day—Comte, Spencer included—who have
"designated as determining the conditions of social phenomena
certain psychological states that are relatively definite and distinctive but which are, after all, only the consequence of these social phenomena."[7] Repeatedly, Durkheim notes, sociologists have
looked to some imagined religious instinct in man to account not
only for the social structures of religion but also for the changing
types of religion to be found in history. Or if not a religious instinct, some other, equally ingrained biosocial predisposition in

man to be used as an analytic constant, as a uniform, persisting
cause, of change in time as well as of structure. It is not necessary
to repeat again Durkheim's arguments against use of the psychological to explain the social, but it is important to grasp clearly
the fact that these arguments are in a great many instances just
as effective against the evolutionary view of society as they are
against the psychogenic view generally.

Psychological states, as we find these commonly attributed,
are "too general to predetermine the course of social phenomena.
. . . When the artistic character of Athenian civilization is related with such facility to inherited aesthetic faculties, we show as
little insight as did the scholars of the Middle Ages when they
explained fire by phlogiston and the effects of opium by its dor-
mitive property."[8]

If, writes Durkheim, "social evolution really had its origin
in the psychological constitution of man, its origin seems to be
completely obscure. For we would then have to admit that its
motivating force is some inner spring of human nature. But what
could this be?"[9] Comte thought it to be man's itch for perfection,
his inevitable, adaptational "tendency toward progress." But
what kind of explanation is it, Durkheim asks, to take the phenomenon and then, so to speak, merely repeat it in substance but
this time as some imagined instinct? Or Spencer's assumed "urge
to happiness" on the part of human beings: How, then, account,
Durkheim asks, for the fact that with the enlargement and
spreading affluence of civilization happiness diminishes? We are
obliged by all the evidence and also by the canons of a *social* science to look for causes, whether of change or of structure, in social, not psychological processes. Any use of a uniform, continuous, and internal cause of change in man's assumed nature is,
from Durkheim's point of view, unacceptable.[10]

But the most original and penetrating criticism of the premises of developmentalism are to be found in Durkheim's consideration of the fallacies of the genetic view of long-run change:
the view which sees one condition contained embryonically, as it
were, in a preceding condition and emerging from that preceding

condition in the manner of growth in the organic world. Or the
view that regards social change and history in the image, not of
growth and its even processes, but of the genealogical relation between generations in the organic world. In each instance a biological metaphor—growth on the one hand, genealogical succession on the other—underlies the attempt to give pattern to social
change and history. As I have elsewhere shown in detail, these
two metaphors have exerted powerful effect upon Western thinking about change and history ever since the early Greeks, and
this effect is scarcely less evident today in the social sciences than
it was in the nineteenth century.

Durkheim, although only briefly, delivered himself of one
one of the most penetrating attacks upon these metaphoric representations of change in society to be found anywhere in the literature of sociology. His attack emerges in his excellent discussion
of what he calls the "social milieu," that is, putting the matter
succinctly, the context which any individual, social relationship,
or cultural trait has in the clustered human beings and social and
cultural elements around it. It cannot be said that Durkheim's
description of "social milieu" is as complete as we should like it,
or as lucid. Social and cultural *context* is, as I have suggested, the
nearest approximation, but Durkheim also stresses the fact that
this context or milieu, though existing in the present for anything or any person, contains the products of what has happened
in past time. That is, for Durkheim, milieu is also a historical
phenomenon, one shaped by the events and changes to be found
in the historical record. There is also an unsatisfactory effort by
Durkheim to relate social milieu to the discussion of population
and social density he had written two years earlier in the *Division
of Labor*. For all its promise as a concept "social milieu" does
not, in sum, emerge as one of Durkheim's more lucid and finished constructions.

Never mind. For purposes here, the usefulness of the concept lies in the fact that it is the springboard for Durkheim's in-
cisive critique of the *growth* and *genealogical* presupposition of
the theory of developmental change so current in his day and
ours. If, Durkheim writes, sociological analysis cannot find causal

elements in the milieu that exists for each social fact—taking "milieu" in the widest possible sense to include when necessary a whole culture or relationship of cultures—then there is no alternative but to go to the past as the genetic source of what we find around us in the present.

> The principal causes of historical development would not be found, then, among the concomitant circumstances; they would all be in the past. They would themselves form a part of this development, of which they would constitute simply older phases. The present events of social life would originate not in the present state of society but in prior events, from historical precedents; and sociological explanations would consist exclusively in connecting the present with the past.[11]

Now, even today the position Durkheim is criticizing and rejecting would be accepted by the vast majority of persons. For, given the conventional thinking of the past three thousand years, what is more obvious, platitudinous even, than the statement that the present emerges from the past, that events are genealogically connected in time with each earlier event in a series generating the later, and that social changes are best seen as emergents from social conditions over long periods of time? But in plain fact, as Durkheim so shrewdly saw, there is *not* this genealogical, this genetic, this maturational relation between the social facts of the present and those of the chronological past.

> It is impossible [Durkheim writes] to conceive validly how the stage which a civilization has reached at a given moment could be the determining cause of the subsequent stage.
>
> The stages that humanity successively traverses do not engender one another. We understand that the progress achieved at a given epoch in the legal, economic, political field, etc. makes new progress possible; but how does it predetermine it? It is a point of departure which permits of further progress; *but what incites us to such progress?*[12]

We cannot, as empirical scientists, Durkheim goes on, admit the existence of some "inherent tendency" in mankind that impels us ceaselessly to exceed earlier achievements in civilization or to increase happiness. Nor, Durkheim continues, can we accept as objectively valid any of the alleged tendencies or directions which have been found for human society, or any of its component institutions, by evolutionists such as Spencer and Comte. Direction in human history, Durkheim is telling us, is a construction of the individual student's mind, not something that exists in fact in the vast complexity of human society. One may believe, if he likes, that the "tendency" of history is toward ever greater democracy, freedom, equality; or, conversely, toward ever greater inequality, crisis, and in the long run degeneration. What must be understood, though, is that such directions are imputed; they are not to be found in the data themselves. Nor, even more important from a methodological point of view, can one assumed phase or stage—that is, in fact, one condition to be found in society—be declared the genetic emergent of some preceding phase or stage—or condition.

> All that we can observe experimentally in the species is a series of changes among which a causal bond does not exist. The antecedent state does not produce the subsequent one; the relation between them is exclusively chronological.[13]

That brief statement must be accounted among the more brilliantly original, and also profound, of the nineteenth century in the social sciences. Not even today can its full implications be said to have been grasped by more than a small number of social scientists. The philosophies of functionalism, of large-scale evolutionism, based alike upon the metaphors of growth and of genealogy, continue to occupy most of the ground today, as in Durkheim's day, so far as the understanding and interpretation of social change are concerned. To most minds, nurtured by the conventional wisdom that is no less strong now than it was when Durkheim wrote *The Rules,* only shock and disbelief can be the consequence of reading the passage just quoted. What? Refuse to admit the genetic linkage of events and changes which have been selected from the infinity of data as crucial ones by the investigator? Refuse to believe that society is an organism with growth its normal means of change? The radicalism of Durkheim's assertion can be measured by the incomprehension and befuddlement it continues to generate in the mind of the social scientist.

Reflecting on it a moment, it is perhaps possible to account in its light for the fact that the evolutionary succession Durkheim had set forth in the *Division of Labor* two years earlier, the claimed succession from mechanical to organic solidarity, was altogether dropped by Durkheim from any future use in his work. One can only conclude that he saw the same fatal weakness in that succession he saw in any produced by Comte, Spencer, Marx, or any of the other 19th-century social evolutionists.

Durkheim concludes,

> Under these circumstances, all scientific prevision is impossible. We can, indeed, say that certain conditions have succeeded one another up to the present, but not in what order they will henceforth succeed one another, since the cause on which they are supposed to depend is not scientifically determined or determinable. . . . Nothing assures us that the overt phenomena express so completely the nature of this tendency that we may be able to foretell the objective to which this tendency aspires as distinct from those through which it has successively passed. Why, indeed, should the direction it follows be rectilinear?[14]

What a devastating blow Durkheim delivers not merely to unilinear evolutionism but also to all pretensions toward what has come in our day to be called "futurology." His attack is twofold. In the first place it is an illusion to suppose that "phases" or "stages" engender one another, that they are anything more than intellectual constructions which we ourselves stamp upon the historical record, and that anything genuinely like growth or genealogy is to be found in the past or in the linkage between the chronological past and the chronological present. Second, even if we enjoy the conceit that we have in fact discerned some line of movement of "history" from past into present, there is not the slightest reason to suppose such a line will continue on into the future. Prevision, then, except in the sense of the kind of premonition and prophecy that sensitive minds have been indulging in for countless thousands of years—and with such widely varying results!—is a delusion.

None of this means that Durkheim is denying the possibility either of propositions of causality or of prediction—taking the latter word in its strictly scientific sense of what is in fact explanation. We considered this in some detail in the first chapter. It is neither causality nor scientific prediction that Durkheim is denying: Only the idea that events and changes have genetic linkages in time and the related idea that it is possible to so construe these as to foretell the future.

THE USES OF HISTORY

Although there are elements in common in the "historical" and the "developmental" approaches to the understanding of the present, with each putting the present in not merely chronological but also genetic relation to the past, there are also substantial differences between the two approaches. Unfortunately these differences tend to become blurred in most treatments of not merely Durkheim but also of Western thought generally. Thus, one finds the adjective "historical" often used in application to the strictly evolutionary treatments we encounter in such profusion in the eighteenth and nineteenth centuries. Little or no differentiation is made between, say, the "natural" histories constructed by writers like Rousseau, Ferguson, Adam Smith, and Kant in the eighteenth century, where the aim was that of reconstructing through reason, supplemented by trait-illustrations drawn from a great variety of peoples, the imagined stages of social, economic, and cultural development mankind as a whole has assertedly passed through, and the "histories" written by those such as Gibbon, Robertson, and Voltaire who were concerned with the concrete, event-by-event, person-by-person records of a given people or area. If by "history" we have any kind of reference at all to what actual historians from the time of Thucydides down to the academic historians of our own day do in fact in their works, we assuredly have something very different in view from what the social evolutionists—stretching in time from Aristotle's *Politics,* with its reconstruction of the "natural" stages of development of the state, down to the works of Comte, Tylor, Spencer, and Morgan in the 19th century—commonly do. It is not enough, as I have indicated in detail elsewhere,[15] to say that social evolutionism is simply history with names and dates omitted or that historiography is simply a more concentrated and detailed form of social evolutionism. Two very different methodologies, constructions of reality, are involved and have been ever since the time of the Greeks.

Very different metaphors of reality underly these two by-now ancient approaches to time and to the relation of past, present, and future. In the evolutionist's construction, it is basically the metaphor of *growth* that is fundamental. From this come the familiar premises of immanence, continuity, direction, and fixed succession of "normal" stages of development. The image of the plant or organism in process of ordered, inner-directed growth is the vital one in the social evolutionist tradition. In Western history-writing, on the other hand, the metaphor of *genealogy* has been the dominant one ever since Herodotus and Thucydides, especially the latter, set themselves to the task of indicating exactly how events and personages could be set in the form of a narrative. To say that the historical—in the strict sense —and the evolutionary presentations are basically the same makes no more sense, in sum, than to say that the two metaphors are basically the same. Granted that both metaphors seek to put past and present into interpretative relation, the contrast between growth in its essential nature and genealogy is nonetheless profound. No less vivid is the contrast between the "historical" and the "developmentalist" approaches to man and society.

Durkheim was both historian and social evolutionist. His two-volume *L'Evolution pédagogique en France,* published in 1938, based on a course of lectures given at the Sorbonne in 1905, is, despite the lead word in the title, much more nearly a piece of history-writing in the conventional sense than it is anything suggested by the word "evolution." It is indeed a excellent work in the history of French education from the Middle Ages on, not without its due evidences of the mind of Durkheim the sociologist, but it remains what it was intended to be: a narrative, historiographic, unilinear treatment not at all different in structure from what many an out-and-out historian was writing then and has written since. To try to harmonize the genealogical treatment of events, personages, and French institutions we are given in that book with the evolutionary treatment of social solidarity that forms the essential structure of the *Division of Labor* would be an exercise in futility. It would be similarly futile, or at best precious, to seek to find very much of the methodology of such a work as *The Elementary Forms of Religious Life* in Durkheim's narrative history of French education, though I dare say affinities between the latter and certain of the propositions contained in *The Rules* can be found easily enough. After all, it is one and the same man involved in both, and while Durkheim does indeed show a masterful capacity for handling narrative history and the techniques of historiography in the study of French education, and for regarding this kind of enterprise as a very different one from, say, his *Division of Labor,* it would be strange if no Durkheimian sociological insights at all had crept into the history of French education.

Durkheim was no Weber in his use of historical materials. Save for the strictly philosophical and methodological sections in Weber's writing, it is almost impossible to find his sociology other than deeply and powerfully suffused with historical materials—in the literal sense, the sense that is recognized instantly by any professional historian as such—drawn from ancient, medieval, and modern sectors, from non-Western as well as Western. What one finds very little of in Weber is use of ethnological types of material, those drawn from primitive peoples, from those without historical record of themselves or others, from those, in short, whose probable history or social change in time can only be inferred from structural relationships or areal locations.

Weber was the historical sociologist, the sociological historian, par excellence. His sociology is simply not imaginable apart from the wealth of historical data he incessantly used in connection with his central propositions relating to religion, law, authority, the city, and other interests. By contrast, one could strip Durkheim's work of all its infrequent historical allusions and nothing of importance would have been taken away from either its argument or its methodological structure. Weber sought his fundamental insights directly from the historical record; Durkheim sought his, basically, from the analytic nature of the social bond, from social structure and process. If the developmental approach is common in Durkheim (and certainly not in Weber!), it is because developmentalism and structuralism—or functionalism or the social systems perspective, as we like—are and have been ever since Aristotle closely connected.

And yet it would be a gross disservice to Durkheim to separate him from what can only be described as major impact upon the writing of history in our time. As I have already noted briefly in two or three places in this book, Durkheim's lectures at the Sorbonne seemed to fascinate young, budding historians, more than a few of whom would eventually reach scholarly distinction and in whose works the imprint of Durkheim's sociological concepts is plainly to be seen. Among these historians are Henri Berr, whose great synthesis of history, the work of many minds under his close editorship, brought social analysis and perspective to world history, Marcel Granet on Chinese cultural history, Gustave Glotz on Greek kinship and political history, and many others. It is well worth noting also that the now famous and still flourishing *Annales* school of historians in Paris was begun in the first instance by Marc Bloch, Lucien Febvre, and Fernand Braudel, all of whom as young men studying in Paris had been fascinated by Durkheim's own ideas and especially by the brilliant articles which had begun appearing in Durkheim's journal, *L'Année,* from the moment of its inception.

One can see why young historical minds of the originality of Bloch's, Febvre's, and Braudel's would have been attracted to Durkheim's work. In this work lay practical as well as imaginative use of concepts—social structure, social function, collective conscience, the sacred, the cult, and others—that could be uti-lized easily by historians willing to go to a different type of ar-chive than that to which the then-sovereign political and diplo-matic historians invariably went. What Durkheim had had to say about the uses of population analysis and social density in his *Division of Labor* inspired one of his own students, Maurice Halbwachs, to further work on morphology, urban ecology, and the like that had, apparently, direct inspiration for social his-torians, such as those who wrote for the journal *Annales,* in turn-ing to these areas for new interpretation of European and other history.

If there is a single idea that, on the record, modern historical theory has acquired from sociology, it is, I think, the idea of so-cial structure. I would not go so far as to say that Durkheim is either the mind first to be concerned with structure in hu-man behavior or that his is the only influence to register itself upon historians. But this has to be said: Durkheim is par excel-lence the sociologist of structure—social structure—and it was in France during his own day (when a fascinating outpouring of in-stitutional histories occurred) and later, after Berr and his *Syn-thèse* and the founders of the journal *Annales,* that much of the most interesting and influential work in social and comparative history has been done. As I observed above, it would be erroneous to cast Durkheim in the role of comparative historian himself, certainly in anything like the degree to which it is possible to cast Weber. Even so, the remarks on classes of data, on compari-son of types, we find in *The Rules* must have had their due im-pact upon minds in Paris which would later turn to comparative history in the full sense. And no one can take away from Durk-heim the creation of concepts which serve the comparative social historian very well indeed.

9 Durkheim and Modern Culture

It is highly unlikely that Durkheim will ever compete seriously as a household name with Darwin, Marx, and Freud, whether among laity or scholars and intellectuals. His influence in the social sciences has been substantial and, as I have stressed, is very likely to become even more substantial during the age ahead of us. But there is very little likelihood of this influence becoming, as has been so conspicuously true of both Marx and Freud in our century, a very part of the culture we live in.

There are solid reasons for this. Marx has become virtually canonized in a number of countries in the world. But even had nations such as Russia and China not become Marxist in official writ, Marx would still have been assured of a commanding position in modern world culture by virtue of his unique relation to the dominant themes of political, social, and economic revolution. It is not different with Freud. We live in an age of extraordinary preoccupation with the self, with the individual conscious and unconscious, and with those aberrant forms of mental life we call neuroses and psychoses. No one needs to be told of Freud's relation to all of this, of the affinity between this preoccupation, to be seen at all levels, and Freud's writings at the turn of the century. As Marx shaped our revolutionary perspective, Freud shaped our psychological perspective. Both have been mighty prophets! For even those vast numbers who never have and never will actually read Marx and Freud, these two minds, very much like Darwin, will be nonetheless powerful, shaping forces. For, to an astonishing degree, they have created 20th-century culture.

Little, if any, of that kind of influence can be claimed for Durkheim. Nor will I make the effort to claim it. What I want to do instead is highlight the relation between Durkheim's central ideas and some of the most dominating themes of contemporary thought and behavior. I repeat: it would be impossible beyond a very limited, even negligible, degree to put Durkheim's writings in causal connection with these themes; they are too diverse in their roots and manifestation, and, as just noted, Durkheim's name was scarcely known at the time these themes were beginning to become luminous in Western, and especially American culture. But lack of causal connection in no way bespeaks lack of intellectual relation. Very often in the history of thought there have been those writing whose influence was then, and remained, minor by comparison with the Platos and Augustines in the West but in whose works we, with the advantage of retrospect, can nevertheless see a striking epitomization of large and powerful cultural forces.

I believe this to be true of Durkheim's thought. Formidably scholarly and scientific though his works may be by the standards of even intelligent general readers, aloof as Durkheim's own mind was, as we have seen, to the interests of the market place, devoted though he was to the problems which arose directly from his scholarly materials, there is yet an underlying affinity between Durkheim's interests and the by-now far-flung interests of modern Western populations. This is what I shall be concerned with in this final, rather brief chapter. Irrespective of causal relation or of household status as a name, Durkheim's thought contains ideas, values, and a general sense of the movement of history which are in many ways closer at this moment to what strikes deepest in the breast of modern man than even the ideas and values of a Marx or Freud.

HISTORICAL PESSIMISM

There is in the first place Durkheim's view of the historical process, that is, its seeming direction out of the past and into the future. We have seen in the preceding chapter Durkheim's almost fierce insistence that no scientific prevision is possible, nor, for that matter, scientific derivation of the present from the past—that is, in genetic terms of necessary causality. All relationships between past, present, and future are strictly chronological, Durkheim has told us. He is, of course, correct. But Durkheim was no more capable than any of us in resisting speculation on meanings of history, on apparent directions taken by Western history. And this is what I want to mention here first. There is a certain melancholy, a pessimism about mankind's development that stands in singular contrast to the rampant progressivism of his age but in very considerable likeness to the currents of melancholy and pessimism which we find around us in so much 20th-century philosophy and literature. Durkheim's thoughts—often nearly concealed in writing with quite different overall intent—on man's increasing unhappiness, his growing moral and social isolation, and his general loss of roots in the social order are certainly among the early, major reactions to the kind of confidence in inevitable progress that we are able to find in so many of Durkheim's contemporaries.

I do not want to leave the impression that Durkheim was a prophet utterly alone in his sense of the moral crisis that was overtaking Western society. For a long time, in our histories, we tended to make the nineteenth century a virtual monolith of faith in progress, secularism, individualism, technology, and large-scale organization. Today we know better. We have become increasingly aware in the scholarship that has spread widely since approximately World War II of those minds in the nineteenth century for whom pessimism, not optimism, was the controlling mood. Tocqueville, Burckhardt, and Weber could regard the future with considerable misgiving; more to the point, could limn that dark future in impressive detail. There were others—Dostoevski, Nietzsche, and Kierkegaard—all of whom found nothing but a black joke in the prevailing belief in moral, cultural, and social progress. Across the Atlantic were Melville, Hawthorne, and, late in the century, the Adams brothers, Henry and

Brooks, for whom entropy, or at best a Brownian motion, would have seemed a fitter metaphor than either growth or progress.

In European sociology a somberness of mind is notable. Weber and Simmel reveal, in explicit statement as well as emphasis, a distrust of, or unease with, modernism. Without succumbing to defeat or total renunciation, they nevertheless display an alienated quality in their work. They saw, or could see on frequent occasions, in the present a tragic inversion of the very forces that had ushered in the modern world, that had liberated man from centuries-old oppression and superstition. It was a subversion in which individualism was becoming atomism and democratic will a new despotism (Tocqueville); in which rationalism was producing a new, bureaucratic type of regimentation (Weber); in which the urban-pecuniary economy was bringing about a displacement of man's own self (Simmel). For the major European sociologists of the period, the direction of Western social development was mixed, to say the least.

Durkheim falls very clearly in the company of Tocqueville, Weber, and Simmel in this respect. Modern development, he writes, "has swept cleanly away all the older forms of organization. One after another they have disappeared either through the slow erosion of time or through great disturbance, but without being replaced." Class, kindred, parish—all have disappeared or weakened under the massive forces of modern individualism and political centralization. Durkheim sees no likelihood of either kinship or religion becoming vital forces in human life once more, and he specifically disavows the state as the means of restoring moral or social organization. According to Durkheim, it is in the establishment of occupational organizations alone that hope lies, but it is a mark of his melancholy view of history that he explicitly places this mode of reform against the tides of "progress" and concedes it to have somewhat more relation to the medieval and ancient worlds than to anything that contemporary history seemed to be spawning. There is a broad gulf between the view of history found in the progressive writings of his day— a view resting on faith in history's capacity to resolve all organizational problems—and Durkheim's almost melancholy envisagement of the modern age.

A host of passages in Durkheim's works supports the conclusion that he considered the cohesive and stabilizing forces of European society to be undergoing disintegration—transitory, perhaps, in the longest view, but not the less real and ominous. Suicide is taken by Durkheim as the index of a very deep flaw in the social constitution; that is, "the general unrest of contemporary societies." In moderate degree suicide is normal, but in contemporary civilization "the exceptionally high number of voluntary deaths manifests the state of deep disturbance from which civilized societies are suffering, and bears witness to its gravity."[1]

He refers to the "currents of depression and disillusionment emanating from no particular individual but expressing society's state of disintegration." Such currents "reflect the relaxation of social bonds, a sort of collective asthenia, or social malaise, just as individual sadness, when chronic, in its way reflects the poor organic state of the individual." Such currents are collective; that is, social. And because they are social "they have, by virtue of their origin, an authority which they impose upon the individual and they drive him vigorously on the way to which he is already inclined by the state of moral distress directly aroused in him by the disintegration of society."[2] Admittedly, a certain incidence of suicide, like a certain incidence of crime, is inherent in the conditions which also produce high culture—the arts, letters, and the liberal professions. But suicide has come to mark in our society, Durkheim concludes, "not the increasing brilliancy of our civilization, but a state of crisis and perturbation not to be prolonged with impunity."[3]

Durkheim's melancholy does not rest on the incidence of suicide alone. In the *Division of Labor*, he had noted the nearly inverse relation between the development of culture and human happiness. States of boredom, anxiety, and despair are relatively unknown in a primitive or simple society, he observed, for the common causes of these states are largely absent. In civilized societies they mount and, with them, endemic unhappiness. One should not conclude, Durkheim emphasizes, that progress causes these states; more likely they are concomitant: "But this concomitance is sufficient to prove that progress does not greatly increase our happiness, since the latter decreases, and in very grave proportions, at the very moment when the division of labor is developing with an energy and rapidity never known before."[4]

Durkheim's attitude toward happiness has little in common with the reigning notions of his day. Far from seeing in happiness the proper goal of individual and social energies, he deprecates it: "Too cheerful a morality is a loose morality; it is appropriate only to decadent peoples and is found only among them. . . . From certain indications it even seems that the tendency to a sort of melancholy develops as we rise in the scale of social types." There is a functional necessity in sadness, as there is in crime:

> Man could not live if he were impervious to sadness. Many sorrows can be endured only by being embraced, and the pleasure taken in them naturally has a somewhat melancholy character. So, melancholy is morbid only when it occupies too much place in life; but it is equally morbid for it to be wholly excluded from life.[5]

One can imagine such a sentiment coming from Tocqueville or Weber, but not from Mill or Spencer.

Historical periods like ours, Durkheim observes, are necessarily filled with anxiety and pessimism. For our objectives are Faustian in scope.

> What could be more disillusioning than to proceed toward a terminal point that is nonexistent, since it recedes in the same measure that one advances? . . . This is why historical periods like ours, which have known the malady of infinite aspiration, are necessarily touched with pessimism. Pessimism always accompanies unlimited aspirations. Goethe's Faust may be regarded as representing par excellence this view of the infinite. And it is not without reason that the poet has portrayed him as laboring in continual anguish.[6]

This is precisely the condition that had led Tocqueville to see increasing frustration and unhappiness as the consequence of democracy, and it is the background that Durkheim sees for the general breakdown in social and moral discipline. That he regarded this breakdown as critical is plain enough:

> Indeed, history records no crisis as serious as that in which European societies have been involved for more than a century. Collective discipline in its traditional form has lost its authority, as the divergent tendencies troubling the public conscience and the resulting general anxiety demonstrate.[7]

There are still other ways of assaying the intensity of the modern malaise that has gripped European society: through the proliferation of philosophical systems based on skepticism and materialism. Durkheim compares the modern age in this respect with periods of decadence in ancient Greece and Rome when, similarly, belief-systems arose that reflected loss of faith and membership in society:

> The formation of such great systems is . . . an indication that the current pessimism has reached a degree of abnormal intensity which is due to some disturbances of the social organism. We well know how these systems have recently multiplied. To form a true idea of their number and importance is it not enough to consider the philosophies avowedly of this nature, such as those of Schopenhauer, Hartmann, and so on? We must also consider all the others which derive from the same spirit under different names. The anarchist, the esthete, the mystic, the socialist revolutionary, even if they do not despair of the future, have in common with the pessimist a single sentiment of hatred and disgust for the existing order, a single craving to destroy or to escape from reality. Collective melancholy would not have penetrated consciousness so far if it had not undergone a morbid development. . . .[8]

Such is Durkheim's reaction to an age that his contemporaries—secularists, individualists, Protestants, and progressives alike—were hailing as the onset or at least the harbinger of a new order, a new freedom, a new morality. Durkheim's is clearly an alienated view of modern culture. He is too much the child of modernism himself, too deeply devoted to science and to liberal democracy, to seek refuge in any of the traditionalisms that vain and reactionary politics sought to impose upon France and on Europe in general. But—unlike a great many of his fellow rationalists, fellow liberals, and fellow democrats—he knew that no stable order could be built directly on the intellectual pillars of modernism: until the values of science and liberal democracy were rooted in social contexts as secure and binding as those in which religion and kinship had once been rooted, and until they were endowed with the moral authority—the sacredness—that these more ancient institutions had once known, European society would continue in the state of crisis that would subvert each and every proposed political remedy.

SOCIAL DISINTEGRATION

It would be impossible to find a sociologist at the turn of the century in whose writings the themes of alienation, estrangement, and moral isolation are as vividly set forth as in the writings of Durkheim. This is not to suggest that Durkheim, in morbid fashion, celebrated these as did some of the *fin de siècle* poets and essayists of his day. Durkheim was the very last to make virtue of any of these states of mind and feeling. Nor, even for purposes of commentary, did he deal with them outside the contexts of the several scholarly problems he was concerned with. He did not ever declare them to be sovereign or universally pervading themes in the West.

But the fact remains that when, looking out on the prevalence of these themes in our own day, we seek forerunners to the voices all around us, it is to Durkheim we go more surely than to any other social scientist at the beginning of the century. He would have rejected utterly the labels of pessimist and reactionary, and nothing I write here must be construed as placing Durkheim in either camp, certainly so far as his political beliefs and his faith in science were concerned. Nevertheless, it is Durkheim, above anyone else at the beginning of our age, who told us that in urbanism, in industrialism, and in the belief-systems founded upon the individual, whether these were religious or secular, there lie the certain seeds of man's progressive isolation from both community and morality. As I have shown in the chapter on deviance, Durkheim's treatment of suicide as a great deal more than that; it was at one and the same time a profound analytical essay on the social psychology of modernity. Suicide becomes for Durkheim a kind of concrete universal. In its widening incidence in the modern West Durkheim saw not just increase in the number of those taking their lives, but also, and far more deeply and ominously, increase in the fragmentations and disintegrations of the social bond which cannot help but leave more and more individuals precariously exposed to the void on the one hand and to the absolute power of the state on the other.

Durkheim is in striking degree the philosopher or sociologist of what we today call social disorganization. There were assuredly others in his day also concerned with this, though usually on a scale so broad and encompassing as to weaken effect. Durkheim in effect takes us to the concrete sectors of modern life—industry, city, electorate—and shows us that in the process of achieving liberation from traditional unities of village, kindred, and class, we have brought into being new forms of authority which do not have, however, the capacity of fusing individual to social order in the degree possessed by the older ones. Egoism—his word for a state of the self we would today replace for the most part with alienation or isolation—is on the increase in modern world, Durkheim thought, precisely because the increasing objectivism of the society around us: that is, the seeming exteriority and remoteness of society from personal life. Such objectivism produces as its counterpart an increasing subjectivism on the part of the individual. In this observation, Durkheim was one with Simmel whose own treatment of the matter is subtler than Durkheim's but without the kind of concreteness and vividness Durkheim was able to give it in the context of his study of suicide. The point is, it is only against a background of perceived separateness and otherness of society that a degree of egoistic preoccupation with self, resulting in suicide for some, mental aberration in others, and that more diffuse state called alienation for a larger number, is likely to become present in a culture.

Side by side with Durkheim's premonitions of the twin forces of social disintegration and individual alienation in modern society's future history lie his deep convictions of the moral nature of the crisis Durkheim saw around him in the West. One need but look at the final chapters of his first book, the *Division of Labor,* to see how profoundly this moral nature lay in Durkheim's mind at the beginning of his career. And it never left his mind. It is in *Suicide,* in the chapter on anomic suicide, that we get the clearest picture of the essence of that normlessness, that disruption of values, which is for Durkheim one of the major consequences of the two great revolutions in modern life, the democratic and the industrial.

Durkheim was not the first to sense the difficulties which affluence brings to moral community. One can go all the way back to the earliest religious prophets for that. And in the nineteenth century there were a number of perceptive minds, among them Tocqueville, to point to the high correlation between increasing material prosperity and what Tocqueville called "that strange melancholy which often haunts the inhabitants of democratic countries in the midst of their abundance, and that disgust at life which sometimes seizes upon them in the midst of calm and easy circumstances."[9] But Durkheim took such ancient insights and gave them prominent place in a general theory of personality and its relation to the moral structure of society.

What has been recently called "the revolution of rising expectations" is a perspective we have no difficulty in finding in Durkheim's treatment of modern anomie. As we observed above in the chapter on deviance, Durkheim gave emphasis to what he called the "remarkable immunity of poor countries" to the incidence of suicide and states of mind associated with its genesis. "Poverty protects against suicide because it is a restraint in itself. . . . The less one has the less he is tempted to extend the range of his needs indefinitely." Obviously, Durkheim is not extolling the virtues of poverty. He is only giving social-psychological cast to the differences between the desires and expectations one finds in the chronically impoverished and those one finds among relatively affluent individuals whose recently achieved affluence has had the effect of stimulating desires or expectations well beyond immediate possibility of gratification. "With increased prosperity desires increase. At the very moment when traditional rules have lost their authority, the richer prize offered these appetites stimulates them and makes them more exigent and impatient of control. The state of de-regulation or anomy is thus further heightened by passions being less disciplined, precisely when they need more disciplining."[10]

As I write these lines I am reminded inevitably of some of the expressions on the subject of the community of poverty and on the general "revolt against affluence" which has seized the minds of a fair number of young, second- and third-generation members of the American middle class. The sense of disillusionment with affluence on the part of so many born to it in our day and the groping for a kind of consecrated poverty in communal structure—as in the communes today in both rural and urban areas—both have their illumination in Durkheim's treatment of anomie, though he did not, so far as I know, predict any "revolt against affluence" for this century.

In sum, it is the very concentration upon the moral factor in human behavior and organization that allows Durkheim to deal as illuminatingly as he does with affluence as a potentially disintegrative force upon the social structure. In one of his essays, the late economist Lord Keynes speculated on what effect the solving of the economic problem for a majority of human beings—that is, their release from any of the disciplines which spring from either poverty or necessity of job—would have upon the social bond. Lord Keynes was not certain. Nor can we be. But if such a time came and if increased rates of social disorganization were indeed the consequence, we should not have to look far beyond Durkheim's writing for sociological and social-psychological explanation. In any event, release or not from the disciplines of economics, we have seen in the West and especially in America during the past quarter of a century what Eric Hoffer has so well called "the effluvia of affluence" to an extent scarcely dreamed of by earlier generations of social philosophers and social scientists. In anomie as in alienation—and paralleling these, moral and social disintegration which, for Durkheim, is the context of each—Durkheim's emphases three-quarters of a century ago give him vivid relevance in our day; beyond the degree, I should say, properly ascribable either to Marx or Freud at the present moment.

TWILIGHT OF AUTHORITY

The affinity between Durkheim and the contemporary cultural scene goes beyond a generally pessimistic view of history and an envisagement of society with widening rents in the social bond and with ever-larger numbers of individuals existing in moral and social isolation. If there is great stress in Durkheim on these, there is equal if not greater stress on such matters as the re-establishment of social and moral authority, on the reactivation of the collective conscience, and on religion in the form of persistence of the sacred, in whatever sphere of life. These too are dominant interests in our day.

Durkheim was, as we have seen abundantly enough, preoccupied by the problem of authority and its roots in the legitimate functions of social life. His early perceptions of the fragmenting effect of modern industry upon social authority were followed very quickly by perceptions of the fragmenting, or at least desiccating effects of centralized political power upon authority. There is no considered theory of governmental bureaucracy in Durkheim, nothing to come close to Weber's writing in this respect, but there is a much more vivid conception in Durkheim of the destructive effect of the modern political state upon the natural social groups such as kinship and village and also upon the more recent types to be found in guild, profession, and labor union. It was precisely his recognition of the atomizing effects of political power upon the social order that led to Durkheim's recommendation, in the final pages of *Suicide*, of new, quasi-occupational groups which would lie intermediate to individual and state, supplying the individual with a form of community relevant to modern economic life and setting up buffers, as it were, to the intrusive role of the modern political state in the lives of individuals.

I am inclined to think that our own discovery, during the past decade or two, of this atomizing, fragmenting power of the modern state is among the more important aspects of the contemporary consciousness. Not often today do we find the centralized political state and nationally bureaucratized approaches to human welfare celebrated by intellectuals as these most certainly were celebrated by Western intellectuals down through about the 1950s. The immense esteem held by the works of Jacques Ellul on the subject of political power and mechanism is perhaps evidence enough of what I say. And it will not be missed that the greatest single difference between the New Left of the 1960s and the Old Left lies directly in this matter of political power. Where the Old Left had generally found political power more or less aseptic, free of the taint attached to centralized economic power, the New Left might have drawn, and no doubt did in degree, its inspiration from Durkheim with respect to the actual nature of the state, though I dare say the cognate inspiration from anarchists such as Proudhon played a substantially larger role. What Durkheim and the French anarchists—and, for that matter, the social Catholics of that day—had in common was apprehension of political centralization united with faith in the restorative possibilities of intermediate occupational groups, thus reinforcing individual freedom and also the fabric of society.

No one will miss in the intellectual scene around us at this moment analogous interests; not necessarily, to be sure, in occupational associations—though the radically changed conception of the function of the labor union in our time has its due share of concern with matters such as social status, authority, and a collective conscience, along with economic goals—but in the whole problem of the creation of a sense of community, and with it authority, in modern economy, city, and political order. The experience with the totalitarian state in our century with its "compressive and levelling" effects, to use the words Durkheim addressed to the national state of his own day, and the ease with which otherwise acceptable social and moral ends can become assimilated and then corrupted by the omnipotent state, has made more and more of us alert to the need for secondary or intermediate unities whose very attachment to their members would be indication of the countervailing force they might have with respect to the political state. Durkheim, as we have seen, was a nationalist to a degree, an aspect that the outbreak of World War I intensified inevitably. No Frenchman has ever been more devoted to the French nation than Durkheim, and even omitting what he wrote under the passion of Germany's military assault on France in 1914, there is clear enough evidence of his respect for the nation as a vital modern form of political community. But Durkheim was also aware of the dangers which lay in any nationalism that could expand in the allegiances of its citizens unchecked by the existence of other, social, economic, and cultural associations lying intermediate to man and the nation.

On the whole, it is the concept of authority rather than freedom that looms largest in Durkheim's thought, but it is for him the authority alone of the kind of conscience, or consensus, that is produced within the social group, the association, or community that is required. It is emphatically *not* the kind of authority that goes with the coercive machinery of the large scale association, whether economic or political. Authority for Durkheim is something inseparable from family, local community, school, occupation, and other of the associations within which man normally lives. It is the breakdown of authority in these areas that results in, not only estrangement and isolation of individuals but the intensification of coercion and power. We have learned this ourselves in very recent times, and it is this self-achieved lesson that makes Durkheim's ideas on the matter, written three-quarters of a century ago, of such surpassing interest, and also relevance, at the present time.

There is, finally, the role of the sacred. If there is any single change in recent thought in the West that is noteworthy, given the so-largely secular character of Western thought since the eighteenth century, it is the vastly increased respect among intellectuals in our time for those non- or prerational elements of life and culture we associate with religion. Durkheim was not himself a religious mind in the ordinary sense; he was indeed a professed agnostic. He at no point thought any given form of religion, any given intensity or institutionalization of religion, eternal. He was well aware of, and gave much of the final section of his book on religion to, the ever-changing boundaries of religion on the one hand and science or philosophy on the other.

But Durkheim nevertheless provided what is probably even to this moment the single greatest testament to the power and also the basic indestructibility of religion that has ever been written by a professed nonbeliever. This lay, as we have seen, in his concentration upon the sacred and the indissoluble relation between the sacred and the social bond. The sacred and the social are, Durkheim argued, but two sides of the same coin. The sense of the sacred proceeded originally from primitive man's sense of absolute dependence upon society. Totemism, Durkheim further argued, has its roots in man's sense of attachment to his clan, with the totem the symbol of this attachment. From the beginning the cult and its indispensable rites of both negative and positive kind have been the molecular elements of religion. And, Durkheim concluded, the preservation of religious creed and sense of identity has throughout history depended upon these social elements, in one form or other. Where there is religion, there is invariably society in the strict sense of the word: society made sacred; the social made sacred.

There is, Durkheim showed us, an eternal quality in religion that arises from the fact that the sacred—the very heart of religion—is for man an unavoidable state of consciousness, of being, indeed. We cannot, Durkheim tells us, live above the level of the purely ephemeral and superficial unless we anchor our lives in some degree upon dogmas, symbols, rites, and relationships which, by very virtue of their deeply constitutive quality in our personalities and communities attain the status of the sacred. The French Revolution, as Durkheim points out, attained its maximum intensity destructively in its law and acts against religion, particularly Christianity. But, hardly had these laws and acts come into being when, accompanying them, there came also into being an intensity of devotion to reason, to the concept of France one and indivisible, that within a very short time was made manifest in worship by the Jacobins, in rites and ceremonies, in liturgy, even in religious sculpture symbolizing what was being worshipped.

No form of community or association we participate in can remain for long external to us. This is a point that Durkheim makes over and over in his writing. Since "society cannot exist except in and through individual consciousnesses, this force must also penetrate us and organize itself within us; it thus becomes an integral part of our being and by that very fact this is elevated and magnified."[11] It is this internalization of what a dualistic philosophy of mind had for so long left outside man that makes for, in Durkheim's view, the indissolubility of the sacred and culture—or society. A completely rationalized culture, that is, one somehow liberated from all dogmas and from symbols of a depth of faith and conviction that transcends, or underlies, the cognitive uses of the mind in their ordinary sense, is as much a monstrosity of thought as a completely individualized community. It is, Durkheim argued, by his sacralization of community and by his internalization of the values of community that man is capable of living at all. The sacred, the traditional, the commemorative, the ritualistic: all of these in substantial degree help form culture, whether high culture or low.

"There are periods in history when, under the influence of some great collective shock, social interactions have become much more frequent and active. Men look for each other and assemble together more than ever. That general effervescence results which is characteristic of revolutionary or creative epochs."[12] Hence the ease with which the most destructive and seemingly nihilistic of movements become themselves within a very short time religious movements, in effect. It is seemingly the fate of all great creative periods in history to be relatively brief, to become shortly as conventionalized, even ritualized, as what preceded them. This is a phenomenon as vivid in intellectual and artistic history as it is in economic, political, and military history.

In our own day, Durkheim writes, "we see society constantly creating sacred things out of ordinary ones. If it happens to fall in love with a man and if it thinks it has found in him the principal aspirations that move it, as well as the means of satisfying them, this man will be raised above the others and, as it were, deified." This is the process that Weber referred to as charisma. It is hardly necessary to call attention to the number of individuals in history, contemporary as well as ancient, who have been raised from being ordinary politicians or generals or priests or technologists to being superlative ones, sacred ones, whom others around them could not or would not approach save through appropriate genuflection or other rite designed to maintain the quality of the sacred in such a being. But, as Durkheim points out also,

> society also consecrates things, especially ideas. If a belief is unanimously shared by a people, then, for the reason which we pointed out above, it is forbidden to touch it, that is to say, to deny it or to contest it. Now the prohibition of criticism is an interdiction like the others and proves the presence of something sacred. Even today, howsoever great may be the liberty which we accord to others, a man who should totally deny progress or ridicule the human ideal to which modern societies are attached, would produce the effect of a sacrilege.[13]

There is no need to specify instances in which Durkheim's brilliant words are apposite in our culture. We have learned that not even science, least of all the secular and revolutionary idols of the modern intellectual mind, is, or ever can be, free of a state of attachment on the part of all of us at one time or other that is but another way of referring to the sacred. Whether among soldiers and politicians, among workers, or among artists and intellectuals and scientists, the social bond and the sacred are, as Durkheim tirelessly stressed, but two sides of the same reality.

Notes

PREFACE

1. There are the classic studies of the 1930s done by Talcott Parsons and by Harry Alpert, both of which did so much to introduce Durkheim to American sociology. It is a pleasure to salute both of these scholars for lasting effect. As I write, books on Durkheim are coming forth in a veritable torrent; some of them: Dominick La Capra, *Emile Durkheim* (Cornell University Press, 1972); Ernest E. Wallwork, *Durkheim: Morality and Milieu* (Harvard University Press, 1972); and, most detailed and comprehensive, Steven Lukes, *Emile Durkheim: His Life and Work* (Harper & Row, 1973). Such a listing does not include Durkheim anthologies with their often valuable introductions or works dealing with several major figures of the age, Durkheim among them. Any serious reader of Durkheim is advised to see all of these. Still other studies of Durkheim are forming.

INTRODUCTION

1. In this brief biographical section I am especially indebted to Harry Alpert, *Emile Durkheim and His Sociology* (New York: Russell & Russell, 1961, first published in 1939 by Columbia University Press); also to Henri Peyre's remarks, "Durkheim: The Man, His Time, and His Intellectual Background," in Kurt Wolff, ed., *Emile Durkheim, 1858–1917* (Columbus: The Ohio State University Press, 1960). The full and authoritative biography by Steven Lukes, *Emile Durkheim*, reached me after my own book had gone to the publisher, too late to be used for this section. It is a pleasure, however, to refer all who are interested in the details of Durkheim's life and times to Professor Lukes's distinguished biography.
    1. Peyre, "Durkheim . . . ," p. 10.
    2. John Henry Newman, in his famous *Idea of a University*, makes this point precisely: if one were obliged to choose, Newman writes, between being surrounded by able teachers but where one had minimal association with a community of able students and being surrounded by able students in such community but with minimal association with teachers, he would be well advised to take

the latter. Over and over in the history of thought we are struck by the creative power lying in small groups of able peers.

3. I have dealt with this aspect of Durkheim and with his relation to the post-Revolutionary line of philosophical conservatives in a series of studies that began in 1943 with my "The French Revolution and the Origins of French Sociology," *The American Journal of Sociology* (July 1943). See especially my "Conservatism and Sociology" in the same journal (September 1952), reprinted in my *Tradition and Revolt* (New York: Random House, 1968).

4. Alpert, *Emile Durkheim* . . . , pp. 64–66.

5. *The Rules of Sociological Method,* tr. S. A. Solvay and J. H. Mueller, ed. G. E. G. Catlin (New York: The Free Press of Glencoe, 1950), p. 113.

6. Goethe's remarks are under the entry for Thursday, May 3, 1827, in Eckermann's *Conversations with Goethe.* The following paragraph from the same entry is worth quoting in full. Although Goethe was referring to the Paris of his own day, the characterization fits Durkheim's Paris perfectly:

> But now imagine a city like Paris, where the most excellent minds of a great realm are congregated in a single place and enlighten and strengthen each other in daily association, strife, and competition; where the cream of all the realms of art and nature on earth stands exposed for daily contemplation; imagine this metropolis, where every stroll across a bridge or square brings a great past to mind, and where a piece of history has been made at every street corner. And in addition to all this imagine the Paris not of a dull and unintellectual time, but the Paris of the nineteenth century, where for a span of three generations such men as Molière, Voltaire, Diderot, and their like have circulated the productive genius in such abundance as cannot be found in a single spot anywhere on earth a second time, and then you will understand how a fine mind like Ampère's, nurtured in such a climate, can well be something at the age of twenty-four.

The reader may substitute for Ampère the names of Tocqueville, Renan, Durkheim, *et al.,* and the point will remain as vivid.

1   THE SCOPE AND METHOD OF SOCIOLOGY

1. *Montesquieu and Rousseau,* tr. R. Manheim (Ann Arbor, Mich.: University of Michigan Press, 1960), p. 3.

2. *Ibid.,* p. 4.

3. *Ibid.,* p. 5.

4. *Ibid.,* pp. 7–8.

5. *Ibid.,* p. 9.

6. *Ibid.,* p. 10.

7. *Ibid.*, p. 12.
8. *Ibid.*, p. 13.
9. *Ibid.*, p. 13.
10. *The Structure of Social Action* (New York: The Free Press, 1968). Two volumes. Volume 1, p. 468. Parson's work was first published in 1937.
11. *The Division of Labor in Society,* tr. George Simpson (New York: The Macmillan Co. 1933), p. 32 and pp. 64–65.
12. *The Rules of Sociological Method,* XLIX.
13. *Ibid.*, p. 6.
14. *Ibid.*, pp. 7–9 *passim.*
15. See especially Freud's *Civilization and its Discontents.*
16. *Mind, Self, and Society,* ed. Charles W. Morris (Chicago: University of Chicago Press, 1934), p. 255.
17. *The Rules* . . . , p. 10.
18. *The Rules* . . . , pp. 102–4.
19. Translated and published in *Sociology and Philosophy,* tr. D. F. Pocock (New York: The Free Press, 1953).
20. *Ibid.*, p. 34.
21. *A Natural Science of Society* (New York: The Free Press, 1957), p. 49. This book was first published in 1948 by the University of Chicago Press.
22. *The Rules,* p. 104. See also Durkheim's "Individual and Collective Representations" in *Sociology and Philosophy,* pp. 1–34 where he expands on this in detail. "No doubt in the making of the whole each contributes his part, but private sentiments do not become social except by combination under the action of the *sui generis* forces developed in associations." P. 26.
23. *The Rules* . . . , pp. 18, 22.
24. *Ibid.*, p. 31.
25. *Ibid.*, p. 35.
26. *Ibid.*, p. 64.
27. *Ibid.*, p. 95.
28. There is no need to elaborate further here. Suffice it to say that the analysis we get of functionalism in Robert K. Merton's *Social Theory and Social Structure,* which seems to me exemplary, is entirely congruent with Durkheim's.
29. *The Rules* . . . , p. 110.
30. *Ibid.*, p. 132.
31. Hanan Selvin, "Durkheim's *Suicide:* Further Thoughts on a Methodological Classic," *American Journal of Sociology,* LXIII (1958), pp. 607–19.
32. *Elementary Forms of Religious Life,* tr. J. W. Swain (New York: The Macmillan Co., 1915), p. 94. It is this passage, or rather the thinking in Durkheim's work it so excellently epitomizes, that made such a strong impression on the minds of Malinowski and Radcliffe-Brown among others in their founding of modern functionalism.

33. *The Rules . . .* , p. 139. Durkheim's pithy truth seems to me particularly relevant right now when the comparative method is so widely being termed a mere alternative to such "methods" as the survey and statistics, each of which is in fact no more than a special form of use of comparative analysis.
34. I have dealt with this at some length in my "Sociology as an Art Form" in my *Tradition and Revolt* (New York: Random House—Vintage Books, 1968).

2   SOCIAL STRUCTURE

1. *Division of Labor,* p. 203.
2. *Ibid.,* pp. 203–4.
3. *Ibid.,* p. 215.
4. *Professional Ethics and Civil Morals,* tr. C. Brookfield (London: Routledge and Kegan Paul, 1957), p. 193.
5. *Ibid.,* p. 159.
6. *Ibid.,* p. 162.
7. *Ibid.,* p. 163.
8. *Ibid.,* p. 165.
9. *Ibid.,* p. 165.
10. *Ibid.,* p. 167.
11. *Elementary Forms of Religious Life,* p. 9.
12. *Ibid.,* p. 14.
13. *Ibid.,* p. 16.
14. *Ibid.,* pp. 16–17.
15. *Ibid.,* pp. 17–18.
16. *Ibid.,* p. 363.
17. *Ibid.,* p. 366.
18. *Ibid.,* p. 366.
19. *Ibid.,* p. 368.
20. *Ibid.,* pp. 11f.
21. *Ibid.,* p. 369.
22. *Primitive Classification* by Emile Durkheim and Marcel Mauss, tr. Rodney Needham (Chicago: University of Chicago Press, 1963), p. 82. This was first published as an article in *L'Année.*
23. *Ibid.,* p. 83.
24. *Ibid.,* pp. 83–84.
25. *Ibid.,* p. 88.
26. *Ibid.,* p. 87.
27. *Ibid.,* p. 86.
28. *Ibid.,* p. 88.
29. *Elementary Forms of Religious Life,* p. 434.
30. *Ibid.,* p. 434.
31. *Incest: The Nature and Origin of the Taboo,* tr. Edward Sagarin (New York: Lyle Stuart, 1963), p. 97.
32. *Ibid.,* p. 100.

33. *Ibid.*, p. 103.
34. *Ibid.*, p. 112.

3 SOCIAL PSYCHOLOGY

1. "Individual and Collective Representations" in *Sociology and Philosophy*, pp. 24–25.
2. *The Rules* . . . , Preface.
3. See *Mind, Self and Society*, p. 229; *The Philosophy of the Act*, ed. Charles W. Morris (Chicago: University of Chicago Press, 1938), p. 153; and *Movements of Thought in the Nineteenth Century*, ed. Merritt H. Moore (University of Chicago Press, 1936), p. 381.
4. See *Elementary Forms of Religious Life*, p. 347; *Moral Education*, tr. E. K. Wilson and H. Schnurer (New York: The Free Press of Glencoe, 1961), p. 71; and *Division of Labor*, p. 279.
5. *Mind, Self and Society*, p. 263. The passage forms a footnote to the text.
6. See Chapter 6 below.
7. *Division of Labor* . . . , p. 279.
8. *Elementary Forms of Religious Life*, pp. 16–17. The same specific theme of the "duality" of man had been pursued 15 years earlier in *Suicide*, tr. J. A. Spaulding and G. Simpson (New York: The Free Press of Glencoe, 1951).
9. *Moral Education*, pp. 67–68.
10. *Ibid.*, p. 71.
11. *Division of Labor* . . . , p. 171.
12. *Moral Education*, pp. 99–100.
13. *Ibid.*, p. 100.
14. *Ibid.*, p. 101.
15. *Elementary Forms of Religious Life*, p. 347. The final words in that passage should be required for all who charge Durkheim with lacking a sense of concrete human beings.
16. *Moral Education*, p. 73.
17. *Ibid.*, p. 53.
18. *Ibid.*, pp. 53–54.
19. *Suicide*, pp. 363–64.
20. Tocqueville, *Democracy in America*, tr. and ed. by Phillips Bradley (New York: Alfred A. Knopf, 1945), Vol. 2, p. 98.
21. *Suicide*, p. 213.
22. *Ibid.*, p. 211.
23. *Ibid.*, pp. 211–12.
24. *Division of Labor* . . . , p. 279.
25. *Elementary Forms of Religious Life*, p. 209.

4 POLITICAL SOCIOLOGY

1. *Division of Labor*, p. 78.
2. On this see, for further insight, Gustave Glotz, *The Greek City*, tr.

N. Mallinson (New York: Alfred A. Knopf, 1930); and my "Kinship and Political Power in First Century Rome" in my *Tradition and Revolt: Historical and Sociological Essays* (New York: Random House, 1968).

3. Readers of *Division of Labor* will, of course, see the long preface to the second edition, which takes a very different view of what I have just described in Durkheim, but—and this is crucial—that preface was not written until *after* Durkheim had reached rather different ideas of politics and of political power in the final part of *Suicide*. This preface is no more than an elaboration of those ideas. See my discussion below, p. 138.

4. *Suicide,* p. 374.

5. *Ibid.,* p. 379.

6. See my "Conservatism and Sociology" in my *Tradition and Revolt* (New York: Random House, 1968). The essay was first published in 1952 in the *American Journal of Sociology*.

7. *Suicide,* p. 388.

8. *Ibid.,* p. 389.

9. *Ibid.,* p. 390.

10. Durkheim deals with these intermediate associations in *Professional Ethics and Civic Morals* also. The subject was obviously a preoccupying one.

11. *Division of Labor,* p. 1.

12. *Ibid.,* pp. 218–19.

13. *Ibid.,* p. 7.

14. *Ibid.,* pp. 26–27.

15. *Ibid.,* pp. 27–28.

16. Durkheim, *Ibid.,* Tocqueville, Vol. 2, Book 2, Chapter 13.

17. *Division of Labor,* p. 29.

18. *Ibid.,* p. 195.

19. *Professional Ethics . . . ,* p. 60.

20. *Ibid.,* p. 61.

21. *Ibid.,* p. 62.

22. *Ibid.,* p. 63.

23. *Ibid.,* p. 63.

24. *Socialism and Saint Simon,* tr. C. Sattler, ed. A. W. Gouldner (Yellow Springs, Ohio: Antioch Press, 1958), p. 5.

25. *Ibid.,* p. 6.

26. See Marcel Mauss's introduction to the first edition, in *Socialism,* as cited, p. 3.

27. *Suicide,* p. 370.

28. *Socialism,* p. 40.

5 RELIGION

1. Volume 2 of this work is concerned almost entirely with the social and psychological elements of religion but there is much in the other volumes as well.

2. Tocqueville, *Democracy in America,* Vol. 2, p. 20.
3. *Ibid.*
4. *Ibid.,* Vol. 2, p. 8.
5. *Ibid.,* Vol. 2, p. 12.
6. Fustel de Coulanges, *The Ancient City,* tr. Willard Small (New York: Lee and Shepard, Publishers, 1874), p. 12.
7. *Ibid.,* p. 30.
8. See above, p. 69.
9. *Elementary Forms of Religious Life,* p. 8.
10. *Ibid.,* p. 3. Durkheim's evolutionary treatments of contract and property in his *Professional Ethics and Civic Morals,* dealt with in Chapter 2, above are further cases in point.
11. *Ibid.,* pp. 3–4.
12. *Ibid.,* p. 47. The italics are Durkheim's.
13. *Division of Labor,* p. 169.
14. *Ibid.,* p. 169.
15. *Elementary Forms of Religious Life,* pp. 225–26.
16. *Ibid.,* p. 37.
17. *Ibid.,* pp. 38–39.
18. *Ibid.,* p. 427.
19. *Professional Ethics . . . ,* p. 171.
20. *Elementary Forms of Religious Life,* p. 44.
21. *Ibid.,* p. 206.
22. *Ibid.,* p. 3.
23. *Ibid.,* p. 226.
24. *Ibid.,* p. 16.
25. *Ibid.,* p. 425.
26. *Ibid.,* p. 416.
27. *Ibid.,* p. 416.
28. *Ibid.,* p. 416.
29. *Ibid.,* p. 417.
30. *Ibid.,* pp. 299–300.
31. *Ibid.,* p. 326.
32. *Ibid.,* p. 347.
33. *Ibid.,* pp. 348–49.
34. *Ibid.,* p. 380.
35. *Ibid.,* p. 389.
36. *Ibid.,* pp. 413–14.
37. *Ibid.,* p. 437.
38. *Ibid.,* p. 430.
39. *Ibid.,* p. 431.
40. *Ibid.,* p. 431.

6 MORALITY

1. *Division of Labor,* p. 32.
2. *Ibid.,* p. 35.

3. *Ibid.*, p. 36.
4. *Ibid.*, p. 398.
5. *Ibid.*, p. 399.
6. We are informed by the translator, George Simpson, in his preface to the English edition that it was Durkheim himself who chose to omit these pages from his introduction when the second edition was published in 1902. Undoubtedly Durkheim's decision sprang from a desire, at least in part, to give prominence to the new introduction he wrote specially for the second edition in which he elaborated his ideas on secondary groups.
7. *Ibid.*, p. 435.
8. *Ibid.*, p. 434.
9. *Sociology and Philosophy*, p. 36.
10. *Ibid.*, p. 38.
11. *Ibid.*, pp. 68–69.
12. *Ibid.*, p. 69.
13. *Ibid.*, p. 72.
14. *Moral Education*, pp. 35–36.
15. *Ibid.*, p. 46.
16. *Professional Ethics*, p. 14.
17. *Moral Education*, pp. 48–49.
18. *Ibid.*, p. 52.
19. *Ibid.*, pp. 52–53.
20. *Ibid.*, p. 54.
21. *Division of Labor*, p. 399.
22. *Moral Education*, p. 71.
23. *Ibid.*, p. 74.
24. *Ibid.*, p. 93.
25. *Ibid.*, p. 114.
26. *Ibid.*, p. 119.
27. *Ibid.*, pp. 99–100.
28. *Ibid.*, pp. 100–101.

7 DEVIANCE

1. *Sociology and Philosophy*, p. 65.
2. *Moral Education*, p. 53.
3. *Division of Labor*, p. 106.
4. *Ibid.*, p. 106.
5. *The Rules . . .* , p. 54.
6. *Ibid.*, p. 55.
7. *Ibid.*, p. 64.
8. *Ibid.*, p. 67.
9. *Ibid.*, p. 69.
10. See especially Vol. 2, Part 2, Chapter 13. "When inequality of conditions is the common law of society, the most marked inequalities do not strike the eye; when everything is nearly on the same level, the slightest are marked enough to hurt it."

11. Both of the quotations are *ibid.*, p. 70.
12. *Ibid.*, p. 71. Italics added.
13. *Ibid.*, pp. 71–72. See also Durkheim's discussion along the same line, involving Socrates, Jesus, and other "moral deviants" in his *Moral Education*, p. 52. There he writes: "To dare to shake off the yoke of traditional discipline, one should not feel authority too strongly."
14. *Moral Education*, pp. 53–54.
15. *The Rules . . .* , p. 72.
16. *Ibid.*, p. 73. Once again making evident his awareness that crime can be both normal and yet repugnant, Durkheim compares it to pain in the organism. No organism is normal without a pain mechanism; pain under appropriate circumstances is itself normal. Yet, understandably, we seek to reduce pain and indeed obviate it.
17. *Moral Education*, p. 179.
18. *Division of Labor*, p. 85. The full sentence reads: "In the first place, punishment consists of a passionate reaction."
19. *Ibid.*, p. 88.
20. *Ibid.*, p. 90.
21. *Ibid.*, pp. 96–97.
22. *Elementary Forms of Religious Life*, p. 311. The whole chapter on the negative cult is built around the thesis along this line first set forth in the *Division of Labor*.
23. *Moral Education*, p. 182.
24. *Ibid.*, p. 186.
25. *Ibid.*, p. 188.
26. *Ibid.*, pp. 139, 140.
27. *Suicide*, p. 337.
28. *Ibid.*, p. 209.
29. *Ibid.*, p. 213.
30. *Ibid.*, p. 214.
31. Such ages as, for example, post-Peloponnesian Athens, imperial Rome, and postindustrial modern Europe, in all of which generalized conditions of hyperegoism may be seen, sometimes creative and buoyant, other times depressed and sterile with "failure of nerve" evident.
32. *Ibid.*, p. 246.
33. *Ibid.*, p. 247.
34. *Ibid.*, p. 248.
35. *Ibid.*, p. 253.
36. *Ibid.*, p. 254.
37. *Ibid.*, p. 225.

8 SOCIAL CHANGE

1. *Professional Ethics and Civic Morals, Incest,* and *Primitive Classification,* all published posthumously, based on Durkheim's lectures and notes, are heavily charged with developmentalist implications;

which, of course, does not mean they are devoid of other implications as well.

2. *Division of Labor,* p. 123.
3. *Ibid.,* pp. 129–30.
4. *Elementary Forms of Religious Life,* p. 3.
5. *The Rules* . . . pp. 110, 111, 113, 116.
6. I have dealt with this in considerable detail in my *Social Change and History* (New York: Oxford University Press, 1969). See especially the last two chapters.
7. *The Rules* . . . , p. 107.
8. *Ibid.,* pp. 108–9.
9. *Ibid.,* p. 109.
10. The importance of Durkheim's criticism of psychological evolutionary origins lies in the fact that these are basically the *only* kinds of absolute origins that can be reconstructed when it is institutions rather than, say, pottery types or pictographs with which we are concerned.
11. *Ibid.,* p. 117.
12. *Ibid.,* p. 117. Italics added.
13. *Ibid.,* p. 118.
14. *Ibid.,* p. 118.
15. See my *Social Change and History* and also my essay "History and Sociology" in my *Tradition and Revolt: Historical and Sociological Essays.*

9 DURKHEIM AND MODERN CULTURE

1. *Suicide,* p. 391.
2. *Ibid.,* p. 214.
3. *Ibid.,* p. 369.
4. *Division of Labor,* p. 250.
5. *Suicide,* pp. 365–66.
6. *Moral Education,* p. 40.
7. *Ibid.,* p. 101.
8. *Suicide,* p. 370.
9. *Democracy in America,* Vol. 2, Book 2, Chapter 13.
10. *Suicide,* p. 253.
11. *Elementary Forms of Religious Life,* p. 209.
12. *Ibid.,* p. 210.
13. *Ibid.,* p. 213.

Index